SOME THINGS ARE N

Martha Royce Blaine

Some Things Are Not Forgotten

A PAWNEE FAMILY

REMEMBERS

University of Nebraska Press, Lincoln and London

© 1997 by the University of Nebraska Press
All rights reserved
Manufactured in the United States of America
⊛ The paper in this book
meets the minimum requirements of American
National Standard
for Information Sciences – Permanence of
Paper for
Printed Library Materials, ANSI Z39.48-1984.
Library of
Congress Cataloging-in-Publication Data
Blaine, Martha
Royce, 1923– Some things are not forgotten :
a Pawnee family remembers /
Martha Royce Blaine. p.   cm. Includes
bibliographical
references and index. ISBN 0-8032-1275-5
(cl : alk. paper)
1. Blaine, Garland James, 1915–1979.
2. Blaine, Martha Royce, 1923–   .
3. Pawnee Indians—Biography.
4. Pawnee Indians—History.
5. Pawnee Indians—Social life
and customs.
I. Title. E99.P3B55   1998
973'.04979—dc21 [B]
97-2187 CIP
ISBN 978-0-8032-4527-3 (pa : alk. paper)

CONTENTS

ILLUSTRATIONS

Preface

THE PAWNEES

For many centuries Garland Blaine's people, the Pawnees, lived in Ne-braska and Kansas in earth lodge villages surrounded by their fields of corn, beans, squash, and other crops. Archaeologists have found Pawnee village sites along the Platte, Loup, Beaver, Blue, Republic, and Smoky Hill streams and rivers.[1] The annual subsistence cycle of the Pawnees consisted of planting fields in the spring, hunting buffalo on distant plains in the summer, harvesting, preparing, and storing their crops in the autumn, and returning to the plains once again as a village and band for the winter hunt. At one time, before the advent of the European colonial powers – the Spanish, French, and English – the estimated population of the tribe ranged between ten thousand people and twenty thousand or more. Their political system divided the tribe into four bands: the Chawi, Pitahawirata, Kitkahahki, and Skiri (Skidi).[2] Each band occupied its own locality, called itself a tribe (*akitaru*), and was governed by a council of chiefs, one of whom was the head chief.

The Pipe Ceremony (Hako) established and maintained friendly re-lations with neighboring tribes such as the Otoes and Omahas in Ne-braska.[3] To accomplish this certain Pawnee band members visited another tribe to adopt a high-ranking member, such as a chief's child, during several days of ceremonies. This action sought to establish a kinlike relationship and build alliances to avoid hostility. When hostile nomadic Sioux bands entered the northern part of Pawnee territory after the mid-nineteenth century, however, war became a constant factor in the Pawnees' lives.[4]

Relations with the United States government, which began with the first treaty in 1818, were never easy and rarely were beneficial to the Indians. They brought about the erosion of Pawnee culture, including kinship, economic, and political systems, and eventually undermined tribal autonomy as attempts to "civilize" the nation's Indians began. The westward movement of land-seeking settlers brought greater and greater demands for Indian land, and Pawnee treaties with the federal government in 1833, 1848, and 1857 called for cession of most of their lands and their removal to a reservation in 1857.[5] In 1874–75 the tribe found itself forced to move from its ancestral Nebraska homeland, with its family graves and spiritual places, to a reservation in Indian Territory.

Here the Pawnees faced even greater loss of lives as illness, hunger, and death overtook them, largely owing to government neglect and mismanagement. As a consequence, by the beginning of the twentieth century their population had decreased to fewer than seven hundred people. Allotment in severalty of their reservation and opening the excess land to white settlement in 1893 served as another blow to the tribe. They gained some redress in coming years with a federal government decision to allow tribes to present to the United States Indian Claims Commission their grievances about unfair compensation for their ceded lands. The Pawnees received their judgment award in 1964, and it was paid in per capita payments to each enrolled member.

The Pawnee people acknowledged a supreme being, Tirawahat, and other sacred beings in the heavens and earth that held power over their lives and the world around them, including the growth of their crops and the success of their hunt. Sacred bundles that carried power in the objects within them originated, it was believed, with the intercession of the sacred beings that appeared to certain individuals in visions or dreams. Each village and each sacred society and its members possessed sacred bundles used in ceremonies devoted to obtaining success in hunting, planting, harvesting, warfare, curing illness, and other aspects of the life cycle. Especially noted in the literature are the postharvest Doctor Dances, when members' magical feats of curing astounded tribal onlookers and visitors.

At present continued loss of the Pawnee language and traditional knowledge has caused the disappearance of most of the old ceremonies, songs, and stories. Language classes have not been able to stem the loss, since English has been the language from birth for at least the past two generations. Although many Pawnees have a limited understanding of the Pawnee language, only a few elders in their seventies and eighties speak it fluently.

Today the tribe has two councils, the Business Council and the Nasharo or Chiefs Council established by the Oklahoma Indian Welfare Act of 1936. The Indian Self-Determination and Education Assistance Act of 1975, as well as other federal legislation, has improved Pawnee life. Government grants and programs support health, housing, elder care, and costs of tribal government. Bingo games and a tribal gas station and convenience store provide a few Pawnees with employment and income. At the Young Dog, Kitkahahki, Memorial Day, Christmas, and Veterans Day dances singers gather around the drum, and dancers are dressed in traditional costumes. Pawnee donations pay for a feast that tribal members prepare before each dance. Several groups play an important role in tribal life, including the Pawnee Indian veterans organization, which sponsors several of the events listed above, including the annual four-day Homecoming in July. Pawnee families from all over the country return to camp, visit, and attend the large powwow, and visitors are welcomed.

Christian church denominations such as the Indian Baptists and the Indian Methodists have loyal members, and the Native American Church is active in the community. Education is valued, and young people can take advantage of grants to attend college. The tribe is proud of having two members who are medical doctors, as well as several attorneys, teachers, accountants, artists, and other professionals. At present the tribe has approximately 2,500 enrolled members, most of whom live and work away from the old reservation area centered at Pawnee, Oklahoma.

In *Some Things Are Not Forgotten: A Pawnee Family Remembers*, Garland James Blaine recalls important tribal events in his and his family's experiences during the years after the Pawnees' removal from Nebraska to Indian Territory by 1875 and continuing through the 1930s. Born 25 March 1915, when he was a young child he had two names. His Skidi kinsmen called him Garland, the "white" name his mother gave him, and his father's more traditional Pitahawirata band relatives called him Kuruks awaki, Little Spotted Bear.

As the story will tell, his parents died before he was two years old, and he lived with his Blaine grandparents, Wichita and Effie. His parents' death was a misfortune for the child, but his life with his non-English-speaking grandparents was fortuitous for Pawnee history. While others of his generation may have been learning English and adapting to new ways, he spoke only Pawnee and absorbed the past with those who were training him to be a traditional chief. He took part in traditional ceremonies with his grandparents, who also participated in efforts to preserve Pawnee culture and language, working with Frances Densmore, Gene Weltfish, and Alexander Lesser.

His early school experiences in a non-Indian public country school were difficult. He later attended Indian schools, including Pawnee Indian School and Chilocco Indian Training School, and he also attended the public Pawnee High School. One school had a set of the *Encyclopaedia Britannica,* and to increase his knowledge of English he decided he would read the entire set. He started the task and claimed he read as much as he could, encouraged by his teacher. At Chilocco he wanted to learn to become a teacher, but the prevailing philosophy of Indian education at the time prescribed courses in agriculture, masonry, and other manual skills. In his fifties, however, he attended night extension courses at the University of Oklahoma, fulfilling a lifelong ambition.

During his lifetime he worked in various places and in occupations that included farmwork, road work with the Civilian Conservation Corps, masonry, roof tarring, and other jobs. In 1941 the newly established United States Tinker Air Force Base in Oklahoma City hired him, and over a thirty-five-year period, until his death, he held increasingly skilled positions such as production control analyst.

Athletics played an important part in Garland Blaine's life. He participated in most popular sports, including football, baseball, and track, in which he won first place in all events at Chilocco. One of his great disappointments came during his stay there. Because of his ability and qualifications, he wanted to try out for the Olympics of that time, but he said his coach was not interested in promoting him and offered only excuses. Garland said, "I listened to him and thought, I don't care. I knew I could win, and I wanted to go. Oh, how I wanted to go."

His interest in sports continued throughout his life, and at one time he coached a softball team. In one game the team played so ineptly that they were being badly beaten. Becoming more and more frustrated, he abruptly changed the lineup. At the beginning of the next inning, he sent the first baseman to right field, the second baseman to center field, the third baseman to left field, and the outfield to the infield. The shortstop stayed where he was, but Coach Blaine told the catcher, "You pitch," and the pitcher, "You catch." "We went on to win," he added.

Garland Blaine lived a bicultural life. His childhood and young manhood, the subject of several chapters here, were largely spent among his Indian people, who taught him that he must learn to live in the white man's world but to value his own. He accomplished this, but he faced the difficulties that members of a minority encounter. As a man, his dignified appearance and reserved but confident manner, enhanced by clever and frequently pointed rejoinders, often made friends of prejudiced detractors and gained new admirers. After entertaining him and the author at dinner, the historian Angie Debo said, "I like Mr. Blaine better than anyone I have met in a long time."

In 1937 the New York World's Fair administration decided that a mounted American Indian honor guard of two dozen young men should be selected to escort important personages and display skillful horsemanship. The announcement went out across the country to federal Indian agencies and schools, and Garland Blaine, at age twenty-two, was among those chosen based on appearance, bearing, character, and ability. The *New York Times* photographed him and noted that he was the only trooper spoken to by the queen of England when she and King George reviewed the troop. Years later he was invited to return to New York as a subject on the television program *To Tell the Truth*. Oren Lyons, another prominent Indian leader, was one of those who played the role of Blaine on the program.

Garland Blaine became head chief of the Pitahawirata band, one of the four Pawnee tribal bands. In a traditional ceremony in 1964 other band chiefs selected and installed him as head chief of the Pawnee tribe. As a tribal leader, he confronted the Bureau of Indian Affairs (BIA) at various times when its innate paternalism and neglectful inefficiency frustrated his people. He corresponded and met with congressmen on various matters important to the Pawnees. As a member of the Oklahoma Advisory Board to the United States Indian Public Health Service, he went to Washington DC when the leaders of various tribes argued before

Congress for Indian Health Service improvements. He became a member of several national Indian organizations and others within the state of Oklahoma in order to serve Indian people. He was a charter member of Oklahomans for Indian Opportunity; a member of the Oklahoma City Human Relations Council, Indian Affairs Committee; National Congress of American Indians, membership chairman, Anadarko District; president of the Pawnee Historical Society; and consultant to the Oklahoma State University and United States Office of Education study of twenty-five nationwide school systems, including Indian agency schools, Indian boarding schools, and public schools.

Probably Garland Blaine's most important contribution to his people was not his position as a tribal leader, but his role in preserving the Pawnee language, narrating tribal history, and describing culture as he had learned and lived it. In 1976 he and his wife, Martha Royce Blaine, were invited to participate in a symposium at the Smithsonian Institution, where both read papers on the origins of the Caddoan-speaking peoples, the language group of which Pawnee is a member. He also served as consultant to Chicago's Field Museum of Natural History for the construction of the almost life-size Pawnee earth lodge and the presentations given by docents. The Minneapolis Museum of Art asked his assistance in the development of a Ghost Dance exhibit. He and other Pawnees worked with linguists in formulating a Pawnee descriptive grammar and recording vocabulary and Pawnee language lessons. Other scholars and young Indians also sought his advice over the years, and the Nebraska Educational Television system invited him to help with a project in which he would be filmed describing Pawnee history and traditional events at different Pawnee sites in that state. Plans called for this work to be used in public school and museum settings to teach about the different indigenous inhabitants of the state.

After Garland Blaine's death in 1979, Paul Olson of the University of Nebraska, who had interviewed him during the filming, wrote: "I will think of the few days that I have spent with him as some of the best days of my life. He was a powerful, charismatic figure and one who embodied as much as anyone I have known the cultural traditions of the people in a meaningful way."

Garland Blaine's first marriage to a Ponca woman he met at school ended in divorce. In 1964 he met Martha Royce Siegel, and they married in 1967. During their years together they made a consistent effort to record on tape or paper information on a wide range of Pawnee subjects, including language expressions long forgotten; songs, from lullabies to warriors' songs; ceremonies no longer performed; values, attitudes, and behaviors, with illustrations; Pawnee relations with people of other tribes and races; and many more subjects covering the spectrum of human activity. He did not always agree with what individual "outsiders" wrote about his people, and his clarifications served a useful purpose, inasmuch as the Indians' view of their history or culture often does not reach the printed page.

Beginning with the sixteenth-century Spanish documents in Spanish and Mexican archives and the seventeenth-century *Jesuit Relations,* compiled by French Catholic missionaries, a large body of information has become part of Pawnee literature. Colonial powers became aware of American tribes through the efforts of their explorers, treaty makers, medal and certificate givers, missionaries, and traders. Later came United States Indian agents, representatives of religious groups, museum agents seeking cultural artifacts, and scholars aspiring to note and preserve traditions and lifeways before they were lost as tribes faced the onslaught of the United States' "civilization" program imposed on its reservation-bound wards. In *The Pawnee: A Critical Bibliography* I sought to bring together and evaluate many major printed sources. Topics are listed under appropriate headings such as archaeology, military affairs, culture studies, United States–Indian relations, and history and ethnohistory. Some well-known chroniclers included are John B. Dunbar, Sir Charles Augustus Murray, Henry Rowe Schoolcraft, James R. Murie, George A. Dorsey, George B. Grinnell, Alice C. Fletcher, George E. Hyde, Gene Weltfish, Alexander Lesser, Robert J. Bruce, Ralph Linton, and Waldo R. Wedel. Recently David J. Wishart, Richard White, Clyde A. Milner, and others can be added to the list.[6]

There is a diminishing amount of information found about tribal history after the Pawnees' arrival in Indian Territory. Particularly lacking are studies by Pawnees themselves, although it is hoped that James Riding In, Walter and Roger Echo-Hawk, Robert Fields, Anna Walters, and others will continue to contribute studies about their people.[7]

Knowing he was one of the few fluent Pawnee speakers, Garland Blaine wanted to continue to preserve Pawnee language, history, and culture, so we cooperated in recording his experiences and knowledge until the time of his death in 1979. In time I felt the need to utilize and present some of this information to give a Pawnee view of life and culture in their Nebraska homeland and the tribe's removal by the United States government to a reservation in Indian Territory (*Pawnee Passage: 1870–1875*).

Subsequently, in this present work, I wanted to relate what happened to the Pawnees after that time, particularly to the Blaine family, describing and emphasizing the most important events that intruded on and altered that family's life, with consequences that carried over into the twentieth century. Documentary sources and other tribal members' accounts bolster and affirm the tragedy of their early reservation life and later times when the tribe relinquished much of its reservation to white settlement. For other topics discussed in this book, the experiences of the Blaine family and others illuminate the reality.

Some Things Are Not Forgotten: A Pawnee Family Remembers is divided into two parts: Part 1, "They Came Before," tells of the grandfather generation of the Blaine family, including Wichita and Effie Blaine and John and Mary Box. I describe their experiences in Nebraska and Indian Territory, including their participation in the Ghost Dance religion, detailing its genesis, acceptance, and performance, and the government's continuing resistance to it; allotment of the Pawnee reservation, the tribe's resistance to loss of the "surplus" land and members' views of white settlement in 1892; the acceptance or rejection of nontraditional ways; and the character of Pawnee–white relations after allotment, when the family faced land speculators and lessees, town merchants, bankers, and others who often saw a way to profit from them.

Part 2, "Becoming Pawnee," describes the experiences of Garland James Blaine as a child and a young man growing up in the milieu described in part 1. They are told in his own words as he recorded them himself or dictated them in answer to my questions. This information is cited as "Garland J. Blaine and Martha R. Blaine Research Notes" (BRN) and includes stories and information given him by his grandparents and others, or his own experiences and observations. Each narrative seeks to give readers a sense of one Pawnee Indian child in his developmental years, as he encounters the wonder of his own world and later the frustrations of the white world. As was his purpose, his words also preserve the past for future Pawnee people, describing some of their older values, stories, songs, ceremonies, and other events that will be forgotten as the language is lost and the old Pawnee world is condensed into a very small experiential space.

As the author I also seek to balance perceptions and broaden knowledge by presenting certain historical and cultural realities as viewed by the Pawnees. Information and insight gained during my thirty years of tribal closeness give me some hope and confidence that this may be accomplished by Star Woman, a name given me by my husband, From the Heavens Two Eagles Come Flying.

THE GARLAND J. BLAINE AND
MARTHA R. BLAINE RESEARCH NOTES

The Garland J. Blaine and Martha R. Blaine Research Notes are a collection of written material and tape recordings gathered between 1961 and the present. Garland Blaine contributed the information found in the collection from 1964 until his death in 1979. Before and after that period, I added to the collection with reports from fieldwork among the Pawnee.

Garland Blaine either wrote, recorded, or dictated his knowledge of Pawnee life to me. Tape recording was used to preserve the bulk of the work. In some instances Garland would initiate the discussion of a topic about Pawnee history or culture. At other times I asked questions and Garland answered them, and the ensuing discussion and clarification of certain statements he made were recorded. Sometimes, as often happens in data collecting, discussion led to related subjects.

Our recording was done at home and often in the car after returning from some Pawnee event or a visit to Pawnee friends or relatives. Recording even occurred on trips out of state or to Mexico, when some view or event aroused a memory. Approximately 125 cassette or reel tapes are included in the Garland Blaine period, and 149 tapes are in the Martha R. Blaine group. Each recording was labeled according to the year, its sequence number in the year, and tape side (e.g., 76.10.1); the name of the person talking; the date; and the subject. The tape's number and contents were listed in a master list year by year, and the tapes are filed by year.

Written and typed notes contain information made at times when the tape recorder was not used. Garland would write down Pawnee phrases and words he remembered while at work or at home. I made notes of small additions to larger subjects previously discussed, or notes about something Garland saw that triggered a memory. It was an active, ongoing process aimed at preserving as much of his knowledge as possible.

All material collected was filed according to the subject. There is a master list of over fifty subjects that has been expanded as needed. Each subject title was written in alphabetical order in a master volume on separate pages. Under each subject was listed the title and date of a tape recording that contained information on that subject. Tape or field note transcriptions are filed in a subject file with other notes written on paper. The Research Notes thus contain all the information that Garland supplied by himself or gave in his discussions with me, as well as the field notes I made independently.

As part of planning for the writing of this book, from the Research Notes I composed a list of all file references to the topics chosen. For example, descriptions about the early days in Indian Territory and early Oklahoma statehood came from stories Garland heard told by his grandparents and other tribal members. Many events in the text came from his descriptions of his own experiences. His memories were recorded during the period given above (1964–79). Although he wrote no family history before that time, he did record songs sung by Effie Blaine, his grandmother, and by himself and others. All the information Garland acquired came from everyday conversations with other Pawnees during his lifetime. Except for a few formal interviews, my contributions to the Research Notes included casual discussions with Pawnee relatives and friends after 1961 when I made contact with the Pawnees.

PAWNEE LANGUAGE USAGE

The majority of the Pawnee words and expressions used in the book are written as Garland Blaine wrote them. It is not possible to transcribe them linguistically as linguists would do because there is no way to hear what was said. His translations are accurate because he spoke the language from his earliest years. Regrettably, he sometimes found nonspeakers' printed interpretations and translations erroneous.

Acknowledgments

This work would not exist without the inspiration and efforts of Garland J. Blaine and all the other Pawnees past and present who have contributed to my knowledge of Pawnee culture and history. These individuals include Viola Blaine McIntosh, Susie Bear Chief Jim, St. Elmo Jim, Albin Leading Fox, Horace Taylor, Henry Stoneroad, Rosanna Yellow Calf Turnbull, Ethel Wilson Riding In, Lynn Rice, Wilson and Virginia Moore, William Howell, William Taft Eaves, Rachel Crow Chief Eaves, Nora Pratt, Clifford Jim, Levi Horse Chief, and Alexander Mathews. I especially want to thank Maude White Chisholm, who has helped and encouraged me throughout the past few years and, while in her eighties, guided me through bushes and briars searching for old Pawnee sites, translated some taped Pawnee-language conversations, and added information that will be found here and there in the text.

There are fond memories of friendship with Waldo R. and Mildred Mott Wedel, and our visits together when they shared their vast knowledge of Pawnee archaeology and history. Garland and Waldo explored the fields around Pawnee locating forgotten mudlodge sites, and Mildred and I discussed aspects of Pawnee ethnohistory.

However, the greatest appreciation is for the contribution of my husband, Garland's, contribution. This is the story of his family, and without his many memories and descriptions of times gone by and the roles played by his paternal and maternal ancestors in tribal history, there would not be a story to tell.

Part One
THEY CAME BEFORE

ONE

They Came Before

Grandparents have an important place in the lives of Indian children. In traditional Pawnee culture the grandparents lived within the family circle, and the grandmother in particular became a respected influence for the child. She fed him at times, nursed him in illness, carried him on her back on a cradle board, taught him through stories and parables, and paid attention to him when no one else could. Garland Blaine's grandparents played a major part in his life as they guided, instructed, and nurtured him after his parents died before he was two years old. This story begins with what is known about the grandfather generations of the Blaine family – how they lived and how they influenced the lives of others who came after them.

The earliest known ancestor is He Who Reveres the Universe, followed in time by the men of nine paternal generations: Only One with Eyes, Tall Slender Man, Man of Meat, Old Man Gray Hair or House Full of People, He Who Reveres the Universe, Overtakes His Enemy (Overtaker) or Wichita Blaine, James G. Blaine, and From the Heavens Two Eagles Come Flying or Garland James Blaine (see appendix A).

Only One with Eyes was a great hunter in Nebraska and was said to have eyes that could see clearly for great distances, like the spyglass the white soldiers carried. When no one else could see it, he could spot a small, pale cloud of dust on the horizon indicating a moving buffalo herd. His son, Pita-kisatski or Man of Meat, had a great reputation for butchering the animals. In the time it took the average hunter to skin one buffalo and load the meat on his horse, Man of Meat could complete three. There is a song that he received in a sacred vision. The spirit that appeared to him at that time made him exceedingly fast and efficient at butchering. He was big and strong, so he could hold up a heavy buffalo leg and cut it. Even when he was an old man, with a "a mere wave of his hand over the meat, it seem to be butchered." A hunter who remembered his skill laughed and said, "While I was still fooling around trying to get started, he would be all done butchering, and his meat back at camp, dried and stored!"[1]

WICHITA BLAINE, TU-TU-RA-WI-TSAT, OVERTAKES HIS ENEMY

When Wichita Blaine was young his grandfather told him that all his grandfathers were born in Nebraska as far back as he knew of them. Wichita himself was born near present-day Fremont on what was called Cocklebur Creek.[2] Its exact location is not known, but it would have been a Pitahawirata village, because his people belonged to that Pawnee band.

When he was old enough to walk around very well the big snow came. It snowed and snowed and snowed, drifting almost as high as the tops of the village mudlodges. The horses had to be found and brought into the dwellings, and some wall supports had to be taken down so they could eat the dried grass in the sod lining. The family was lucky there had been good crops that year, because they had a lot of dried corn and pumpkins in their storage caches and a good reserve of dried buffalo meat. If they had not had enough food they would have had to eat their horses, because they could not get out to hunt.[3]

In the Nebraska winter of 1857–58 there was indeed such a snow.[4] Old settlers' accounts testified that people died stranded in the snow or in their houses without food or heat. If 1857 was the year, then Wichita's statement that he had learned to walk well would place his birth in the mid-1850s.

When he was very young his mother died. He often wanted his mother and cried because she was dead. His father, He Who Reveres the Universe, composed this song in his sorrow:

> This is sad. This is painful.
> When I am thinking [of the small child crying for his mother]
> Tirawahat is over all. Look to him.

Wichita had vague memories of the people living in his family's mud-lodge, including his grandfather, his father, and an old lady who might have been his grandmother. He thought the old lady had a brother there. Then there were two other men, but he forgot who they were. There may not have been other women in the lodge, because marauding Sioux often killed women working in the fields.

His grandfather often took him riding and showed him landmarks the Pawnees used in their journeys. Sometimes they walked to the cleared place in the village where men played the hoop game.[5] When they returned to their mudlodge there was a hide shield in front hanging on a tripod. The shield was painted with a heronlike marsh bird with long legs. The bird may have represented his grandfather's or father's spirit animal, which protected him in battle.

There were dangers in the child's life. When he was about six years old he was allowed to go by himself to get water from a spring. He could carry only half a bucket at a time, and once as he was bending over to fill his bucket, someone grabbed his hand. It was an enemy from another tribe. He dropped the bucket, jerked loose, and ran up the hill. The man stumbled, but followed. The boy ran as fast as he could with the man behind him. He kept yelling, and as he neared the first mudlodge at the village edge, men ran out with their bows and arrows. They ran back down the path, but the stranger had disappeared.

Winter was hard in some ways. When the cold was intense, the young boys in a mudlodge would sit on the earth floor with their blankets or buffalo robes. Each would be given a short wood ember five or six inches wide, and they would put them on the floor beneath their legs with their knees drawn up. Then they pulled their blankets around them very carefully, and the embers' heat kept them warm. Little girls sat close to their mothers or fathers, wrapped in the same blanket or buffalo robe.

As white settlers depleted the supply by loading their wagons with stolen Pawnee reservation timber, wood became scarce and had to be carried long distances.[6] So as not to be detected when they were away from the village, warriors always used as small a fire as possible for keeping warm or cooking. They always wondered why the white people in wagon trains and other places built such big fires. "Big fire and they still can't keep warm," they'd scoff. You always knew where they were at night.

In the winter Wichita and his friends would go to the river and chip out pieces of ice about three feet long and two feet wide. The pieces were very heavy, but they managed to chip the ice so it curved up in front. Someone would weave willow twigs into a mat to lay on top, while someone else gathered grass to cover that. One boy would find a hollow reed long enough to go through the ice, spit into it, place the end against the ice, and with suction draw it up and down until the ice cooled the spit. That was painstakingly repeated until a hole appeared all the way through the ice. The last step was to thread a strap through the hole. Then the boys got on the sled, held the strap, and rode down the bank and onto the frozen river on their "horse," whooping all the way.

In the summer, when no tasks had to be done, the village boys ran to the river to swim. Wichita continued to carry water from the spring, bring in wood for the fire, and help the feeble old people walk to the village outskirts to defecate. Most of all he remembered being sent to herd the family horses at some distance from the village. This was a wonderful time. Uncle the Wind blew the grass in waves as far as the eye could see. The boys were watchful, learning to be alert by listening to birds and other sounds that might warn them of an enemy approaching to steal the horses. They made what Wichita called "twerps" – rawhide strips three to four feet long with knots tied in them, attached to a sturdy stick about two feet long. Blackbirds would circle, fly down, and gather on the ground to feed around the horses. If a boy got close and lay very still, he could lash out with the twerp and kill one or, if he was lucky, even two birds. Then they scooped up river clay, wrapped the birds in it, roasted them in a fire, and ate them.

When Wichita Blaine was about ten or twelve his father remarried, and the child went to live with his grandmother. One day his uncles asked him to go with them to trade at a nearby town outside the Pawnee Nebraska reservation. They used to ride there on a flatcar with their hides and skins. On the way back they sat on the flatcar waiting for the train to depart. Wichita was thirsty, and he decided to jump off and get a drink. They had received a metal bucket in trade, and he was filling it from a horse trough when the engine whistle blew one long and three short blasts signaling it was leaving. He quickly pulled the bucket from the trough and ran as fast as he could to catch the train. Someone reached as far as he could but he could not grasp the boy's hand, so he began to trudge back home. It took him almost two days to reach the village. He went into the mudlodge, but there was no one there. He sat down in a dark place wondering where everyone was and if they were angry with him. The hours went by, and finally an aunt came into the darkened lodge and saw him. We thought you were dead! she said. They feared that since he had to walk through enemy country he might have been killed. Then his aunt said, "You will have to be a man to hear what I am going to say. We have all been gone because we have just buried your grandmother." That was why no one had been there all day, and the boy had been afraid to find out why. It was an unhappy memory all his life that he had not seen his grandmother then, because she had raised him. After she died he lived with two of his paternal uncles, and later he told this story about them.[7]

One day He Who Reveres Goals and Water along the Trees walked to the fields beyond the village to get their horses.[8] They expected to find them grazing, but the horses were gone, so they knew they must search for them. They began to look, traveling at some distance from each other but keeping each other in sight. The day wore on, and the horses had not yet been found. Late in the afternoon one brother thought he heard singing, very faint but recognizable. He had now lost sight of his brother but thought he must be singing, so he began to travel toward the sound. Far away on a hill he saw a figure he thought was his brother. He hurried on, following the sound of the singing.

It grew dark, Mother Moon appeared, and he stopped to spend the night. While he was asleep he dreamed that a tall warrior came to him. He wore a buffalo robe with the fur inside, a buckskin shirt and leggings, and a wolfskin hat that indicated a warrior. The man revealed that he was the one that the brother heard singing, and that he had brought him here. The warrior told him he had taken the horses and started the brothers on their search. He explained, "I brought these horses here; they are there," gesturing toward a distant village. He then pointed to a hill and said, "On top of that hill is a wallow. If you go there you will see how large it is. I fought there all day and another, and I was surrounded on all sides. Many of us fell, and in the end I did too."[9]

What the spirit man instructed the uncle to do is no longer known. He may have told him how to make certain things for a sacred bundle, but the uncle would have kept this knowledge to himself and acted on it. Two songs came to him in that vision. The first song tells about following the singing. The second speaks of the brother he was following. It also tells of the Iruska warrior society they belonged to and says it was not his brother he saw but someone who comes and goes and appears and reappears on the horizon.

Wichita Blaine had a little bag, a little bird bundle with yellowhammer feathers in it, plus a bag of paint and other small things he would show his grandson. As he showed them he talked about his uncle's seeing the warrior. Then he sang the two songs his uncle had learned during his vision. He said his uncle had given him this bag and told him that if he wore it in his hair when he went to battle he would never be killed. He wore it when he was in the United States Army Pawnee Scouts, and he returned home safely each time.[10]

Many men, including Wichita's uncles, had more than one name in their lifetimes. One of his three uncles had another name, Leading Chief, and another uncle's name was translated as Warrior Disheveled Chief. After a ferocious battle a warrior's hair would be tangled, his arm swollen from the bowstring's repeatedly striking it, his mouth swollen where he had been biting his lips. His eyes would look wild, and he might seem more like an animal than a person. His uncle probably gained this name after surviving a battle where he had shown great bravery.

When Wichita was a young man, after the Pawnees agreed to removal from Nebraska, the government sent the tribe to the Wichita agency in Indian Territory. The two uncles who reared him stayed there after the rest of the tribe went to their new reservation in north-central Indian Territory in 1875.[11] A few years before the United States government allotted the Pawnee reservation in 1892, they rejoined the tribe with their families.[12] The surname Wichita was given to some family members. The uncle He Who Reveres Goals, who reared Wichita, became Tom Wichita, but instead of Blaine Wichita, his nephew's name appeared in the records as Wichita Blaine, apparently because some government clerk had inverted it.

EFFIE BLAINE, TSA-STU-WIRA-HI-KAT, TO LEAD A HORSE IN

Effie used to say that she was born a long time ago in Nebraska before the village went buffalo hunting one year.[13] It may have been in the spring or the autumn; her pregnant mother and her aunt stayed in the

Pitahawirata village while her father and uncle went with the others on the hunt, traveling south and west toward the hunting grounds. Her family descended from a line of chiefs, and one ancestral village was near the Smoky Hill River in Kansas.[14] Here lived Kihega (Ki-hi-ki), who had seven sons, one of which was her great-great-grandfather. Left-handedness was a characteristic feature of this family; one ancestor was Left-Handed Man Who Acts Chiefly, and another was simply Left Hand. Some other ancestors were the Chief Who Embraced the Horses and the Chief Who Stops Intermittently in Meditation.

Kihega is not a Pawnee name but a Siouan-language family word meaning chief or leader. Effie Blaine said her ancestor had acquired this name when his village took the Pipe Ceremony to an Otoe village. Here, as was customary, his village entourage adopted a chief's child with several days of ceremony. He had been given the name during that visit by his Otoe-speaking hosts.[15]

Not many memories remain of Effie's childhood in a Pitahawirata village.[16] Each day she accompanied her mother, aunt, and some old ladies to get water, maybe half a mile away, she thought. As far as you could see there would be village women and girls walking. They carried metal buckets that looked like they were made from the same yellow metal bullet casings were made from, a different color from iron or silver. Buckets made of brass therefore came to be called in the Pawnee language "containers for food or water made of bullet metal," or bullet buckets.

Sometimes the women and girls would go along certain streams and pick armfuls of grass or reeds for weaving mats for the mudlodge floors and bed platforms.[17] They spent much of a day in the fields planting the corn, weeding it, then harvesting it after returning from the summer hunt. Corn, squash, pumpkins, and beans were dried and stored in underground caches.[18] At other times Effie would play with other little girls in the village. She remembered that they sometimes ran to the top of a nearby hill on the Nebraska reservation and waited for what she called the Pony Express rider to come by on a road below. They would yell, jump up and down, and wave, and he would look up and wave back.[19]

One day a stranger came to the village. He was either a Mexican or a Spaniard, and very old. They heard that he had been everywhere and had lived in Sioux, Comanche, and Wichita country. He had been captured several times and lived among his captors. He carried herbs and was successful in curing people. They always wondered who he really was.

Her father was Resaru pitku or Two Chiefs, a name he chose when he became a chief in Nebraska.[20] He also had other names; one was Resaru-arusa-ueti-kahkis or the Chief Who Embraced the Horses, and another was Warrior Horse.[21] Later he called himself Leading with the Bear, Kuruks-sirakitawi. The village of his birth is unknown, but when all four bands lived on the Pawnee reservation in the 1860s and 1870s he was one of the Pitahawirata village chiefs. When the Pawneees were removed from the reservation by government order, each chief led his part of the band to the Wichita agency in Indian Territory. Later they traveled to the new Pawnee reservation where the Pitahawirata, Chawi, Kitkahahki, and Skiri (Skidi) bands settled in different camps around the agency.[22]

Effie claimed that she and her family came with the first Pawnee group removed from Nebraska in 1873 to the Wichita Indian agency. At that time she said she was old enough to ride a horse all the way. She also said that if she had not been at the Wichita reservation she would have been with other family members during the August 1873 tribal hunt when over one hundred Pawnees were massacred by an overwhelming number of Brulé and Oglala Sioux near the present Trenton, Nebraska.[23]

Leading with the Bear's daughter said her father was tall with coal black, slightly wavy hair. He was nice-looking, she thought. Like many other Kihega descendants, he was left-handed. He told her he was born soon after his people met with white people, perhaps at a treaty council.[24] When he was a young man, he was ill one day and stayed in the family's mudlodge. The tribe was on the hunt, so not many men were in the village. The Sioux chose that time to attack, and the people could hear their crowlike calls as they came riding toward them. His sister got his horse ready, and he ran out of the mudlodge, but the enemy was already there. As a Sioux rode down on him, he froze in his tracks, unable to move. His sister made the woman's ululating sound and cried out, "My brother, let me see you this day protect us." He recovered, jumped on his horse, and yelled the Pawnee battle cry, "The Pawnee tribe and you, my sister, where the sun stands today, I will protect my tribe." He fought and survived that attack. "I became a man that day," he told his daughter years later.[25]

Effie also remembered that when they came from Nebraska her immediate family consisted of her father, her mother, a brother, an uncle, and her grandmother. Visitors came to their mudlodge, and the men would ask her father to tell about his war experiences. He would say, "It was God's will that I should be successful on the warpath. Once I named myself Leading with the Bear because I was blessed with a vision.[26] While I was traveling there appeared to me in a dream a gray-haired person. It was my contact with him that caused me to bring in many horses.[27] I have had a long life. When I grew up I would sit among the old men and give heed to the wisdom of their words. They would say, 'A man's life is not a happy thing. When a man is born they say, "It's a boy," and everyone says regretfully that it would have been better had it been a girl. For it is the proper destiny of men that they should go out on the warpath and be killed. It is a bitter thought that this child will some day have to lie dead on the plain.' My father spoke and would say that these old men spoke bitterly about life."[28] This was believed because during the 1830s to 1870s the Pawnees were in conflict with several Siouan bands and other tribes. Often the enemy would attack and burn villages, scalp and kill women working in the fields, and attack the tribe on the hunt. Defending the band and the tribe and counterattacking in vengeance constantly made life a harrowing experience for Pawnee men and men of other Missouri River village tribes subject to enemy depredations.

A former United States Army Pawnee Scout, Leading with the Bear was ill when Maj. Frank North and Capt. Luther North went to the Pawnee agency in 1876 to seek men to fight the Cheyennes.[29] Effie remembered she was outside the tipi one day and saw a man coming on foot. He may have been leading a horse. She said he was not very tall, and he looked sick – his skin was yellow and his eyes were big.[30] Because all the men were absent, she ran inside.

The man came to the tipi and said in perfect Pawnee, "My child, is this where ——— lives?" He gave a name that Effie did not recognize for a minute. She had not heard her father called that for many years. She raised the tipi flap and replied, "Yes, you can come inside and see my father." Her father looked up, saw the man, and cried out, "Here he stands. Pari resaru [Pawnee Chief] has come." He had given him that name after a battle some years before.[31]

Major North called him by his old Pawnee Scout name.[32] Effie's father got up, they clasped hands, put their chests together, and patted each other. Each felt bad to see the other not looking well. Her father said, "You do not look well, Grandfather [a term of respect]." "I do not feel well," North replied, "but I have come to see the Scouts who are still living.

I have also come to recruit some men to go and fight your enemies." They talked for a while and her father asked him to stay for supper. "I cooked the meal, and they ate," Effie remembered.

"Afterward he thanked me and turned to my father, saying, 'you are getting heavy [old]. It is good to know you are still here and your children can see you. Have a strong mind and think good thoughts. Don't weaken, look to God. He is the one who's in charge of us.' Father then talked to him in the same manner, and they said goodby. He said he was going back to the agency, and he did."

The next day Wichita Blaine went to the agency to join the Scouts, and he stood in line with his uncle, He Who Reveres Goals. North pointed to those who could go. As soon as North came to them, his uncle said, "This is my nephew. We are ready to go." North replied, "You cannot go, but your nephew can go." The uncle answered, "Let me go. He is young. If anyone is to die, let me die." North said, "No, you are wise; stay here and teach the young people what you know." But the uncle and a lot of others followed as far as they were able to go toward Coffeeville, Kansas. One old man bothered North, begging him to be allowed to go, and kept crawling onto the train. North finally strapped him across the back. The old man said, "You have shamed me." North replied, "No, you have shamed *me*. Here you are an old man and I have to strike you, an old man, so you will know you cannot go." Many other men standing there said, "Grandfather, let us ride with you a little way." It was hard for North to refuse them, but he had to. So many wanted to go because life was hard on the reservation, they were hungry, and they wanted to be warriors and feel successful again.[33]

Leading with the Bear died sometime before the 1890s.[34] Family accounts say that at one time his camp or village contained one or more mudlodges near a Camp Creek branch and that he died and was buried near there. Garland Blaine remembered seeing a small family burial ground when he was a child. There were no markers, just mounds of earth. A later search did not find it.

Effie Blaine said that after her father died there was no one to take his place, since her brother had died too, so his part of the band would go to Eagle Chief's camp for the sacred dances. A third Pitahawirata chief, White Horse, also had a camp on Camp Creek where his band members lived.

Effie had been a good rider since childhood, and she prized horses. She once said that she liked to ride the kind of horse that quivered under your hand when you walked up and touched it. Other horses were too tame.[35] Although men received horses during tribal ceremonies when individuals were honored, women were not acknowledged in this way. But Effie was given three horses during her life. After she received the second one, Old Man High Eagle said to her, "Granddaughter, here I am a warrior. I have done all these things [and he named them], and nobody has ever given me a horse, and here you are, you have two horses given to you." She is said to have replied, "Oh, Grandfather, if I should ever receive another horse I will give it to you."[36]

Time passed, and at a ceremony or gathering either Sitting Bull or White Horse rose and said, "There is something I want to do. I want to be among the first here to give this woman a horse. She already has had two given to her, so I will give her this horse to be the third." Effie took the horse and blessed the giver as she should. Then she saw an old man in the audience, and for some reason she led the horse over and gave it to him, saying the proper things as he accepted it.

Later she returned to her tipi and prepared the evening meal. People came and sat down, including High Eagle. He begin to speak slowly: "There I was and my granddaughter got her *third* horse. I sat there and thought, there is *my* horse. I could see my granddaughter lead the horse to me and help me get on, for I am an old man." He paused and looked at Effie. She suddenly realized what she had done and said, "Oh, Grandfather, I am sorry. I don't know what happened to me. . . . I saw that old man, and . . ." High Eagle was not really hurt, but he did not let her forget she had broken her promise.[37]

Sometime in the late 1870s or early 1880s Wichita Blaine and Effie married. When and where they met is now forgotten. They may have known each other as children in Nebraska, or they may have met in Indian Territory. In the traditional Pawnee social class structure the children of chiefs married other chiefs' children. This seemed to be true here. The details of the courtship are missing, but at the traditional wedding ceremony both sets of relatives attended, and Wichita's uncles had gathered the horses to present to Effie's kin group. "They Gave Each Other Things" is the Pawnee expression for this event.[38]

JOHN BOX, RU TSI RA SU RE SA RU, MAN TREATED
ROYALLY, KIWAKU-PAHUT OR RED FOX, GOOD SUN

John Box was Garland Blaine's maternal grandfather.[39] His grandmother, Mary Box, Beautiful Stand of Corn, died 7 July 1893, and he
never knew her. Their people, the Skidis, built an early village northeast
of the Pawnee agency on Skidi Creek, consisting of tipis and mudlodges
more or less in a circle. This village appears to have been built near the
present Pawnee City Lake.[40] A Pawnee showed me where she lived as a
child near the old village site. She pointed to a high ridge above the site
where once stood the mudlodge of her grandfather, Frank Leader, the
keeper of the Morning Star bundle.[41]

In 1914 John Box's brother White Eagle, a band chief, was granted
permission to visit his Nebraska birthplace. He was very old at the time
and was accompanied by David Gillingham, said to be his son. The
Pawnee agent sent a letter to the Arikara Indian agent at Elbowoods,
North Dakota, asking him to care for the old man when he arrived. It was
thought he might have kinsmen there. White Eagle made the journey,
stopping in Nebraska on the way, and returned safely.

In 1976 Garland Blaine, who called White Eagle "Grandfather" in the
Pawnee way, also returned to Nebraska for the first time to see the village
sites and sacred places of his people. He had been told as a child that
his mother's people came from a village on Ash (Ashe) Creek. He was
shown the place White Eagle had pointed out as his village, on the old
Cunningham place near Fullerton. One of the group's hosts brought a
handwritten note from an elderly Nebraska lady. It said: "The old chief's
son visited our farm around 1914. He was getting old himself. The creek
at our home was Ashe Creek. He said that the village on the high bank
was his fondest memory. The one I saw was White Eagle and he had an
interpreter as he did not speak English."[42]

At the time of the 1976 Blaine visit, Mr. and Mrs. Babb had lived
on a farm just north of the Cunningham site for many years.[43] Mrs.
Babb said she was a little girl when White Eagle came to visit. She
pointed out the village site and showed where the village cornfields
had been. Once "you could find things there, but not any more because it had been plowed over for so many years," she said. When the
head chief of the Pawnees walked into these cornfields in 1976, he
prayed in his language, telling the spirits of his people there that he

had come back to tell them their people were living far away to the south and that he felt blessed to be here among his grandfathers and grandmothers.

While visiting the same village site, White Eagle said he had been born there eighty-three years before (1831), the year the shooting stars covered the sky. It was said that a memorable meteor display had occurred in 1833, which would be close to the time he claimed to be his birth year at the old village site.[44] He also told Wichita and Effie Blaine during one of the visits they had together that as a young child he had seen the Morning Star Ceremony. He told this story.

> They took this girl, who had to be a virgin without blemish, to two old ladies, who combed her hair and dressed her and fed her well. Then nothing was done for a time. It could be five days, two weeks, until a certain phase of the moon came. On a certain day, she was tied on a scaffold. A group of old men faced east, standing by the fire. One had a long stick made of *bois d'arc* that he put in the fire to char it. Then he took it and rubbed it on all the joints of her arms, legs, neck, and groin. He then approached her and opened the rectum and vagina to see "if there were any seeds within." If so, then he would announce to the people that they would have bountiful crops for that year. After this, only boys before puberty were taken by their fathers, who helped them hold small bows and arrows to shoot the girl. White Eagle remembered his father making arrows for this ceremony, and he and his father participating in the final act. Even small babies were helped to hold the bow. All took part in this. There was no status order. They shot until there was no place remaining for an arrow to penetrate, and the victim bled to death. At this time it was done secretly by this particular Skidi village, and none of the other bands knew about it. The Skidi chief said many of the people had never taken part, and they hoped the crops that year would be bountiful if it were performed. It is estimated that this would have occurred in the late 1830s.[45]

During one of the visits to John Box and White Eagle, Wichita learned a song White Eagle sang, which belonged to this ceremony.[46] As for the other bands, Wichita always declared that they did not approve of the Skidis' Morning Star Ceremony. He repeated the story of the time that the Chawi chief Pitaresaru had stopped it in Nebraska by killing the girl as she hung there.[47]

John Box, who was also born at the Cunningham site, was younger than his brother White Eagle and was said to have been born about 1844. His and Mary's children included Garland Blaine's mother, Maggie. John Box served as a United States Army Pawnee Scout under Capt. Luther North, and in a 1867 roster he was listed as Red Fox. In the 1869 campaign his name had been changed to Good Sun.[48] The origin of the name Box is uncertain, but a family story says that at one time he was asked his name, and in English he tried to say Fox. He was misunderstood and was thereafter listed as John Box rather than John Fox.

John Box accepted the government's "civilization" program and took up farming and stock raising on the Pawnee reservation in Indian Territory. He also cooperated and agreed to the Indian agent's nominating him for the position of judge of the Pawnee Court of Indian Offenses in September 1892. At the same time, Wichita Blaine was nominated as a private in the Indian agency police.[49] Previously he and John Box had also served as agency teamsters.

By the time his children were grown, and some years after his wife Mary's death, John Box lived with and then married Lizzie Washington, also a Skidi band member.[50] Lizzie's granddaughter remembers them as an interesting old couple. John came to live at Lizzie's place, and they each had their own belongings. She had a barn and he had a barn. He slept in his bed, and she slept in her bed. A family story tells that Lizzie's favorite grandson, six or seven years old, often visited her and slept in her bed. One cold night he woke up and saw the old man coming toward the bed. He yelled out, "EEEEEEeeeeeeee, there comes that old John Box again trying to get in this bed." The old man turned around and went back to his own bed. "He was just trying to get warm with Grandma, and Charles had to tell the whole the world," the storyteller laughs.[51]

At about this time the old man began to drink more than he should. He would hitch up his team and drive into town, drink at some unnamed saloon, and then in a tipsy state would go out and slowly climb up on his wagon. It was said his team would start and take him home unguided. "Here comes John Box," one of Lizzie's female relatives would say. After he got off the wagon, he would go and lean against the barn. "Look at John Box, pretending he is Jesus on the cross again," she would add.

The old Pawnee Scout would be standing against the barn with his arms outspread, looking at the sky.[52] Unfortunately his drinking caused him to be arrested by the Pawnee City marshall on 2 November 1911. He pleaded guilty. In 1915 he faced the same charge again. His deposition said:

> I, John Box, . . . on or about the 27th day of November, 1915, I bought of Burl Meador, at his pool hall in the City of Pawnee, several drinks of a beverage dispensed by him in such place, called cider; that to the best of my recollection, the number of such drinks taken by me, did not exceed six or seven; that [as] a result of my taking such drinks, I was made intoxicated, and I did not at such time drink any other intoxicating liquor or beverage of any nature and further, that I firmly believed that the drink dispensed to me by the said Burl Meador, as stated above, was an intoxicating beverage.[53]

Later records indicate that he was "cured," had signed the pledge to abstain from alcoholic beverages, and was capable of handling his own funds.

According to Lizzie Washington's granddaughter, who used to sit on the porch and listen to John Box tell stories, "John Box and White Eagle hated white people." She told about a time when both of the old men needed money, so they caught some rabbits and took them to town to sell to white people. At one house the lady opened the door with a broom in her hand. In halting English, they asked if she would like to buy a rabbit. She talked roughly to them and told them to get off her porch – she didn't want their dirty rabbits. The granddaughter added, "They were old men then, they were chiefs, she shouldn't have treated them that way."[54] But it is probable that any antipathy they held toward white people arose many years before this incident, probably during the early years in Indian Territory.

TWO

The Early Years in
Indian Territory

The movement of the Pawnee from Nebraska to the Indian Territory has been disastrous in its results.

Barclay White

The government takes better care of the wild Indians who killed white people than they do the peaceful Pawnees.

Ter-re-re-cox

Wichita Blaine said that times were very hard after the family came from Nebraska to Indian Territory in the 1870s. Before the Pawnees' removal from Nebraska, in October 1874 the chiefs held a council with Barclay White, superintendent of the Northern Superintendency of the United States Indian Office. They unwillingly signed a series of resolutions that surrendered the last of their Nebraska land and included their agreement to settle on individual allotments, or farms, on their new reservation in Indian Territory.[1] This agreement reflected the United States government's policy of "civilizing" the American Indians by endeavoring to place each Pawnee family on a separate homestead rather than allowing them to live in kin-dependent groupings in earth lodge villages.

When all the people, including the Blaine and Box families, arrived by the winter of 1875, the Pawnee reservation contained unplowed land and virgin timber. The people lived in tipis and canvas shelters clustered around the newly constructed agency buildings. Pawnee agent William Burgess urged each band to move away from the agency to new locations, where land would be plowed for next spring's crop plantings.

After the bands settled in separate band locations, they began to build small groups of the traditional earth lodges, or mudlodges, as the Pawnees call them. Timber from the woods around them formed the large interior supporting posts, and they used other natural materials to complete the dome-shaped structures. The Pawnees tried to find sites on river terraces like the ones where they had built their traditional Nebraska villages. They found there were few such geographical features on their new reservation. Black Bear Creek bore little similarity to the deeper and wider Platte and Loup Rivers in Nebraska. It was a small stream, and Camp Creek and Skidi Creek were even smaller. The only village that had a setting like Nebraska village sites stood on top of a bank above the wide Arkansas River, which served as the reservation's northern boundary. The small community abandoned its few mudlodges in 1878 after an epidemic killed its chief and most of its inhabitants.[2]

Wichita Blaine described a smaller type of earth lodge. Individuals, particularly the elderly, who had lost most of their family and were caring for a grandson, a niece, or some other relative would go into a wooded area and build a smaller, less well-constructed mudlodge for two, three, or four people. Four center poles instead of eight supported the roof. Sometimes there would be just one structure, but more often up to twelve little lodges were clustered together. The dwellings' location made it easier for feeble old people to gather wood and fetch water from a nearby stream or occasional spring. Another shelter, called the half house, was constructed of saplings bent into a partial dome and covered with skins or canvas. In winter small families built this type of house in the forest when hunting for game.[3]

After the people were settled in band enclaves or on individual pieces of land, an ominous situation emerged. Figures given in Pawnee agents' annual reports reveal that year by year after 1875 the death rate far exceeded the birthrate (see table 1). Disease, hunger, starvation, and suicide accounted for the rapid population loss after arrival in Indian Territory. The act of suicide had never been condoned in earlier times; the Pitahawiratas believed that people who committed suicide never entered the place where their dead lived together in a village.[4]

Government mismanagement accounted for the Pawnees' dire condition. In their 1857 treaty, in exchange for ceding all their remaining

Table 1. Pawnee Population, Births and Deaths

Year	Population	Births	Deaths
1875	2,200		
1876	2,026		
1877	1,523		
1878	1,438	45	85
1879	1,440	33	160
1880	1,306	49	51
1881 (n.a.)*			
1882	1,251	25	27
1883	1,212	17	56
1884	1,142	58	72
1885	1,045	38	103
1886	998	28	77
1887	918	45	125
1888	869	54	106
1889	851		
1890	804	53	79

Source: Annual Reports of the Commissioner of Indian Affairs.

Note: The accuracy of the figures cannot be determined. An annual census determined the number of living Pawnees who would receive the annual per capita payment of goods or money (or both). There is often a discrepancy between one year's deaths and the following year's population compared with the previous year's figures.

*Not available.

Nebraska lands except for a reservation, the government promised the tribe $30,000 in perpetual annuity, subject to the president's approval. At least half of the annuity was to be paid in goods such as food, blankets, and metal utensils. In December 1875 the agent said the Pawnees could not be paid their annuity and no money could be spent on food because some tribal members had not yet arrived at the new reservation and so the annual census that determined per capita annuity distribution could not be made in time for congressional appropriations. Thus in 1876 Congress failed to pass the appropriations bill that enabled the Pawnees to receive the much-needed funds promised them by treaty. Consequently the Pawnee people continued to face desperate conditions.

When asked about these early years, Pawnees recall their grandparents' telling them that in some tipis or mudlodges the family members still alive would be too sick to bury those who had died. One woman recalled that in her village they dug a long trench out near the present North Cemetery and "just piled the bodies in it to bury them." A member of another band said that bodies thrown into Black Bear Creek floated and got caught in a pile near Rocky Ford.[5]

During this difficult time, Wichita and Effie Blaine grieved over the loss of two small sons. As members of the agency police, Wichita and others accompanied the agency doctor when there was an epidemic. They all wore wet handkerchiefs over their noses. They went to a tent and called out to the family living there; if no one answered, they went in and sometimes found the whole family dead. They removed the bodies, then pulled the tent down on top of its contents, piled brush on it, and set it afire. Many precious things burned, even sacred bundles.[6]

The Pitahawiratas still remember accounts of efforts to prevent illness and death from disease in those times. When disease and death came, extended family members living in the same mudlodge divided into smaller units and lived in different dwellings, sometimes in "little houses," or *tsakahpahas*.[7] At times like these they tied *parakaha*, a fragrant herb, to water buckets. Each person was told to go outside the mudlodge for a few minutes of fresh air in the morning. The women brought out the blankets and buffalo robes and shook them vigorously; the entire structure was aired, and the dirt floor was completely swept. The material they swept up was called sickness, and the Pawnee expression for this action translates as "sickness you must put it out forcibly." It was believed that dust or dirt from the air could get into the stomach and cause illness. They would see dust motes moving in a shaft of sunlight and say, "See, that is sickness."[8]

Effie Blaine declared to her family that trash caused sickness. If someone was ill Grandpa Blaine would say, "*Uri*, I bet they had a dirty house." The first thing in the morning, everybody in the household got up, and someone swept out the house or mudlodge, wherever the family lived. Effie said, "Sickness, push him out." Just before sundown she had the house swept again. If it was not done until after dark, the person sweeping would get a tongue-lashing. They closed the windows of the house or the canvas flap of the mudlodge entry at night to keep out sickness.[9]

There were other causes of disease and death. In the new place where they lived the Pawnee doctors, members of sacred societies who had visions during which sacred beings revealed to them how to cure illnesses, could not always find the plants and roots that grew in Nebraska, where they had learned their art and assembled their pharmacopoeia.[10] The medicines needed were specific to certain ailments. Dried and prepared, they were placed in little cloth or skin packets in medicine bundles exclusive to each doctor.[11] When the tribe came to Indian Territory each doctor, including Wichita Blaine, brought his sacred medicine bundle. If the plants could not be found in the new reservation's fields or forests when the medicine was gone, it curtailed a doctor's ability to cure.

Pawnee agents deplored the tribe's use of traditional practitioners, but the Pawnees continued to go to them for many years because they believed their knowledge came from Tirawahat (the supreme being) and other sacred beings. The figures appeared in dreams or visions and taught the doctors rituals and procedures to cure specific illnesses. Since the curing methods came from a sacred source, they were believed to be efficacious. With the onslaught of many new European-introduced diseases for which there was no immunity or medicine, however, even the doctors succumbed to the deadly diseases. With fewer doctors to believe in and to treat them, more Pawnees died. Although, the Pawnees accepted smallpox vaccinations from agency physicians, for the most part in the early years they did not use their services.

Persistent hunger also descended on Pawnee households in the early years. When prolonged hunger and malnutrition were followed by illness, the sick or hungry women or men in the family could not prepare the ground, plant, weed, harvest, and store crops. They lacked the strength to do the hard work necessary to complete the long process. Malnutrition was an important factor in the terrible death toll in the years after the tribe entered Indian Territory.

The government had removed the Pawnees to a new reservation without ensuring the means for their survival. Warned of the disastrous situation, in 1876 the Indian commissioner noted that the "Pawnees [were] compelled by hunger to leave their reservation and seek among border settlements such scant subsistence as they were able to pick up."[12] Tribal members made their way north as far as Montgomery County in southern Kansas. William C. Masten, mayor of Coffeyville, reported that a number of Indians were prowling around the town "seeking aid" in April 1876. Sheriff J. T. Brock of Independence, Kansas, declared that many Pawnees were entirely without food. They claimed there was nothing to eat on their reservation and were bothering the town's citizens. He asked, "Cannot something be done?"[13]

The Pawnees responded to their constant shortage of food with certain strategies. Not only did they go to white settlements and submit to the denigrating act of begging, but they asked to be allowed to hunt buffalo as they had done for centuries. Government policy stated that in order to become civilized the Indians should no longer hunt buffalo but should take up the plow and raise their own food. In this difficult situation, however, the agent gave permission in 1875. But their efforts were in vain. After traveling westward, they discovered the herds were too far away to be reached. Small parties found and killed a few buffalo in the summer of 1876, but not in sufficient numbers to supply adequate food. In 1877 the hunt was again a failure. In February 1878 Agent J. D. Miles at the Cheyenne and Arapaho agency reported there were 420 Pawnees at his agency, returning from an unsuccessful hunt and without food. He received orders to issue enough food to last the ten days it would take them to return to their own reservation.[14]

When the people were starving the hunters would travel in all directions and never see a buffalo. They went farther and farther and stayed longer and longer, but there were no buffalo to be found. By now the white buffalo hunters had almost destroyed the great herds on the plains, and for plains and prairie Indians this major food source had almost been destroyed.[15] Once again the chiefs received permission to go on the hunt. Near Camp Supply, in northwestern Oklahoma on the North Canadian River, they sighted a herd. One hunter had a serviceable gun, and the others carried bows and arrows, the traditional weapons used so as not to spook the animals with the sound of gunfire. The exhilarated hunters triumphantly killed 150 animals, prepared the meat and hides, and returned home by the way of the Ponca reservation, where they shared some of their bounty with their friends.[16]

In the beginning there was some game on the reservation, including deer and turkey. In 1878 government trader T. E. Berry asked if he could sell the Pawnees ammunition so they could hunt for small game. Quaker agents did not favor distributing guns or ammunition to the Indians. In addition, government regulations prevented such items from being sold or distributed as annuity goods. Disregarding philosophical beliefs, Quaker agent Samuel Ely informed the commissioner of Indian affairs that if the destitute Pawnees had ammunition it would help them obtain subsistence.[17] Approval came, and the trader sold ammunition.

In time the reservation was hunted out, and the destitution and hunger of Wichita Blaine's family drove him to steal a cow from a white man's

large herd near the Cimarron River in the southern part of the reservation.[18] He got on his horse and rode south toward the river. Once there
he waited in the woods until dark. Then he singled out a cow, drove it to
a creek that ran into the river, and killed it with a heavy blow to its head.
He retraced his steps, brushing out with a branch the signs of the path
he had taken to drive the cow from the herd. Then he returned to the
animal, skinned and butchered it, and let the blood run into the creek,
hoping all traces would be obliterated. To leave no evidence, he had to
carry away all parts of the animal on his horse. He started back along the
creek, throwing off first the hooves, then later the head, and last the guts.
He finally turned north toward home and arrived at sunrise. His family
shared the meat with his two old aunts, Julia and Susie, and other older
relatives. For a while there was enough to eat.[19]

On 28 December 1877, agent Charles H. Searing received a note from
the agency physician, J. L. Williams, "The man and his family that are
at my office for medical treatment is actually suffering for the want of
something to eat. Can you give them some 'Bacon' and flour?"[20] By this
time a commissary with a lock had been built. It contained food and
other items purchased with Pawnee annuity funds. Limited amounts of
food were now being issued weekly to Indian families. In January 1878
the amounts given were three pounds of flour, four ounces of sugar,
two ounces of coffee, and three and a half pounds of beef, reduced
from five pounds.[21] In February the agent reported a broken commissary
window; 100 pounds of flour and 291 pounds of bacon had disappeared.
Previously the Pawnees had received a beef ration; now each received
three-fourths of a pound of salt pork. The Pawnees remember white
slabs of pork, mostly fat with little lean meat, green with mold and bad
tasting. It was so distasteful that in disgust the people threw the fatback,
as it was called, into the creeks to use as stepping stones.[22] The coffee
ration decreased with the order to give two ounces every other week.
Pawnees still remember their people borrowing used coffee beans from
one another. Shaking their heads, they recalled that the coffee looked
almost like clear water because the beans had been used so many times.[23]

In the last part of 1877, the commissioner of Indian affairs sent Joseph
Hertford to replace the agency clerk and to report secretly on Pawnee
agency affairs.[24] He arrived on 6 November 1877 and immediately began
to describe the starvation that existed there. The rations per person were

insufficient, and he declared that the agent should be instructed to issue greater quantities. He added that he and the agency physician had visited the camps and villages and found dire need. At one dwelling they found a starving child placed outside on the woodpile because the sick family had no food and knew the child was almost dead.[25]

Hertford claimed he had seen beef purchased for the Pawnees with Pawnee funds served on employees' tables. He sent the commissioner a penciled list he found in the agency office. Ten employees' names appeared, with the number of pounds of beef each had received. Supposedly the agent received eighty and one-half pounds.[26] Hertford also suspected that the agency traders, Walton and Moore, received Indian beef and sold it to non-Indians. While visiting the store he also observed that the agency doctor bought eight pounds of sugar for one dollar at the store, whereas an Indian woman who came was charged the same amount but received only two pounds.[27]

Now convinced of employee dereliction and fraud, Hertford noticed that the amount of supplies supposedly issued to the Pawnees did not always match the tickets, which showed the Pawnees as receiving more than the amounts actually distributed to each family.[28] He continued his observations and reported them in carefully written letters to Commissioner E. A. Hayt.

The Pawnees' search for a source of food seemed futile. In May 1879 a severe drought destroyed their crops. Whenever the corn died from lack of rain, the Blaine family went into the field, sat beside the stiff dry plants, and mourned because they were thought of as people dying. If the corn produced only a few ears, each member of the family went through the fields saying, "Mother Corn, do you have anything for me?" hoping to find an ear or two. They walked slowly through the entire field two or three times, looking for dried ears they might have missed.[29]

In their acute need, Pawnees continued to go to neighboring border towns, such as Arkansas City, Kansas. Here they begged for food or money, or at annuity time, after clothing and other articles were issued, they sold their clothing for whatever it would bring. A letter from a merchant in that city declared that probably "5/8s" of all Pawnees who came to town sold what they had. He complained that allowing this to continue was bad for local clothing merchants' business.[30] In the early 1880s the practice continued, and the agent wanted to abolish the annuity clothing issue as a solution to the problem. It annoyed him that Pawnees sold for $1.50 blankets that cost the government $3.50.[31] These blankets and clothing were sorely needed for covering and warmth, but the need for food was greater.

A few Pawnees survived because they worked for pay at the agency and received food subsidies for their labors. One was John Box, an agency teamster. Other men served as assistants to the farmer, carpenter, and other white employees. Some Pawnee employees in these years were Merritt Sherman, David Richards, Johnny Wright, Clark Ricketts, Abraham Lincoln, and John Bowman.[32] Other Indian employees were freighters, driving wagons to Arkansas City or Coffeyville, Kansas, to pick up agency and school supplies and annuity goods.[33] These freighters and the agency police force, consisting of one captain, two sergeants, and five privates, were often traditional chiefs or leading men. The agent hired them to maintain their goodwill, and he hoped to use them to maintain his influence over the people. John Box, a Skidi chief, exerted influence among his band along with his older brother, White Eagle, who because of his age held the dominant position of authority as a band chief.

Soon after Hertford arrived, however, he discharged John Box.[34] Baptiste Bayhylle, the agency interpreter, accused Box of hitting some agency animals over the head with a stick. At this time Bayhylle, a Skidi mixed-blood, aspired to be head chief of all the Pawnees. Hertford wrote to the commissioner calling him by this title and requested that he be officially placed in this position.[35] He wanted this because he used Bayhylle as a source of information and needed him as an ally. Bayhylle may have concocted the accusation against Box, who probably became aware of the scheme and told Bayhylle he had no hereditary right to be a chief. After this John Box, his brother White Eagle, and others signed a petition in 1878 to have Hertford removed from the reservation. The agent, well aware of Hertford's efforts to find fraud, wrote the petition and urged the Pawnees to sign it. That apparently ended the interpreter's pretensions and also Hertford's attempts to better agency conditions. He was recalled soon after that, having investigated malfeasance in the Pawnee agency, the task he had been sent to do.

The government allowed four Pawnees to join William F. Cody's Wild West show. They were Ralph J. Weeks or Little Warrior; Eagle That Flies High; Follow the Sun; and Weeks's wife, Growing Grass That Sprouts in the Spring. They left the reservation 10 September 1878. Cody agreed that the Pawnees were to be fed adequately and not allowed to drink spirits.[36] Pawnees who obtained paid employment or rations at the agency and in Wild West shows were a minority.

Droughts continued, and so did the government's failure to meet its commitment. In the fall of 1878 no annuity payment arrived at the expected time, although Congress had passed the appropriations bill that provided funds. By spring, as bureaucratic mismanagement continued, no annuity came; resentment and anger grew as the agent allocated fewer and fewer cattle for tribal beef rations. The chiefs, who could count as well as anyone, demanded that the agreed-on twenty-nine head of cattle per week be divided among the bands. By May they observed that the tribe was already short 200,000 gross pounds of beef for their people.[37]

On 10 April 1879 the chiefs and leading men met with agency clerk J. W. Phillips. The agent was away on business, but the leaders did not want to wait for his return to voice their concern and anger.[38] Each man got to his feet and in no uncertain terms stated his views on the plight of his people, as the summary of their words indicates:

> *Ter-re-re-cox* (Skidi) warned that they were tired of waiting for their money. It was almost time for the second annuity. If they did not receive it soon, they would leave. The government took better care of the wild Indians who killed white people than they did the peaceful Pawnees.
> *Chu-cah* (Chawi chief) said that the Pawnee had stood for such conditions long enough; that they should not have to beg because the annuity money was rightfully theirs.
> *Eagle Chief*[*39] described how the people were starving.
> *Te-re-re-co-wah* (Pitahawirata chief) threatened to take his band away from the reservation.
> *Curly Chief* (Kitkahahki chief) said, "if we start once, the Great Father will never get us back. We would rather die with a ball through us than sit down here and die like chickens."
> *Comanche Chief* (Skidi chief) sternly said that it was not the Pawnees' fault that the present trouble existed and they should be paid their annuity.

*Good Chief** had visited all the tribes that fight the government, and they are treated well. "But we try to make our living and it seems that the Great Father prevents us. Beef is our principal living and we have none."

Pipe Chief (Chawi chief) repeated what had been said.

Frank White (Chawi) reminded the clerk that many men present had been US Army Scouts and had rendered loyal service to the United States and should not be treated in this shameful manner.[40]

The forcefulness with which the Pawnee leaders displayed their feelings and delivered their arguments alarmed the agent when he returned and heard the council results. A few days later some Cheyennes came to the reservation, and this event increased agency fears that something was about to happen.[41] Pushed by concern about a possible uprising and the chiefs' threat to take their people and leave, the agent sent a telegram to the commissioner demanding that the annuity be sent immediately or that troops be sent to prevent the tribe from leaving. Finally authorizing what should have been done months before, the commissioner immediately gave the order for the agent to purchase food and other necessities for the Pawnees.[42]

Having won a rare victory, in a council that soon followed the Pawnee chiefs became even more forceful, demanding that the employees not use beef belonging to the Pawnees. They stated that each band wanted the cattle it was entitled to and that their funds had paid for. Since the agent was away purchasing the promised supplies, the clerk pledged that the employees would no longer be allowed to use Indian beef.[43] With emotions calmed, the agent believed the crisis had passed. Nevertheless, Effie Blaine said that some of her band, the Pitahawirata, did leave the reservation and started to return to Nebraska. How many left and what happened to them is now unknown.[44]

During the early years, not only was the physical survival of the tribe in peril, but the entire social organization faltered. The deaths of experienced tribal leaders and religious figures contributed to the disaster. Luther North reported that over half of the Pawnee chiefs died soon after their arrival in Indian Territory.[45] These men had coped with the government in treaty times and after and had stood up to their agents in Nebraska and Indian Territory, demanding fair treatment. More often than not, however, they failed to defeat the government's policies and continuing pressure to change the ways of their people.[46] Still, they were the first line of defense for protecting their people's lives and traditions. For this reason the United States government tried to eliminate their power, by employing them as Indian police, for example, in hopes of influencing and controlling them so that they in turn would influence their people to accept the government's "civilizing" policies. These efforts often failed; some chiefs stood aloof and did not accept the agent's offer of food and pay for government service.

Even with the best efforts of the remaining leaders to ameliorate tribal disintegration, conditions continued to deteriorate, as the following 1884 statement by J. W. Smith indicates: "The Pawnees receive no subsistence from the government and are entirely dependent upon their own re-sources. They are very poor. Cash annuity [per year] averages $13 each and it doesn't go far. A large portion of the tribe is in a chronic state of hunger. The Pawnees are gradually dying out. At the present rate of decrease in ten years there will be but a handful left."[47]

This prediction nearly came to pass. In less than twenty-five years their numbers decreased from approximately 2,200 to fewer than 700 in 1900. Only in the middle of this century did the population recover to the former number, and that necessarily included members born of intermarriages with other tribes and non-Indians. As Garland Blaine explained many years later, "As our tribe became smaller, a man might be related to all the eligible women, and therefore there was no one to marry. So many men and women of my generation had to marry into other tribes, such as the Poncas, Otoes, Osages, Ioways, Creeks, and others."[48]

THREE

Allotment Comes

History supplies little beyond a list of those who have accommodated themselves
with the property of others.

Voltaire, *The Philosophical Dictionary*

I do not like the idea of the allotting agent laying us off and the president issuing
the order to open our country. It does not seem right to me.

War Chief, Pawnee

Effie Blaine's father died sometime after Major North's visit in 1876.
Afterward the family and other members of that portion of the band
apparently allied themselves with the other Pitahawirata groups living
near Camp Creek south of the agency.[1] After the tribe's removal from
Nebraska to Indian Territory, some of Wichita's uncles and probably
Wichita himself lived among the Wichita tribe for some time. Evidence
suggests that Effie and Wichita married in the middle or early 1880s,
before they appeared on the 1886 Pawnee census as man and wife. Only
small details are known about where they lived and what their living
arrangements were. They may have lived in the Pitahawirata village near
Camp Creek south of the agency or on piece of land he may have selected
in the area.[2]

In Nebraska the Quaker Pawnee Indian agents had ardently advocated
the idea of individual land allotments or farms for the Pawnees. They
believed that if the people embraced farming, it would enable them to
survive and retain land in a world that would continue to demand more

Indian acreage for white settlement.[3] To carry out their goal, they decided to survey part of the Pawnees' Nebraska reservation and divide it into six hundred ten-acre lots. After this was done, agent Jacob M. Troth urged the Pawnees to move onto these individual plots.[4] The Pawnee chiefs refused. They knew that their constant enemies, the Sioux, would welcome an arrangement in which each family, separated from others, would be vulnerable to attack. Adequate defense depended on a community of village warriors, instantly ready to repulse the enemy.[5]

In October 1874, under difficult conditions, including coercion, Pawnee chiefs and leaders reluctantly signed a series of government-prepared resolutions aimed at removing the tribe to Indian Territory. Still intent on instituting allotment, resolution 2 stated that the new reservation would be "allotted in severalty, 160 acres to each head of family and 80 acres to each unmarried person over 18 years of age," available to those Pawnees who wished to claim allotments. In the "Act to Authorize the Sale of the Pawnee [Nebraska] Reservation, April 10, 1876," section 5 authorized the Pawnees to take up allotments on their new reservation.[6]

By 1877 and 1878, with various inducements such as farm equipment, some Pawnees agreed to select individual homesteads on the new reservation and move there. Nevertheless, most preferred traditional communal life with its cooperation and shared work patterns. Successful yields from Mother Earth could be obtained by female kin members helping one another in the village fields, aided by relevant rituals before, during, and after the growing and harvest seasons.

John Box was one of the men who decided to accept the offer of land when he was offered farm equipment and stock. In the summer of 1878 he had selected land and had planted six to eight acres of corn, potatoes, and vegetables. The agent, seeing his progress toward "civilization," reported that he was neat and clean, wore citizen's dress (white man's clothes) and "[spoke] English quite well."[7] In September of that year the agent again praised him by saying that he was getting to be quite a farmer and deserved to have his stock increased.[8] There is no mention of Wichita Blaine's accepting the agent's offer to take land and accept the trappings of farm life. Most of the men accepting the agent's offers belonged to the Skidi band. Even in Nebraska, agents reported that the Skidis differed in their acceptance of the "civilization" programs. Many accepted the new agricultural innovations, such as the plow, whereas the other bands tended to follow traditional practices.[9]

In 1880 the commissioner of Indian affairs stated that the Pawnees were not moving very fast along the road to civilization. Few of them wore "civilized dress" or had exchanged their tipis for houses. "Farms are principally worked by the bands in common," he reported.[10] As was often the case, Pawnee agents stayed only a short time, and in 1881 Dr. E. H. Bowman, a former army surgeon, came as agent and continued to advocate Pawnee allotment. On investigation he found some Pawnees already settled on farms, but he discovered no records describing each allotment's boundaries. In addition, these persons had no documents validating their selections.[11]

Bowman looked around and decided he did not approve of what he saw. The Pawnees used what he called "squaw patches" (band fields), and certain "lazy loafers" hung around when he thought they should be out doing their own farming. He criticized the earlier establishment of communal band farms and said they should never have been allowed.[12] He apparently did not understand, or ignored, the fact that in the early reservation years large fields worked communally were the best solution for obtaining critically needed subsistence. They were better than small, widely dispersed fields where the prairie sod had to be broken by agency equipment because the Indians had none. Additionally, the road system was inadequate, and it was easier to prepare several large fields for each band than many small ones scattered here and there. Bowman soon realized that the village chiefs and religious leaders impeded his progress in convincing people to take up life on individual farms. At this time lack of food weakened many Pawnees, and in many families productive members were ill or dead. Tribal leaders understood that band fields produced more food by using traditional methods than did small, widely spaced family plots, situated on newly plowed ground in places without shelters, tools, or enough women to ensure the crops' success. In addition, Pawnee social and economic constructs, based on religious beliefs many centuries old, determined subsistence patterns and roles. Radical changes would diminish the small amount of control the Pawnees had over their lives and futures if they ignored traditional beliefs and practices. Many believed unsanctioned changes would also increase the number of deaths and other calamities they had endured since leaving their sacred places and Nebraska homeland.[13]

In 1881 band villages continued to exist. The Indian agent visited the Pitahawirata village and ordered the men who were freighters to go to Arkansas City, a town in Kansas on the Territory border, to pick up goods for the agency. If they did not leave, he would take the government wagons away from them.[14]

On discovering that no boundaries were recorded for farms of the few Pawnees living on allotments, Bowman asked that a new survey be made. The commissioner's office instructed him to retrace and reestablish section and subdivision lines. Several stories of his efforts remain. One source said he had heard that all Pawnees were "desirous of being a Chief, so Major Bowman told them that any who would go out and select a tract of land might be ruler or Chief over it, and that the agent would send out a farmer to assist him in farming it."[15] It is highly unlikely that every Pawnee would dare presume to be a chief, but a number of Pawnees selected allotments and built mud lodges or cabins on them. They were later designated as the allottees of 1881 and 1882.

The allotment sites chosen by the individuals listed in table 2 show that most were in what had been called Skidi band land north and northeast of the agency. A few lay west of the agency in the Chawi band area. It appears no individuals chose allotments south or east of the agency in what would be considered Pitahawirata or Kitkahahki lands. Skidi band members constituted the greatest number of those tribal members accepting allotments.

On 26 May 1882 Agent Bowman met with the Pitahawirata band members, and they agreed that he could go and select allotments for them in the "south part of their reservation, and "start them aright in the way of Farming."[16] The record of these allotments has not been discovered, but it is possible that the documents were lost or not completed. Many may have been allotted land but did not move to or use these selections for various reasons. Others like Wichita Blaine may have left their village and moved to their land later. This is suggested by the fact that in 1890 Wichita received a hoe planter, a whiffletree, and 650 pounds of wheat seed. The next year the agency gave him window glass as well as nails and oat and corn seed. By the first quarter of 1892 he had broken or plowed eight acres for cultivation.[17]

Before that time, in the last part of the 1880s, selection and improvement of allotments slowed. There was not enough equipment to plow the land or material to complete log cabins or houses for those who had

Table 2. Names of 1881 and 1882 Pawnee Allottees

David Ah ka pah kish	Henry Sargeant
Big Bear	Running Scout
Battiste Bayhylle	Spah lah oo loo looks (female)
John Buffalo	George Susas
Ce lu ooh tah luh ooh	Skeedee Tom (Ah kah tah)
Coo rux ruh ruk koo	Seeing Eagle
Comanche Chief	Sitting Eagle
Chucah	Eli Shotwell
Joseph Esau	Sun Chief (1883)
Eagle Chief	Tah rah hah
Richard Fields	Te ra rah e ticks
Henry Geneva	Ter ra re cox
Good Lon	Te re tak coo sah
Kickapoo	Tah we loos teh sah
Knife Chief	War Chief
Lay tah cot tah wah coo augh	George Washington
Loo ku tah lah ooh	We te lay sah lus pek
Richard Lushbaugh	James Wood
Lone Chief	Peter Wood
Lame George	Ralph J. Weeks
Pah te waugh tah	White Eagle
Pipe Chief	Young Elk

Source: Identification and Description of the Lands Covered by Selection and Allotment, Act of March 3, 1893 (27 Stat. 612) for the Pawnee Indians.

recently selected allotments.[18] In addition, allotment boundaries had not been determined for many Pawnees listed in table 2 and others. Thus those tribal members who had decided to leave the camps or villages to settle on their allotments could not do so and found it necessary to stay and use the band fields to grow their crops. Nevertheless, the agent claimed he saw evidence that the village system was disintegrating, a desirable result as far as the government was concerned.[19] Allotment weakened the chiefs' power and decreased the cohesiveness of purpose found in close-knit villages.

Two years later, in 1886, the United States Congress considered passage of a universal allotment act. The agent at the consolidated Ponca, Pawnee, Otoe, and Oakland (Tonkawa) agency contended that the Pawnees "will be more easily led into taking their lands in severalty than any tribe in my charge."[20]

However, this was not totally true after passage of the Dawes Act in 1887. In 1889 the agent reported, "This tribe has a few progressive men, who are untiring in their effort to induce the tribe to accept the lands in severalty. They meet with strong opposition from their people."[21] Most Pawnee families continued to build mudlodges or live in tipis and to camp together for ceremonies and weeks-long visits. Within the Pawnee tribe factions developed opposing the 1887 Dawes Allotment Act and rejecting its implementation.[22] The chiefs requested permission to go to Washington DC to discuss this and the sale of surplus reservation land that would remain after completing individual land allotments.[23]

Unknown to the tribes involved, the United States government had other plans for the Pawnees and thirteen other tribes on surrounding reservations – the Absentee Shawnees, Potawatomis, Iowas, Sacs and Foxes, Kickapoos, Cheyennes and Arapahos, Wichitas, Kiowas, Comanches, Apaches, Otoes and Missourias, Poncas, Tonkawas, and Quapaws. Congress established the Cherokee Commission by an act of 2 March 1889 to discuss with the Cherokees the sale of the land known as the Cherokee Outlet (see map). The commissioners were to request that the Cherokees allow the government to settle these tribes within the Cherokee lands east of 96° longitude. Most tribes listed lived on reservations west of that line on land that the Cherokees and the other members of the Five Civilized Tribes relinquished to the United States in post–Civil War treaties.[24] (The Pawnees agreed to purchase their reservation from the Cherokees in the area west of 96° longitude with funds received from the sale of their Nebraska reservation.) Now the government wanted to move thousands of tribal people onto the remaining Cherokee lands in eastern Indian Territory.[25]

Needless to say, the Cherokees' principal chief, Joel B. Mayes, wrote a strong refusal to commissioners Lucius Fairchild, A. M. Wilson, and G. W. Sayre. Part of his reply stated:

Now these fourteen tribes have been settled on land of the five civilized tribes west of 96 degrees under treaty stipulation and executive orders, and their lands have been marked out to them where they have made homes in good faith in the Indian Territory in accordance with the treaties entered into with the five civilized tribes . . . and now to indicate the remotest idea of the President's picking up these fourteen tribes of Indians that have located on lands of the five civilized tribes in the Indian Territory and "dump" them all down

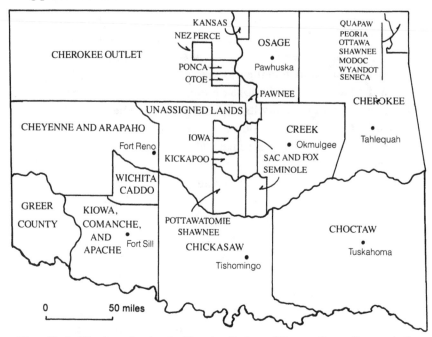

Map of Indian Territory showing the Cherokee Outlet and Pawnee, Ponca, Otoe, and other Indian reservations before allotment in the 1890s.

on the lands of the Cherokees east of 96 degrees among the homes of the people is preposterous in the extreme, and contrary to treaty stipulations as many of them already have deeds to those lands they occupy from the Cherokees. . . . Your commission very well know that there are no unoccupied lands east of 96 degrees upon which a tribe of Indians could be located.[26]

The government abandoned its plan, but the underlying motive was apparent. Ostensibly, if the United States government could have removed all the tribes mentioned to the Cherokee lands, large areas of Indian Territory would be emptied of native people. Then their vacated reservation lands would be made available for non-Indian settlement or, possibly, placement of other tribes. It was part of a continuing pattern of duplicity with which the Cherokees were quite familiar. One wonders how the government planned to persuade the fourteen tribes to accept such a scheme.[27]

The Pawnees and members of the neighboring tribes visited each other from time to time and exchanged views and information. As a result of the Pipe Dance or Hako adoption ceremony and other intertribal visits in Nebraska, some Pawnees, particularly the leading men, had "brothers" in nearby tribes such as the Poncas, Otoes, and Omahas. This relationship could become as strong as a kinship bond and could last their lifetimes.[28] After the tribes arrived in Indian Territory, contiguity of their tribal reservations enabled the brothers to visit one another occasionally. At times an entire group of tribesmen sojourned with another group. Effie Blaine attended Otoe and Pawnee encampments when she was a young woman; at such times new brothership bonds were created.[29] On a certain day the tribes' "brothers" and leaders and their families exchanged gifts of blankets and horses and other things.[30]

She also participated in the visits the Poncas made to Eagle Chief's camp near Camp Creek. They came in wagons and on horseback from their nearby reservation and stayed a few days or a week as guests of the Pitahawirata band. Wichita and Effie's son James, who was born in 1889, was beginning to walk at the time of one visit, and one of the Ponca leaders "adopted" him and gave him a Ponca name.[31]

This would have been shortly before allotment, and the Pawnee and Ponca leaders probably discussed additional land loss through allotment and the sale of the surplus reservation acreage to the government. The Poncas and Otoes opposed allotment and continued to do so for many years. The Pawnee leaders listened to their reasons, and their own reluctance and opposition likely were reinforced by these discussions. Although initially they said they accepted the law, they had lived long enough to know that the government always wanted more and more of their land. Now it seemed possible that all of their Mother Earth would eventually be lost to them.

On 6 September 1890 President Benjamin Harrison authorized allotment of the Pawnee reservation. On 20 December 1890, a letter to the commissioner informed him that the Pawnees accepted the law but were not ready to take allotments at that time.[32] Leading the twenty-one signers were Sun Chief (Chawi), Curly Chief, (Kitkahahki), Eagle Chief (Pitahawirata), Roaming Chief,[33] War Chief, and Good Chief.

Despite major tribal resistance to allotment, the government proceeded to appoint allotment agents. For the Pawnees and other tribes at their agency, Miss Helen P. Clarke became the agent on 17 March 1891. She had taught at the Indian Industrial School at Carlisle, Pennsylvania, and her mother was Sioux, which may have figured in her selection, since her appearance and background might make her more acceptable to the tribal people she would deal with.

Clarke arrived at the agency in April 1891 and hired four people to assist her: an interpreter, a surveyor, and two chain men to help the surveyor.[34] She was charged to allot 160 acres to heads of families, 80 acres to each single person over eighteen years of age, and the same amount to each orphan under eighteen and those tribal infants born before the president's proclamation that abolished the Pawnee reservation. Soon after her arrival, she and her crew took to the field to begin work.

The Dawes Act or Allotment Act provided for allotment of reservation land to individual tribesmen and for United States government to purchase the remaining acreage.[35] To make the acquisition easier, the president received authority to appoint a commission "to negotiate with the Cherokee Indians and with all other Indians owning or claiming lands laying west of the ninety-six degree of longitude in the Indian Territory for the cession to the U.S. of all their title, claim or interest of every kind or character in and to such lands."[36] The government was anxious to deal with the Cherokees in order to acquire the Cherokee Outlet,[37] then it would negotiate with other tribes that occupied reservations in that area to purchase their surplus lands. After that these lands would be opened for white settlement.

The Cherokee Commission, as it was first called, consisted of three appointed members. Later two of the original three could not serve, and David H. Jerome remained as chairman of the group, along with Judge Alfred M. Wilson of Arkansas and Warren G. Sayre of Indiana. It began functioning in May 1890 and became known as the Jerome Commission.

Allotment was in progress when the Jerome Commission arrived at the Pawnee agency on 31 October 1892. To say the Pawnee chiefs were eager to do business would be an exaggeration. In fact, after opening preliminaries on 31 October and 1 November, Curly Chief of the Kitkahahki band intimated that the Pawnees were in no hurry to sell their surplus land. He remarked, "Our land is money, our timber [is] money. It will not run away." He then suggested that the commissioners go deal with the Osages first.[38]

The commissioners refused. They informed the Pawnees sitting there that the government knew what was best. It was the Indians' friend and would always see to their best interests. The law declared that the surplus land would be sold to the government and to no one else. Finally, this sale with all its benefits would set the Pawnees on the white man's road, and that truly would be greatly to their advantage.[39]

On the second morning, more Pawnee leaders attended the meeting. The commissioner explained that after allotment there should be over 200,000 acres of surplus land that the United States would buy. Then the Pawnees would have enough money to build houses, put up fences, and start farming. Besides, there was nothing the Pawnees could do with all that extra land, Jerome declared. If there was reason not to farm their allotments, then the Pawnees could lease their farms to white men. The commission believed the mention of money from the land sale and leasing would appeal to the poverty-stricken Pawnees.

Now the Pawnees began to speak. The Chawi Sun Chief, apparently the head chief, said that not all the chiefs were there, and that he wished to think about the matter. Working for time, he declared that allotment should be completed before they discussed any sale. The Pawnees had paid the Cherokees for this land, and it was their decision about its sale. He too suggested the commission go elsewhere and deal with tribes who had finished their allotment.

The commission had been instructed to obtain the Tonkawa and Pawnee surplus land as quickly as it could.[40] Wilson told the assembled Pawnees the government planned to open the Cherokee Outlet and the Pawnee surplus land in it for settlement the next spring, because "thousands of white people were pushing Congress to get homes" and "the great father had to take care of all his children." One can imagine how these words fell on Pawnee ears.

He implied that if the matter of sale was not settled before then, the settlers would swarm in anyway and "be troublesome."[41] Unfazed by the calculated pressure of these words, Eagle Chief rose to speak. He declared he did not favor selling the surplus land because as the years went by there would be a natural increase in tribal numbers. If the Pawnees sold the land now, there would be no land for their grandchildren. He repeated what Curly Chief and Sun Chief said: the commission should go away and deal with tribes where allotment had been completed.[42] He reiterated that the

Pawnees owned the land by purchase from the Cherokees and had the right to decide about its sale.

Ignoring these remarks, Wilson asked to discuss the price of the surplus land before allotment was completed. This question suggests that there was to be an open discussion and agreement between the commission and the Pawnee leaders regarding price. But that was not the plan. Jerome then explained that the government offered the Pawnees $1.25 an acre to be made in two payments of $30,000 each. The sale proceeds would be placed in the United States Treasury and earn annual interest.

Curly Chief was the first to reply. He refused the offer of $1.25, saying that the Pawnees had never been hostile to the United States although other tribes were, and for this reason they wanted to be paid what they asked. In addition he stated firmly that every Pawnee should receive 160 acres in allotment, rather than some getting just 80 acres.[43] Sun Chief added that the government made offers for its own benefit, and the Pawnees wanted to do the same. He would not sell for $1.25.

Jerome responded that their land was not worth *that* much and added sanctimoniously, "You are getting all the meat and [want to] give us the bones." Baptiste Bayhylle, a Pawnee interpreter, countered by saying that people who buy a horse want to get it for the lowest price they can. The government was the same. He continued that the Pawnee land was worth more than the commissioners stated. Their land in Nebraska was now worth $20 an acre, and the Pawnees had received very little from the government when they were forced to sell it. He accused the commission of working for the white men who had no homes, and he wanted the commission to treat the Pawnees with justice.[44]

Now all the other chiefs and leaders who had not yet spoken spoke in turn, saying that $2.50 an acre was the price they wanted. Charles White, Roaming Chief, Young Chief, War Chief, Walking Bear, Lone Chief, Jackson, and Chowee Jake all repeated that the Pawnees had never attacked the United States. They had been on friendly terms and had served the country as United States Army Scouts. To the government $2.50 was not very much money, so it should pay that small extra amount. Since the white man could make a living on the land, it must be worth $2.50 an acre.

The next day, 4 November, the Pawnees returned determined to obtain the price they thought they should have. The commissioners, who had been through the process with other tribes, had learned the necessary tactics to deal with the government's wards. They knew they held the ultimate power, and their statements revealed their attitude. Sometimes they acted like a father cajoling his children with statements that meant, "Believe what we say, we know what is best for you, so do not argue." At other times they would make threatening statements or belittling, scolding, or sarcastic remarks. Often they emphasized the Pawnees' need for money. Their words made it seem that there would be a lot of money from the surplus land sale. With it and the continuing interest earned on the main portion of the sum, life would be easy indeed – and the Pawnees would no longer live in constant poverty.

Jerome told the Pawnees there were tribes that received less than $1.25 an acre, but they were willing to pay that much to the Pawnees because the commissioners felt sorry for them, even though their rocky land was poor and not worth so much.[45] He continued, "Your greatfather knows better what is good for you than you do yourself."[46] Then he reminded the Pawnees of all the good things the government had done for them, as if they should be grateful, ignoring the fact that in exchange for thousands of ceded acres, the government often reneged on its commitments.[47] As he spoke, the chiefs sat there remembering the years of hunger and illness and death their people had endured. They recalled the loss of their native home and sacred grounds and inadequate government adherence to treaty agreements.

Curly Chief did not conceal his anger as he rose to contend that some tribes may have received *more* than the commissioners said. He was not eager to take allotment, and if the government did not want to give the Pawnees what they asked for their land, then it could "just drop the matter right here." Jerome sternly replied that allotment was the law, and buying the surplus land was the law, and if the Pawnees did not want to conform, then Congress would make a law seeing that they did. He reminded them that the government controlled their land and property (and the money held in trust from previous land cession sales). He appeared shocked to hear that the Pawnees did not appreciate all the government had done for them.[48] Argument over the price per acre continued at each meeting. At one point Sun Chief told the commissioners, "I want to tell you that a long time ago when we used to trade our lands, we did not know what money was when we traded with the white man; we did not know that they were cheating us. *This* is different now. We all know what the value of money is from one cent up. And when we are making a trade with the white man, I do not think they will take advantage of us."

On 9 November, after a lapse of four days, the council resumed. The Pawnees came determined to receive the price they had now decided on. They no longer asked for $2.50, but demanded $1.50 an acre. Jerome, pleased with their retreat, said he would like to give them what they wanted but could not. Curly Chief said that $1.50 was the price, and that was all he would say on the matter. In a conciliatory tone, Charlie White thanked the commission for being patient, adding that the government could make money, but the Pawnees could not make land.[49]

The annual annuity was a matter of great importance to the Pawnees. Their 1857 treaty obligated the United States government to pay tribal members in money and goods as part of the agreement by which the Pawnees ceded land in Nebraska.[50] Now Curly Chief requested that the annuity be paid totally in cash and not half in unsuitable or unusable goods, such as clothing that did not fit. Jerome replied that it was necessary to settle one thing at a time. The commission's assignment was to acquire surplus lands at the government's price, and other matters were extraneous.

On 10 November the council resumed, with both sides fixed in position about the price per acre. Curly Chief led the discussion, saying, "We paid for this land, and we have the right to price it. I will not come down." Other chiefs rose to agree with him. War Chief declared that he wanted the commissioners to go back and tell the great father what the Pawnees had said. With some irritation, Jerome asked if they thought the commission could come and go at the Pawnees' request. War Chief replied, "That is what I said, and the land won't run." Jerome warned the assembled leaders that if the commission should leave, it might come back and offer them only $1 an acre. He then began what might be termed browbeating, with the implication that the tribe had better take what they could while they could.

Not at all threatened, Eagle Chief replied sternly regarding the United States perfidy in its relations with the Indians. He included the remark, "I have seen those tribes that make contracts with the government, just like you want to make with us – and they make a failure. They get the money and spend it and are poor. I am telling you. I have seen the tribes of Indians in the East that have dealt with the Government before and they are in poor condition. I saw harness that they made themselves out of gunny sacks because they had no means to get harness with."[51]

Jerome responded to the repeated Pawnee argument that they wanted to keep the land, or at least get their own price for it as an investment for their unborn children's future. He said that white people did not all stay on their farms and become farmers. Some of their children became carpenters, or perhaps shoemakers, and others followed other trades and left the farm. That is what could happen to the Pawnees. Not all their children might become farmers or stay on the farm. Therefore they did not need any land other than what they would receive as allotments. He added that white people did not get free land. If they wanted land they had to go out and buy it. He conveniently overlooked the impending great Oklahoma land rush, when lands taken from the Pawnees and other tribes would become free farms and homes for thousands of white families.

On 12 November the council resumed. Sun Chief stood. Slowly and deliberately, speaking in the manner of Pawnee chiefs, he informed the seated commissioners that the chiefs had decided to allow the young, educated, English-speaking men to deal with the commissioners. They were Mr. Coons, Mr. Rice, Mr. Morris, Mr. Townsend, Mr. Matlock, Mr. Morgan, and James Murie. Several reasons may have dictated this change in Pawnee tactics. To the chiefs their responses to the commissioners were logical and just. Not fluent in English, they could not be certain whether their remarks were correctly translated into English. Conversely, they did not know whether the commissioners' replies were accurately translated into Pawnee. They thought that the interpreters' intermediate position put the Pawnees at a disadvantage, a situation that had existed whenever they dealt with the United States government. Pawnee leaders often claimed that the final printed versions of treaties and other agreements did not state exactly what the Pawnees had been led to believe or what they had consented to in the original councils with the government.[52] The young, educated, English-speaking Pawnees could catch the meaning, nuances of speech, and inflections of voice that might enable them to respond more precisely to both the commissioners' and the Pawnee chiefs' points of view. Then they could translate them more accurately.

On 14 November 1892 Jerome acknowledged a group of young men in "civilian" dress, or the clothes that white men wore. Samuel Townsend handed him a written report of their conclusions. Apparently the young Pawnees were abreast of events occurring among tribes beyond the boundaries of Indian Territory. They claimed that the Sioux had received $1.50 an acre for their lands. Furthermore, the Cherokees received that much for the little strip of land (Cherokee Strip) lying north of the Cherokee Outlet. The commission had claimed in previous meetings with the Pawnee leaders that the government had never paid more than $1.25 an acre. Now the Pawnees knew otherwise and wanted the commissioners to know they knew it.

Dodging the accusation, the commissioners explained that the Pawnees did not understand each individual tribal land transaction, the complete situation, and the reasons for the discrepancies in prices. Then, taking another tack, the Pawnees said that sometimes the government gave land away, but sometimes it sold it. If it was sold, the Pawnees should receive more than was being offered. To prove the point, Townsend said that the Sisseton (Sioux) land sold for $2.50 an acre.

Reaching for an argument, Jerome replied that where the government sold land, if it charged more than it paid the tribes, it did so to cover expenses. For instance, clerks' salaries continued even while unsold land lay idle. Expenses went on and cost the government. Therefore it could not offer more money for land than it could sell it for.

Harry Coons replied that the government could afford to pay the Pawnees a quarter more than it was offering despite its arguments against doing so. Jerome retorted that there was no good reason the Pawnees should get "$1.50 per acre for your land lying along side of Oklahoma [Territory] when it was paid for at $1.25 – and when your land is not as good."[53] Coons replied that he knew the tribal lands referred to in the western part of the territory. They were dry and not always able to produce crops, whereas the Pawnee land could always do so.

The Pawnees traditionally discussed a matter in council until they reached a consensus. The trained attorneys who confronted them used methods and tactics that the Pawnees found ambiguous, deceptive, and alien to their ideas of proper discourse. In these circumstances they were unable to control the direction and flow of the discussion. Conditioned by years of authority and control by agents, schoolteachers, and other government figures, they had participated minimally in decisions affecting their political and economic lives.

1. United States Army Pawnee Scouts. Seated, left to right: Wichita Blaine, High Eagle, Robert Taylor, Billy Osborne. Second row: Walking Sun, Leading Fox, Rush Roberts Sr., Dog Chief (Simon Adams). (Author's collection)

2. Effie Blaine and her children. James G.
Blaine is standing. Date unknown. (Author's
collection)

3. United States Army Pawnee Scouts, including
John Box, standing second from left, High
Eagle, standing third from left, Captain Jim,
seated left, and James R. Murie, seated center.
(Courtesy of Nebraska State Historical Society)

4. Pawnee mudlodge in Indian Territory, about
1886. The Pawnees use this term instead of
"earth lodge." (Courtesy of Oklahoma
Historical Society)

5. Pawnee street scene early in the twentieth
century showing the Katz Department Store.
(Courtesy of Sue Guthrie Blair)

6. Myra Eppler, left, first row, and her class at
the Pawnee Indian Boarding School. Others are
identified as Gertrude Rapui, a white girl who
later married a Pawnee. Second row, un-
identified. Third row, Katie Tilden and Maggie
Box. Fourth row, Francis Smith and Mary Lone
Chief. Fields, Box, and Smith all had guardians.
(Courtesy of the Nebraska Historical Society)

7. Early Day oil fields near Pawnee, Oklahoma, drilled on reservation land near Pawnee Bill's ranch. (Courtesy Nebraska State Historical Society)

On 16 November the commissioners began to apply more pressure. They knew the Pawnee leaders' concern about their children born after the Dawes Act had received the president's signature. They said if the Pawnees agreed to the government price, then those children could be included in the allotment process. If they did not consent, they would not receive allotments. The government was prepared to pay the Pawnees a certain amount of cash immediately. Then, hoping to completely overcome their opposition, they announced that if the tribe accepted the government's price per acre, it would consent to give the total Pawnee annuity in cash.

There were more veiled threats. If the Pawnees did not sign the agreement to sell their surplus lands for $1.25 an acre, then Congress would decide the price. They intimated that the process could drag on for a long time. Every day they put off signing, the Pawnees were losing interest money and the allotment rights of the little children were diminishing. He reported the dire consequences when the Utes did not listen to him. They refused to sell the government 12 million acres: "They said they would do no such thing." After that the Colorado settlers drove them out, and they lost their land and had to go over into Utah.[54]

The chiefs now began to speak again. Curly Chief, now in his sixty-sixth year and apparently not intimidated or not believing the threats, said the Pawnees did not now oppose selling the land. However, they wanted the commissioners to go home so that the tribe could increase and get more allotments. Annoyed at Curly Chief's stubbornness, Jerome said, "The law does not give them [newborns] any, that is just what I have been trying to tell him. In that paper is the only thing that gives them allotments." Still not retreating, Curly Chief repeated that the Pawnees had always been loyal, that the chiefs would not sell for $1.25, and that the commissioners should leave unless they would agree to the price.[55]

That the Pawnees served in the United States Army Scouts carried a great deal of weight with the Indians. They could not understand why the government showed so little regard or gratitude for this sacrifice. Sergeant Peters said he was one of the first to enlist, and now it was obvious that he was poor, in ragged pantaloons, shirt, and moccasins. He lifted his head and said, "I get nothing from the government. You commissioners should listen to the chiefs." White Eagle, a Skidi chief, spoke: "We know you have visited other tribes. The chiefs made up their minds to go to a certain price and stand there. We are not selling salt, but something worth something. You should not try to scare us – talking about the western Indians. We *helped* you put them on reservations. I am now nearly blind, I have no pension, but white soldiers do. The commission should take pity on us and give us what we ask."[56]

Harry Coons told the commissioners that the chiefs were sensible men and were trying to do the best for their people, but if the commissioners were trying to scare them into trading, they could not be intimidated. Now they wanted to take the paper with the government's proposition that the commissioners had brought and adjourn to discuss it.

A week later the council resumed, on 23 November. During the previous week the chiefs had met with their bands and the young men to discuss the "paper" and decide what to do. They were frustrated with their inability to persuade the commission to agree with them. Earlier they had told the commissioners they wanted to go to Washington to see the great father to discuss their side of the issue, but a previous request and this request to visit President Harrison were denied.[57] Had they known his pronouncements on allotment and Indian land acquisition, they would have been even more discouraged with the obdurate stance of the commissioners. In his third annual message to Congress, 9 December 1891, the president said:

> The good work of reducing the larger Indian reservations by allot-
> ments in severalty to the Indians and the cession of the remaining
> lands to the United States for disposition under the homestead law
> has been prosecuted during the year with energy and success. In
> September last, I was able to open to settlement in the Territory
> of Oklahoma 900,000 acres of land, all of which was taken up by
> settlers in a single day. . . . Since March 4, 1889, about 23,000,000
> acres have been separated from Indian reservations and added to
> the public domain for the use of those who desired to secure free
> homes under our beneficent law.[58]

The 23 November meeting opened with Jerome asking to hear what the chiefs had to say. Sun Chief replied that they had discussed various matters but that today he was ill and would let Curly Chief speak for him. Curly Chief said, "I am coming to the place where we can agree." Remembering the past, he stated that the government did not always do what it promised, and that was of concern to him. When the chiefs made the last agreement with the government, it told the people that the government would always pay in gold and silver. Now he heard that it would pay in paper, and the Pawnees did not want that.[59]

Eagle Chief had apparently retreated from his strong position of demanding more money than the government would give for the surplus land. He asked, "Do you refuse $1.50 an acre for the land? Do you think you could give me $1.50 an acre?" Replying firmly to this plea, Jerome said he had told him from the beginning what the price was and that he was not able to change it. Eagle Chief continued that he had heard the Iowas and Tonkawas had not yet received any money from their agreement. "If you serve me that way and I give up my land, it would probably be a long time before I get any money."

Both Jerome and Sayre explained that the Pawnee contract said they were immediately to be paid $60,000 in gold and silver. This amount would come from the total land purchase price as soon as Congress ratified the agreement. The annuity would also be paid in metal currency rather than partly in goods and partly in money as before.

Indicating that some chiefs had shifted their position, Brave Chief said they had been a long time coming to an agreement. When they did sign, they wanted the commissioners to stand and swear before God. Then the Pawnees would know they were truthful. "When you stand up it is to show us that what is in that paper will continue as long as the Government lasts."[60]

However, War Chief, a dissenter, remarked, "The government sent you here, so we ask you to take pity on us and give us $1.50 an acre for our land. I do not like the idea of the allotting agent laying us off and the President issuing the order to open our country. It does not look right to me." Showing ambivalence, he added, "If we get the money and get quite a sum and make good use of it, we can be comfortable. I do not disbelieve the doings of the government."[61]

Bolstered by War Chief's remarks, Eagle Chief again rose. He said that he had not been offended the day he was absent and heard that the commissioners spoke harshly to his people. He had not been angry because the commissioners and chiefs had important business to discuss, and anger had no place there. It was true that he had not made up his mind to accept the offer, but "I am working for my people's interest. You are trying to buy this land so that you may be rewarded. It is all right for you to want to stay here all winter because you get $16.00 in one day, and I am here, too, but I do not get one cent." He added sardonically, "You ought to let the councils go on for a long time, the longer the councils go on, the more money you make. Tomorrow we will come back and bring all the people and let them vote, and if the people say sell the land, then it goes, but I won't say let it go. If the majority say sell it, then it goes."[62]

Jerome responded to Eagle Chief, including in his remarks the statement that the commissioners could make a lot more money doing something other than government work. Looking at the assemblage, he said, "I want him to understand that every day that I stay and work with the Indians in the Indian Territory, I lose more money than he says I am getting." The Pawnees said nothing.

More talk followed, with the commissioners reiterating how much better off the Pawnees would be with the extra money they would have. They reminded the leaders that if the annuity money was all in cash, they would be far ahead. Of course it would be in cash only if they signed to sell their land for $1.25. It did not escape the leaders that the annuity, whether paid in cash or not, had nothing to do with the present land sale. They recognized the offer as a bribe and pointed this out to the commissioners. Nevertheless, having the annuity in cash was a powerful selling point. Knife Chief said they had been trying to get the payment method changed for a long time. Another declared that the commissary was full of their goods, but they had to go to the agent like beggars to get food that was lawfully theirs. He repeated that the clothing the agent ordered was too big or too small, and they could not wear it. Curly Chief added, "I have seen white men go into a store and try on five or six suits. They do not take the first one, they get one that fits."[63]

Although Sun Chief was ill and had not intended to speak, he said he felt that he must for his people's sake. Some of his remarks follow:

> Grandfather, you can look in the room and see that there are not enough people here. I have a band of men. Of course it is my duty to look after them and their interest. You have been standing upon a quarter you are talking about. For my part, I have been standing on the ground we are talking about. It is true, Grandfather, that you are coming towards us and we are coming to meet you. Now let us be slow and make this agreement carefully, so it is right. One of my

sub-chiefs spoke and seemed to be opposed to selling the land at your price. I do not feel hard toward him. He is here taking it all in, but tonight that chief will think the matter over, because I have just as good as consented, but I do not want to sign the paper tonight. We will get the Young Men in here tomorrow and then vote and read the paper over and commence signing.[64]

When the head chief said these words, it meant the matter was settled. He agreed to sell their land at the government's price, and he expected other band chiefs to consent also. He was ill and may have been tired of the struggle.

On the morning of 24 November the participants gathered. Jerome invited any Pawnee who wanted to speak to do so. Ralph Weeks, who began his education in the agency school in Nebraska, was the first speaker. He addressed the three men as "Honorable Cherokee Commission." Speaking politely, he thanked them for their patience during the proceedings. He had little to add to what the chiefs and others had said, but he declared, "We are but a remnant of what was once a strong tribe; it seems but yesterday that we were boasting of our strength. Today, we are a fast disappearing people." Continuing, he added that the Pawnees could not be left behind on the road to civilization. They must adopt the dress, manners, and ways of the "highest type of American civilization."[65] Eagle Chief, the Pitahawirata band chief, stood and said that his kinsmen Mr. Weeks, his uncle; William Morgan, his nephew; War Chief, his uncle; and Sun Chief, his relative (all Chawis) had talked to him and asked him to agree to the commission's proposition, and "that whatever they do, I will follow."

Sun Chief came into the room with his band leaders. He turned to the oldest chief, Curly Chief, and asked him to speak for all the chiefs. Curly Chief then delivered the last speech made by a Pawnee before the loss of the lands they believed they should not have to sell. They had argued, tried to persuade, pleaded, and asked for justice, but to no avail:

Now Grandfather, I come before you today. Today I understand is the Great Spirit's day and the great father's day. I want you to listen and after you have heard what I say, I hope you will be in favor of what I want. You know yesterday evening that I was coming towards you and I was about to reach you.

I want you commissioners to stand up and then I want to ask my people who are in favor of taking allotments to stand up and you can see for yourselves those that are in favor of selling the land. Those that sit down are against it. (All stand up.) The Tribe left it to me to decide this important question: alone I could not have the heart to decide it, so I asked my tribe, and you see what they say – the land belongs to them. Now Grandfather, today is a day that is set off for prayers and thanksgiving – you see that we will sell the land. We will sign the treaty when you give us $100.00 a head. I am looking after the interest of the young men that have not implements to work with. They want this so they can start improving their places. What is left we will leave in the Treasury to draw interest annually. The other parts we agree that you have fixed right.[66]

He added that they all agreed to this at the tribal meeting and feast that morning. So, without the usual argument, Jerome agreed to this request and changed the "paper" to read $80,000 instead of $60,000. When this was done the chiefs and other men slowly lined up to sign the document.

Of the 203 men in the tribe over twenty-one years of age, 158 signed the document, including Wichita Blaine and John Box. Jerome said that some men were not present because they were away at school. Others were away at work, and some who had not attended the councils were indifferent and would be satisfied with whatever the others decided.[67] He might have added that some continued to oppose the government's taking their land and so stayed away and refused to sign.

President Harrison transmitted the signed agreement to Congress on 4 January 1893. On 3 March 1893 it was ratified by Congress.[68] The Pawnees accepted $1.25 an acre. They had four months to finish selecting their allotments. They were to receive their annuity in coin and not in paper warrants, and $80,000 would be divided and paid per capita. The rest of the surplus land sale money would be placed in the United States Treasury at 5 percent interest, to be distributed to the tribe annually.

Allotment was completed in the summer of 1893. The Blaines – Wichita, Effie, their son James, and their daughter, Carrie, two months old – received 160-acre allotments separated from one another by several miles. Effie's was not far from the site of her deceased father's camp. Her son's and daughter's allotments lay about two miles southeast on

the northern edge of the present village of Maramec, and Wichita's land
was some three miles east of his children's in a wooded area. It was not
far from that of Tom Wichita, the uncle who had raised him.[69] Many
families chose land so that each individual's allotment bordered another's
selection. The Blaines did not do this, except for Wichita's two aunts,
whose land lay next to Effie's. The allotments of John and Mary Box and
their five children lay scattered several miles apart. The reason for this
dispersion is not known. In some cases nationwide allotting agents made
arbitrary assignments when individuals did not or would not make their
own selections.[70]

There were 820 Pawnees listed, many of whom now had English names
given them by Miss Clarke. The tribe retained 112,710.14 acres in allotments, with 840 acres set aside for schools and cemeteries; 169,320
surplus acres remained of the original 283,019,98 acres of the Pawnee
reservation.[71] On 19 August 1893 President Grover Cleveland declared
by proclamation that "all the lands acquired from the Cherokee Nation
of Indians, the Tonkawa tribe of Indians and the Pawnee tribe of Indians
by the three several agreements aforesaid will at the hour of 12 o'clock
noon (central standard time) on Saturday, the 16th day of the month of
September, A.D. 1893, be opened to settlement."[72]

It has been said that the 1893 run was the biggest horse race in the
world. Some 100,000 persons rushed in by horse, by wagon, and on foot.
They overran, claimed, and occupied former Pawnee lands and other
ceded tribal lands.[73] Wichita Blaine said all you had to do was look across
the road to see a white man and his family. "They were that close. They
put up fences so that we could not hunt, and we had to go the long way
around to visit our families and friends. They made it hard."[74]

After allotment, John Box continued to follow the white man's road and
expanded his life as a comparatively prosperous farmer with a growing
family. He and his wife, Mary, had a new house and new barn built, planted
crops, and cultivated a beautiful orchard. Then one day a terrible storm
destroyed much of what he had built and planted. Addie Troth Yellow
Calf, his niece, said this about the catastrophe:

> John Box had one of the most beautiful farms on his allotment.
> There was a big house, barns, orchard, and vineyard. The house
> stood on a rise and commanded a beautiful view. One day a tornado

came, and the family just had time to get down into the storm cellar. They were quite frightened by the sound outside. When it passed they came up out of the cellar. They looked around. Everything was ruined: buildings down, the trees broken – all gone. When he saw this, John Box tore off his white man's clothes, except some underwear, and ran to the top of the hill while the family watched in fear. He stood on the hill and yelled and shouted and shook his fist at the sky. His wife explained to the frightened children and niece that he was angry and asking Tirawahat why he had done this. He'd tried hard to follow the white man's road and worked hard, hard. Now everything was gone. When he came down the hill, he said he would never farm again and that he should not have tried to be like a white man. Addie never forgot and would vividly describe his standing on the rise against the sky, stripped, with his hair in braids blowing in the wind, shouting and gesturing wildly.[75]

Some Pawnees' experiences also indicated that allotment and loss of their land brought misfortune. Some became poor when they lived isolated from the former village or camp life with its shared efforts to support each family. Illness and death of family members continued and impeded efforts to farm and become self-supporting. Whether Wichita Blaine accepted as his allotment the same land he had recently farmed is not certain. His allotment lay several miles from Effie's, and where they decided to live is unknown. They sometimes stayed with Lulu Otter, their kinswoman, and camped with her on her allotment east of Pawnee. There were no buildings, and they lived in tipis. In the evening the relatives sat around, and Wichita would sing Pawnee songs.[76] Even in the new world of plows, houses, and fences, they needed the traditional and sacred world that these songs represented.

As it turned out, the greatest beneficiaries of allotment were not the Pawnees but the white men who acquired their land in the years that followed. Financial need and other reasons often caused the sale or loss of family land. Only a small percentage of the original allotments remain in Pawnee hands.[77]

FOUR

The Spirits Come

I am lonely. Here he comes. Mother [Moon], here he comes. You will be saying,
Son, here he comes. You will be saying, here he comes.
                    Pawnee Ghost Dance song

Now you go home and be good Indians and quit dancing.
                    Pawnee Indian agent, 1892

The Pawnees suffered population loss far greater than population re-
plenishment after coming to Indian Territory. Coming in a time of great
sadness, the Ghost Dance allowed Wichita and Effie to cope with their
sorrows. They had lost two little boys about four and five years old, who
suddenly became sick and died. Wichita would try to forget his sorrow by
working hard in his fields. He would work all day until after dark, then
come home and cry in the shed. In the evening he and Effie would go
up on a little hill and weep. Their family came and tried to console them
to no avail. After a month Wichita's uncle came and told him it was not
good to pursue anything like this; he would make himself sick. It was a
bad sign to be put under such an influence. But Wichita continued to
mourn for about another month. Every evening when he came home,
he could imagine the little boys running to him as they used to; there
were just too many memories. He and Effie continued to go up on the
little hill to weep and console each other. So his uncle came over again
and talked sternly to them, telling them forcefully not to pursue this any
more. Then he said, "Why don't you go and see this new dance, this Spirit

Dance? Why don't you go over there? This way you will see other people and you will hear songs, and who knows, something good might come of it. They say that sometimes people who go to these dances see their loved ones in their dreams."

Reluctantly, Wichita and Effie decided to go, visit with other people, and maybe dance a little. They could hear the drum from where they lived, so the dance must have been at the old Eagle Chief camp on a bend of Camp Creek. One evening they went to the Ghost Dance and believed in it, and they continued to attend for many years.[1]

The Pawnees were not the first tribe in the territory to accept the Ghost Dance. A Northern Arapaho, Sitting Bull, brought the dance to the Southern Cheyenne reservation in Oklahoma Territory in the fall of 1890. He advised the people to accept allotment and sale of their surplus land in order to obtain much-needed funds. Even though they sold the lands, he prophesied, the Messiah would return their land to them.[2] Later, Pawnees who accepted the Ghost Dance hoped their land would be returned to them, if they believed and took part in it.

The Ghost Dance or Spirit Dance received intense government scrutiny, and there were attempts at suppression. Fear grew that its performance could instigate Indian rebellion and uprisings on the reservations. It originated in the western United States, where it flourished among some tribes, including some California tribes in the 1870s. In Nevada in 1889 a Paiute, Wovoka or Jack Wilson, dreamed he journeyed to the spirit world. There he saw God and received the message that he must return to his people and teach them to live peacefully together and with the whites. Certain rituals performed in a peaceful way would cause God to bring back the happy days of the past. There would be no overwhelming illnesses or oppression from the white man. Game would be restored so there would be food. They would see their spirit relatives again, and the Indian people would be free to live as they had before the white man came. At this time in American Indian history it was a powerful message.

When Wovoka returned to his people, he began his teachings and devised a ceremony accompanied by songs and dance. Within a short time one tribe after another heard about the man called the Messiah or prophet. They also heard about the wonders brought by performing the Spirit or Ghost Dance. Some tribes sent envoys great distances to visit Wovoka to learn his message firsthand. On the Pine Ridge Reservation, the Ghost Dance performance alarmed the overly apprehensive Indian agent and the military, and the great tragedy of Wounded Knee resulted. There on 29 December 1890, army troops massacred over a hundred men, women, and children because of their participation.[3]

It is not surprising the Ghost Dance religion spread so rapidly from tribe to tribe over the mountains and across the prairies and plains. By this time its adherents, mainly restricted to reservations, lived a life totally alien to tradition. They found their daily existence one of frustration, hunger, persistent illness, death, and debilitating anomie.

After Wounded Knee, Indian agents were alerted to the possibilities of violence. Responding to a letter of 8 January 1891 from the commissioner of Indian affairs, Pawnee agent D. J. M. Wood replied that he had visited the Indians at a dance and reported, "I know there has been no Ghost dance here or at any of our [sub]Agencies."[4]

At this time, besides the high number of serious illnesses and deaths, the Pawnees were beset by numerous difficulties with the whites around them, who raided their forests for timber, attempted to graze their cattle on the reservation, and stole Pawnee horses. A Stillwater newspaper reported that Curly Chief and some other men were camped outside the town, "bold and defiant." Agent Wood said that was a lie, because Curly Chief – "a kinder man you could not find" – was in Arkansas City on the Kansas border at that time. Another newspaper announced that Indians had shot Wood. He reported that that too was false. As part of the alarm, whites in the area were said to be arming themselves so the Indians could not scalp them. It was Wood's opinion that if the whites and the newspapers would let the Indians alone and mind their own business, "they will enjoy life much better and sleep more sweetly at night." All 1,730 Indians under his agency – Poncas, Otoes, Missourias, Tonkawas, and Pawnees – were going peacefully about their business in spite of all the clamor and accusations directed against them.[5]

Some of these alarms may have been caused by fears the Ghost Dance aroused in the white population. They had heard that the whites were going to be pushed aside and would disappear, and that the land would be left in the hands of its original owners. The Indians believed such an event would be an act of their supreme being, an idea the non-Indians did not accept. Such a catastrophe would be brought about by Indians on the warpath, not by God, who surely was on the side of the whites in the settlement and development of the country. As has been said, "They came to identify God, freedom and acquisitiveness with the image of the continent they were seeking to possess. If there had been room for the Indian in such a scheme, they would have included him."[6] But there was no room. The belief in Manifest Destiny increased with every mile the settler, land speculator, and profit-minded individual pushed westward across and onto Indian land. This philosophy, with its disregard for the native inhabitants, contributed to the problems that eventually led to the acceptance of the Ghost Dance religion. Messianic movements such as the Ghost Dance, whenever and wherever they arise, are the outcome of a stressed society. In the case of the Native Americans, such movements have the goal of reviving or maintaining "distinctive elements of Indian culture."[7]

In Wovoka's vision of his visit to a Spirit Land village, he saw deceased members of his family and tribe living peacefully and happily together. They pursued the cohesive, balanced life of their ancestors before its derangement and destruction by whites. He watched the dead dance, play their games, and do all the enjoyable things that were once possible. When he returned home and told of his experience, he began to gather converts and explained that he had been instructed to teach a dance. Those who took part in it would see once again the members of their families who had died.[8]

This revelation was extremely important among those tribes, like the Pawnees, who had lost so many family members. Many Indian societies believed that at death the individual traveled to Spirit Land, where he was warmly welcomed by deceased members of his family, among whom he would live happily in an earthlike village. The Pawnees believed this, and their mythology contains numerous references to interaction with the spirits of their ancestors. They could return from Spirit Land and reappear in human form to seek out their kin. A Skidi myth says that the dead take their belongings to Spirit Land and lead a life they enjoy. Games there are the same as on earth. People hunt buffalo, and there is no sickness, only happiness. Each family has a village, and all descendants of that family go there when they die.[9]

Sometimes the dead cannot be seen, but they return and their voices can be heard. Once Wichita Blaine and other United States Pawnee Army Scouts visited an abandoned village site in Nebraska. In the evening's stillness, they heard voices and village sounds as if the people were still alive.[10]

In early January 1891 Lt. H. L. Scott, Seventh Cavalry, stationed at Fort Sill, reported hearing that the prophet Sitting Bull would be coming to a dance to be held some fifteen miles from Anadarko, "to give the feather to the Wichitas, as they term it, about the next full moon." He explained that this meant that when Sitting Bull visits a tribe, he selects seven men to whom he gives an eagle tail feather. He then teaches them the songs and "doctrines," and they become leaders of the dance for that tribe.[11] Sitting Bull had not yet arrived, and the tribesmen danced day and night, awaiting his coming. Already some converted Caddos claimed to have healing powers, to be able to foretell events and find stolen or lost property. The "Wichitas seem to be pupils of the Caddos," according to Scott.[12]

Some time later, Sitting Bull arrived at Keechei (Kichai) Creek, where the Wichitas and Caddos eagerly awaited him. He had traveled two hundred miles and brought about twenty young Arapahos with him. Lieutenant Scott's description of him says:

Sitting Bull was found to be a most interesting Indian, partly from his prominence in spreading this religion and partly from his personality. He is above the average Indian in intelligence and is the most graceful sign talker that I have met in the southwest; he is 37½ years old, has rather a light complexion and (what is unusual in an Indian) gray eyes, he is said to be a full blood Arapaho, is about five feet eight inches high, unostentatious in his manner, dignified in his bearing and while his face is by no means handsome yet his smile is very winning, and my opinion formed before seeing him began to change in his favor almost immediately.

It is very difficult to get an opportunity to talk with him quietly on account of the persistent manner in which he was followed about, all sorts of people wanted to touch him, men and women would come and rub their hands on him and cry which demonstration he received with a patient fortitude that was rather ludicrous at times.

While he by no means told us everything he knew, it was easy to believe that he was by no means the rank imposter that I had before considered him, he makes no demands for presents while at these camps, this trip entailed a ride of 200 miles in the winter season at the request of the Wichitas, for which I understand that they paid him fifty dollars before starting, but everything that was given him while at this camp was a voluntary gift prompted entirely by the good wishes of the giver, one would present him with a buckskin, another a calico shirt or a blanket, etc. He took but little property away when he left, and I saw but one horse that I thought he had not brought down with him.

Upon being asked concerning his religion, he said that all I heard must not be attributed to him as some of it was false; that he does not believe that he saw the veritable "Jesus" alive in the North, but he did see a man there whom "Jesus had Helped or inspired, this person told him that if he persevered in the dance that it would cause sickness and death to disappear." He avoided some of the questions about the coming of the buffalo, etc., and under the circumstances it was not possible to draw him out further and the subject of religion was then dropped with the intention of taking it up at a more favorable time, but this time never came. . . . A great many of the doings seen at these dances, are the afterthoughts of all kinds of people. . . . These are not the teachings of Sitting Bull although he refrains from interfering with them through policy. He took no part in the humbuggery going on, but danced and sang like the humblest individual there. . . . He is largely sincere in his teaching and there is this to be said in his favor, that he has given these people a better religion than they ever had before, taught them precepts which if faithfully carried out will bring them into better accord with their white neighbors and has prepared them for their final Christianization, and for this he is entitled to no little credit.[13]

It was during these days when Sitting Bull stayed among the Wichitas and Caddos that Frank White, a Kitkahahki who was there, became converted to the Ghost Dance religion. He fervently believed in the message of Wovoka and participated in the Ghost Dance. During it he had a trance in which he saw the Messiah and the village that Wovoka described. The people in the village danced in a circle with hands joined and sang songs. Some songs that came to him in the trance were in the Pawnee language.[14] When he became conscious he revealed to the leader what he had seen and heard. After this he became known as a prophet and, filled with messianic fervor, decided to return to his Pawnee people.[15]

He may have returned with a group of three hundred or more Pawnees who were said to have visited the Kiowa, Comanche, and Wichita country in the late summer of 1891. According to a newspaper report, they had been guests of Lone Wolf, the Kiowa leader; Quanah Parker, the Comanche chief; and Chief Towakoni of the Wichitas. They began their return home with "about 150" horses given them by their hosts. They were also said to have been "supplied with enough cattle to allow them several feasts on their road home."[16]

The first official government acknowledgment of a Ghost Dance performance on the Pawnee reservation came in November 1891. In his monthly report for October agency clerk Charles Hill observed, "During the latter part of the month what was called a ghost dance, was reported as being in progress in the Petahawerat band on Camp creek. I at once sent an order that it be discontinued, and the Indians dispersed."[17]

James Murie claimed that Frank White first took the Ghost dance to the Pitahawirata band. When he arrived in the fall of 1891, he revealed his vision and his mission to relatives and friends. He is supposed to have said, "The kingdom is coming soon now, so the people must prepare. This that I have is called ghost dancing. You must stop working because when the kingdom comes, you won't take plows or things like that along. That's not ours."[18]

Wichita and Effie Blaine's uncle's statement that there was a new dance where the dead could be seen in dreams seems to confirm its early performance in that band. It was known as one of the most religiously conservative bands, and Christianity had made few inroads. This family belonged to the Pitahawirata band's Kawarakis division, which claimed to be the original receiver of Pawnee religious belief systems and saw its responsibility as advocating and maintaining the ancient beliefs and rituals. To acknowledge his belief in the old ways, Wichita Blaine arose each morning, went outside, faced the east, and prayed. The smoke from his pipe carried his prayers upward to Tirawahat.[19] White may have approached this band understanding its resistance to white ways and its tolerance for Indian-inspired beliefs.

White first gathered a small group of singers to teach them Ghost Dance songs. They were mainly Arapaho and Wichita songs from the original source, with a few Pawnee songs composed by White. These singers, four women and three men, were to assist White in the dancing.[20] According to Murie,

> As soon as they could sing a few songs they went to a camp to dance. They selected a space east of the camp and started to dance. Whenever the prophet shouted, the dancers dropped to the ground in a trance. Some of the dancers began to mourn and others shook all over, for a mysterious spirit took possession of them. They danced a short time. The prophet told them of his experiences. He told the people that if they made up their minds to dance and see the Messiah and their dead relatives, they would fall and see them; that the principal thing in the dance was to mourn and see the Messiah and their dead relatives, they would fall and be humble in spirit. He then sent them home.[21]

Now that White had introduced the Ghost Dance to a small core of tribal members, he moved to establish his position with others. Respecting Pawnee tradition, he accepted several chiefs' invitation to a council on Camp Creek to make his new role known to them. He needed their approval for the introduction of a nontraditional procedure, because they and the leaders of the sacred societies maintained authority over social and religious activities. Having listened to him to ascertain the authenticity and sincerity of his belief, they agreed that he could hold a dance for the entire village. White had followed tradition. It was customary for a Pawnee who claimed to have had a sacred vision to present himself before certain sacred society leaders to tell of his experience and have the authenticity of the vision verified or rejected according to their perception of his veracity. The leaders accepted White's account of his visionary experience and were satisfied with his appeal. A special tipi erected near the dance ground became the place for White and his singers to stay.

After this acceptance, White spoke and asked those interested in participating to bring paint to the special tipi the following day so their faces could be painted for the dance. Those who came to the tipi to be painted brought gifts for the prophet, as was done whenever someone sought information or sacred knowledge belonging to another. With their faces painted, the group, led by White, left the tipi. He and the singers joined hands with them, and they began to sing and dance in a circle. Anticipating that something of great importance was about to happen, other people began to gather around the edge of the dance ground. As they watched the rapid side stepping of the dancers and heard the words of the songs, the psychological effects soon could be seen. According to Murie, "Some did not get into the ring for an unknown spirit took possession of them and stopped them. They raised their hands to the skies and began to cry. In the ring the dancers began to tremble; some seemed crazy. When the prophet went to them, they fell to the ground. Late in the evening, they quit dancing, and they feasted." After that they danced again until about ten o'clock. Completely absorbed by the experience, men and women ended the day with mourning, crying and "having shaking fits." Before sunrise they began dancing again.[22]

Thus did many Pawnees quickly accept the Ghost Dance. James Mooney, a student of the movement, said, "Of all these tribes the Pawnee took most interest in the new doctrine, becoming as much devoted to the Ghost Dance as the Arapaho themselves."[23]

Wichita Blaine told his grandson about his participation, saying,

Yes, it is true, I used to go to these dances. When I first started, as you have been told before, when Grandma and I had lost our two little boys, who would have been your uncles, we were very sad. My uncle urged us to go to this dance. We went a few times and would dance. One day, in the early afternoon, they were dancing and I sat down near the ring where the dancers were. I lighted a pipe and smoked a little bit, then put the pipe out, put it back in its bag, and laid it down on the ground beside me. And just about that time, it looked like something happened. Someone spoke to me. Someone said from above, "Son, look this way." And I raised my eyes up, the clouds rolled swiftly back, and the sun shined. A big bright bolt of sunshine came down, opening up the clouds. As it came down toward the earth, I immediately dropped my eyes to the earth, where the sun had struck the ground. There were my two boys standing there. They looked so happy, and I never felt as happy as at that time – at any time during my life. I was so glad to see them. All my sorrow left me. I expected the two boys to come running towards me as they used to always do. But they just stood there and smiled right at me.

I got up and started to walk toward them. They looked so happy to see me coming. As I walked toward them, I looked up and there was a ring of people revolving in a circle coming downward. They came down and down. I stopped. These people came down and they were in a circle. And as the circle revolved they gradually encircled my two boys. Then the circle went back up, and my two sons slowly rose with them. In my heart I knew they were where Tirawahat is. It was just like the way we believe, just the way we have always believed, that when we die, we go back to Tirawahat. As I said, all my sorrow left. This was a blessing that God gave me, a vision that he let me see my boys. When I came to, my vision became a song. When I became strong enough to sit up and got my breath, I sang this song: "Father said, you must come and you will see / Father said, you must come and you will see."

When Wichita came to he was surprised to find that he was lying on the ground and there was a man sitting with him, holding his head in his lap. He related what he had seen, and this man announced it to the people.[24]

It is possible that Wichita Blaine and others who held seats or positions in the sacred societies and possessed sacred bundles influenced others to participate in the Ghost Dance.[25] Sacred society members' interest in the new ritual may have been generated because the older curing rituals and appeals to the sacred beings were not preventing the tragic loss of lives. After Pawnee arrival in Indian Territory, the traditional societies continued to function as best they could in order to maintain the relationship with the sacred beings that was considered necessary for Pawnee survival.[26]

As the years went by, both Wichita and Effie Blaine created songs received in Ghost Dance visions. One is called "The Yellow Star."

> The Yellow Star has noticed me,
> Furthermore it gave me a standing yellow feather,
> That Yellow Star.[27]

The wondrous star came to Wichita Blaine and told him, "I am the star which you see in the sky at night." In his vision, the star appeared to him as a woman holding a yellow painted eagle feather. She handed him the feather and told him that all the stars in the sky are people. She gave him the right to have a yellow feather to use in mesmerizing people in the Ghost Dance.[28]

Held in awe, Frank White controlled the dance, its performance, and any features added to it. By waving a feather, he could induce a trance in a dancer, who sank to the ground unconscious. If a vision resulted, White interpreted its meaning. The dancer was also expected to bring the prophet a gift after this event. Any suggested change in an individual's dress or decoration received in a trance had to be approved by White. If a person had a vision in which he was instructed to give a dance, he must have White's consent.[29]

In a short time, White added more ceremony and individual roles to the basic forms he first used to introduce the ceremony. Seven singers became an integral part of the dance. One song that resulted from their participation said,

> There they stand with beautiful voices.
> Those with beautiful feathers in their hair.[30]

Effie Blaine remembered that at a dance the seven would slowly and reverently come out of the special tipi, walk around and stop in front of a woman, and say, "You have been selected to bless this dance." She would then be led into the tipi; her face was painted, and she became holy for that day.

At the end of a Ghost Dance, Effie Blaine said the people would be in a circle and would all move to the center. Then they would go back, then dance into the center again. As they backed out toward the edge of the circle, they held their arms up. The last time when they all met in the center, each person bent over as if there was a heavy burden on his back. Then they would take off their blankets or shawls and shake them as if to cast off their heavy sorrows. As each one straightened up, he would smile or have a look of peace on his face. Then the dance ended, she said. This act of shaking the shawl or blanket as a final movement in the Ghost Dance came from the Arapaho closing song. It said,

> Crow [or Raven] holloa at me.
> When he makes me get up to dance.
> He told me now to stop.[31]

The seven singers wore eagle or crow feathers in their hair. The Pawnees said that the eagle can reach great heights and can see all below, while the crow is able to find things. These two birds came to represent the two sides in the hand game that came to be associated with the Ghost Dance. Murie said the game resulted from a dancer's vision in 1904.[32]

By December 1891 the agent found that the Pawnees now neglected their farmwork to attend the Ghost Dance. To exert his control over their actions, he stopped the agency mill from grinding their wheat for food. The clerk received instructions to tell the Pawnees this, and that if they did not plant grain (winter wheat), they would not have food. Also, he was to say that the Messiah would not come, that they were being deceived by Frank White, and that they were to stop dancing, disperse, and get busy on their farms. The agency police were to be told emphatically that the United States government did not pay them to attend the Ghost Dance or perform in it. They were hired to maintain peace and order and to follow civilized pursuits. Any man following the Ghost Dance would be relieved of duty. Wichita Blaine did not become a member of the police until fall of the following year, so at this time in 1891 he participated in the dance.[33]

Understandably, members of the Indian police force were drawn in two directions. They received certain status and authority as well as rations and pay. Nevertheless, the men faced the fact that some of their family members were devoted participants in the Ghost Dance that the police were expected to stop. They, like other tribal members, lived a government-controlled reservation life with all the adversities, resentments, and cultural conflicts that accumulated over the years. The Ghost Dance offered emotional release for these negative feelings, and the police were not immune to its persuasive message. As an example, in January 1892 William Morgan, Kitkahahki, became a private in the police force, taking the place of William Hunt. In June word reached the agency that Hunt had become a "new prophet."[34]

Agent Wood received an "insider's view" of the Ghost Dance in a letter dated 6 December 1891, composed by James R. Murie (1862–1921), a half-blood Skidi who had been educated at Hampton Institute, Virginia. He returned to the reservation, and through the years he worked at the agency and the school. He is recognized for his observation and recording of Pawnee culture and history in collaboration with several scholars.[35] At this time, in 1891, he was about thirty years old and was considered one of the tribe's progressive young men. His revealing letter discloses his bicultural position and conflict:

Dear Major:

I have for some time been thinking of writing you a short letter in regard to the so-called Ghost Dance. No doubt what you have heard is that I took part in the dance – understand not that I believed in it, but that I was curious to find out what good there was in it, and if it was wrong [illegible] if good and God's work wanted to help it make it a success, but if wrong to help run it down and expose it. You know the way to find this or that out, I just go into it myself and find out. I was with them 3 days, and it had no effect on my mind or physical power, nor my will power. I saw while with them that those who are weak minded were effected and thrown to the ground. All through the dancing they are told to have one mind upon Christ and the deceased Ghost relation. Major I am glad to say that I found some good true hearts who only put their trust in *our* God and his son, Christ. They would not put their whole trust and faith in this unknown God. After dancing these few good hearts came to my tent and wanted my opinion upon the Ghost Dance which I gave them the following. "My boys and friends be true to the God and Christ whom we learned to love while at school for he is our God, and the only true God. Pray to him that the sins of our people may be forgiven. That our relations may see that we are not under the influence of this young prophet.[36] The power used in this dance is caused by all of us joining hands and going around in a circle, jumping up and down and exciting the electrical power that is in humans and when that power has worked a certain height the power of mesmerism is tried upon them and they are thrown down upon the ground thence go into a trance and their mind naturally going to that happy hunting ground. It is not the soul leaving the body as they claim, but the mind wandering off. The Indian who must be a smart one who understands the two powers – the power of electricity and the power of mesmerism, and knowing our Indians to be superstitious connected [not to?] the religion of our dear Saviour Jesus Christ – making the dance a powerful organization. O what a shame it is that my poor people should be led in this way by an untutored Indian. Where is the Preacher and the Missionary? What are they here for? Ah, my heart aches to think about it. Ah, if I had only prepared to preach to my people I should today feel proud that I had a battle to fight for my Saviour. Do not think dear Major that I am not working for Him for I have used my influence to his cause and proclaim His good name. Again I thank God that though this Indian is not educated he can use his influence to good cause. He does not want them to be immoral he says it's wicked; does not want them to steal and has established love, peace and good feeling among these people. The Ghost Dance is now in progress. My family went and I stayed home to look after my property; and to study my Bible more. I pray that God may strengthen and bless you in the work you are engaged and to forgive the sins of my people and from my heart I look to Heaven and say, "Father Thy Will be Done."

I remain your Bro. in Christ,

Jas. R. Murie

Major please keep this letter as I may go to that dance again and if I learn any more I want to add it to your letter and finally make a report of it to some newspaper.[37]

This remarkable letter reveals a great deal about the man who believed that the "white man's road" was the one to follow. At one time he traveled to Nebraska and unsuccessfully sought reconciliation with his white father.[38] At this time and later, he seemed to want to identify with the non-Indian culture and sought attention and approval from its members. His idea of writing about the Ghost Dance for a newspaper indicates some of this. His request that the agent forgive the sins of some of his people perhaps reflects his setting himself apart from them and their non-Christian practices. His strong words about leading his people on the true path of Christianity may have been sincere, but they also appear to be aimed at obtaining the agent's approval. Then his plan to attend the Ghost Dance again and report to the agent what he has seen seems self-serving and disloyal to his family and other Pawnees who knew the agent's determined opposition to their rituals and dances.

On 19 December 1891 Agent Wood, sufficiently angered by the Pawnees' stubbornness in continuing the Ghost Dance, wrote the following short letter to Frank White:

Sir:

Reports have reached this office that you are upon the Pawnee reservation engaged in leading the Pawnee Indians away from civilization, and introducing certain customs that are considered by our Government as obnoxious to good Government. You will therefore cease your unlawful practices and return to your home at once and save me further trouble.[39]

When Wood demanded that White go home, he referred to the Kiowa agency, where he had been told White had lived. He sent a letter to the agent saying he had been informed that White had been carried on the Wichita roll and therefore was under the control of the agent there.[40] He informed the agent that he has asked White to leave the Pawnee reservation and wanted to be informed when he arrived. However, White chose not to leave.

News of the Pawnee Ghost Dance and its charismatic leader reached surrounding tribes. In late December 1891 some Delawares, Osages, and Otoes came to attend it.[41] The agency clerk appeared unconcerned about the dance, reporting that the Pawnees were peaceful and the main negative effect was that they did not attend to their work. However, the Indian Office in Washington DC received a letter complaining about the Pawnee dance, its Messiah, the Indian judge, police ineffectiveness, Pawnees not working and "beggaring" themselves by gift giving during the proceedings, children being taken out of school to attend the Ghost Dance, and the giving of Lucy Meacham, a schoolgirl, to Frank White for a wife. This, the letter claimed, was an act "forcing to prostitution a girl who should have had the protection and assistance of the government." All in all, the writer concluded that the Pawnees had been turned from an industrious people back to a barbarous state.[42]

Wood immediately responded to the Washington authorities, clarifying the situation and discussing and attempting to disprove each accusation and so-called false statement with copies of letters to and between himself and clerk Hill, Frank White, and others. He took great care in discussing the Lucy Kuhns Meacham–Frank White situation and his role in it, explaining that Lucy had returned from Haskell Indian school in Kansas the previous year and lived with her sister, Minnie Carrion. He later heard that Lucy was about to marry a white man named Debbs, considered an undesirable type that "we refused to tolerate on the reservation."

Wood called Lucy and her sister and brother-in-law into the agency office to discourage her from marrying Debbs. He advised her to continue her schooling instead. Lucy replied that she did not want to go to school and she would not. At this point in the correspondence, Wood said that "Such girls upon reservations are subject of especial notice and conquest."[43]

Not long after, she married a Pawnee, Scott Meacham, age twenty-five. It was rumored that her sister, Minnie, had interfered, and Lucy was not with Scott at this time. The agent then talked to Scott and told him to try to win his wife back. Apparently Lucy would have none of it and said "she would not live with him." When he heard this the agent confessed he did not know what to do. Confining Lucy to keep her away from the prophet was impractical, and sending her back to school by force was impossible. Confessing defeat, he added that he had found that in such cases "it was impractical to care for such girls when they desired no care," and he did nothing about her alliance with Frank White. A child, Helen P. White, was born in 1892.[44]

Returning to the subject of the Ghost Dance, agent Wood assumed a tolerant attitude toward the movement. On reflection he did not believe the situation was as bad as the secretary of the interior indicated. The Pawnees *had* done their work, since the Messiah instructed them to work as the agent told them and to be honest and pay their debts. The Indian police the agent sent out to stop the dance were afraid of Frank White because he told them, "Attempt to arrest me, and I touch you and you die." The police came back from this unsuccessful assignment saying that their people told them, "White men dance, we dance." He concluded that he would not take any position toward the Ghost Dance that he could not enforce, and he thought that the Pawnees would dance themselves out if left alone. He realized that the Indian Office wanted the dance stopped, but if the only way was to send in the military, he would not suggest that because "it would undoubtedly end in another Wounded Knee disaster."[45]

The Pawnees were now well aware that the government did not approve of the Spirit Dance. "My mother said we used to do it when the snow was up to our knees," one elderly Pawnee remembered, "and even though it was winter, we began to hide around to do it. We wanted to receive a blessing." It would be performed in remote areas away from the agency. There were several secret dance sites along the Arkansas River, Camp Creek, and Black Bear Creek. Some Skidis went up near Ralston and found seclusion in the woods. They would sing softly and shake the gourds so that the sounds would not carry far. At one dance, held some distance north of the agency, one old man who was deaf tended to get louder and louder as he sang and danced in the circle. "We would try to quiet him, but he would not pay any attention. You could hear him for miles! And he kept it up all night long. We just knew somebody would come," another Pawnee remembered.

Although Wood had hastened to assure the secretary of the interior that there was little to worry about concerning the Pawnees and the Ghost Dance, the next day he went to the Pawnee subagency and called a council of the tribal leaders. Aware of the probable reason for the council, Frank White, some chiefs, and an estimated one hundred Pawnees arrived. The Pawnees asked Wood what the government wanted them to do. Some of them became angry as he listed what the government expected. In the first place, they had to stop the Ghost Dance, go to work on their farms and improve them, plant their corn, and "beautify their homes." Assuming the kind father approach, he told them to have good family relations, to respect the laws of the government, and to go home and be good Indians.[46]

The Pawnees listened to all this, and their spokesmen said they agreed to what had been said, except they would not stop their dancing. Dancing was the Indian way to worship God.[47] They believed he would come soon and save the Indians *and* the whites, whom they wished to treat as brothers. Wood replied that the kingdom of God was not at hand, and it was not necessary to dance to worship God. God should be worshiped in the heart, and there were both a true and a false Messiah, implying that Frank White was the latter.[48]

At this several speakers stood and angrily said that they would "die before they would stop the dance." Confrontation and antagonism increased until Wood looked at White and ordered him to leave the reservation at once. Incensed at this command, someone stood up and retorted, "He is a Pawnee and has lived on the Wichita reservation for three or four years, he *is* a Pawnee and wants to live with his people now." After six hours the council ended, and the agent said that when the Pawnees left they seemed calmer but still determined to continue the Ghost Dance.[49]

When Wood had time to contemplate the day's events, he concluded in a report to the commissioner of Indian affairs that he did not believe it wise to forcibly stop the Pawnee Ghost Dance. It would die out by itself in time. "Stir the fire [as he had done that day] and it burns more brightly. Stir up the feelings of Indians and oppose them in what is to them a divine practice, and like men of old they will die for their faith." On the other hand, if Frank White was forced to leave the reservation, the Pawnees would return to their customary ways and all would be well. He erroneously believed that it was Frank White's presence that caused the Ghost Dance to continue, and not the conditions the Pawnees faced, for which the Messiah's message promised succor.

In early March 1892 the clerk reported that he heard rumors now and then that the Pawnees had their Ghost Dances, but when he investigated he found this was not true.[50] Now a conspiracy of silence surrounded the dance, and people gathered secretly to dance far from the agency.[51]

Wood continued to look for some event that would make it possible to finally get rid of Frank White. Although in his correspondence to Washington he appeared to discount the importance of the Ghost Dance, he resented White's audacity in defying his orders to leave the reservation. He also saw his own authority diminishing as he watched White's increasing influence over the people. Although the Pawnees feigned obsequiousness when the agent spoke to them about doing their work, he knew they had no plans to do as he said, and he took offense at their growing independence. Without White's presence, he hoped he could exert his authority more effectively.

Wood heard that on 23 March the Otoes were holding a Ghost Dance with Frank White in charge. Now the agent had his pretext. The "Messiah" had gone too far. Wood feared the increasing momentum of White's influence if neighboring tribes invited him to lead the Ghost Dance. He quickly informed F. W. Miller, the clerk at that subagency, to tell the Otoe chiefs and headmen that the Ghost Dance "will no longer be tolerated" and they must go to work on their farms. He ordered that the Otoe Buffalo Black who assisted White be arrested, and that Frank White be told to leave the reservation. If he returned to the Otoes, he would be taken to Agent Wood's office under guard.[52]

Wood did not wait for that to happen; instead, he sent a United States deputy marshal to the Pawnee agency to arrest White on the morning of 25 March 1892. As soon as he arrested him he took him to Guthrie, the capital of Oklahoma Territory, about fifty miles away,[53] where he was put in jail.[54] Wood had instructed Hill what to do, and he subpoenaed John Morris of the Pawnee police and others as witnesses to White's Ghost Dance activities.

The Pawnees were dumbfounded when White was arrested and taken away. Tribal leaders immediately went to the agency office to talk to the clerk about what they should do. They wanted to have White released on bail if it could be done. Previous experience in Nebraska, where several tribal members were confined in a white man's jail without trial for many months made them dread White's confinement in such a place.[55] They asked Hill to write to Agent Wood to take care of bail, but he informed them the agent did not have that power. White was in the hands of the United States courts, and Hill threatened, "they might make him stay in jail for *ten* years, and they would have to go, too, if they did not completely give up the Ghost Dance." With this appalling news, the Pawnees asked Hill to write to the great father in Washington and tell him they would never do the Ghost Dance again. When he heard this surprising announcement, Wood thought he had won his battle to get rid of both White and the Ghost Dance.

White and Buffalo Black appeared before United States commissioner John W. Boles, and witnesses gave evidence. The two men were accused of insurrection and sent under guard to the federal prison in Wichita, Kansas, to await trial in the United States district court. With this turn of events, some Pawnees and Otoes, not as compliant as they had been at first, reportedly threatened to kill some government employees and their fellow tribesmen who had testified against the two Ghost Dance leaders.[56] However, Hill informed Wood that after a few days passions had cooled and everything seemed calm.

In a short time Wood received a telegram saying a writ of habeas corpus had been issued for White and Black. Returned to Guthrie, they appeared before Judge E. B. Green, the Oklahoma Territory chief justice. Witnesses Harry Coons, James R. Murie, and John Morris, who had arrested White, were not asked to testify. All three men were Skidis, and their previous agreement to testify against White angered the South Band members present.

Judge Green lectured the two men sternly, saying that the Ghost Dance was foolishness and would lead to trouble. The Messiah would come someday, but certainly not in the Ghost Dance. They were forced to promise that they would never take part in the dance again and that they would obey their agent's orders. They would be peaceful, harm no one, and settle down and do their farmwork. Two Pawnee South Band chiefs, Eagle Chief, Pitahawirata, and Curly Chief, Kitkahahki, who attended the hearings, also had to promise to abide by these conditions. If any Pawnees or Otoes took part in the dance, they would be arrested and treated more severely. Although White and Black were released, they were told they could be tried at some future time.[57]

Triumphantly, Wood instructed Hill to keep a careful eye on White, to watch for any signs of the Ghost Dance, and to take careful notes. He was to enlist dependable observers, and if White "proves detrimental," he would be forced to leave the reservation.[58]

In the middle of May United States commissioner George N. Phillips came to the Pawnee reservation, and he asked Frank White to sign the following letter addressed to Agent Wood. Dated 16 May 1892, this document would permit Frank White to be arrested or deported if he did not abide by the conditions imposed in it.

Sir:

I, Frank White, a Pawnee by birth, and a full blood, being born on the Pawnee reservation, have the honor to say that my intention in coming back to the Pawnee reservation is to reside with my people and to make the Pawnee reservation my home, and that I promise and swear that I will not incite my people to practice the Ghost Dance in any manner, but that I will encourage them in every manner that I can to cultivate their farms and to enlarge and beautify their homes and that I will do all I can to preserve order in the tribe and assist in every possible way to benefit my tribe, that I will open a farm of my own and settle down to an honest life among my people, striving to set before them an example worthy of emulation.

[signed] Frank White

Subscribed and sworn to before me this 16 day of May, 1892

George N. Phillips,
U.S. Commissioner[59]

White's thoughts when he signed it are unknown, but it is certain that the Ghost Dance continued, according to the Pawnees and the government correspondence that ensued.

The clerk's correspondence does not reveal much concern about the Ghost Dance during this summer, 1892. There were some new developments, however. Frank White's influence appeared to be diminishing, and a new prophet, William Hunt, a former member of the police, made his appearance. He did not believe in dancing but took a different approach to meeting people's needs. He practiced the laying on of hands to cure the sick.[60] Several individuals claimed he cured them, and people were said to listen to him when he told them that White had misled them. Confronted with a loss of influence and power, White sent a message to the agency office requesting that his rival be arrested. Informing the agent of these events, the clerk said, "I am willing to lean back and watch them have it out for a while at least, I think it will result in good."[61]

Other prophets made themselves known. One was Colonel Meacham, a man about thirty years of age, whom Hill called a "lesser Prophet."[62] Little is now known of his Ghost Dance activities, but it turned out he was one of the young men who had made serious threats when White was arrested. In an effort to prevent White's removal to Guthrie, he and others took their guns and went to the train station. The agent, foreseeing such an action, had already wired to Fort Reno for assistance.[63] When the train arrived and troops got off, the Pawnees saw they were outnumbered and did not attempt to rescue their prophet.[64]

The Ghost Dance movement gave many Pawnees, particularly young men, courage to confront and challenge the control the government held over them. The movement's claim that the whites would soon disappear added boldness to their encounters with the whites. White claimed that the wind would blow away all the white people and the Pawnee "half-breeds" such as "Behaile [Bayhylle], Dorf Corian [Dolf Carrion], Harry Coons, James Murie, Rice, and Papan because they don't believe in this dance" but believed in the white man's church.[65]

A year after Frank White introduced the Ghost Dance to the Pawnees, he found his influence and control lessening. Some who had participated early in the movement no longer took part. Some resented that he had made himself rich because he received many gifts from believers. Although it was traditional for Pawnee sacred society leaders and doctors

72 THEY CAME BEFORE

who treated the sick to receive payment, they were expected to display the highest standards of behavior. White did not do so. He began to charge people five dollars to paint their faces. He consumed both liquor and peyote, which he claimed made him wise.[66] The use of peyote began to increase at this time among many tribes, following "the anti–Ghost Dance frustration of anti-white sentiment."[67] During a traditional Doctor Dance, White came supported on either side by two of his followers. The people gathered there noticed his intoxicated state, but someone said, "We can't say anything, because he is the Messiah."[68]

Until this point, few dared to show independence by claiming they had received the call through a vision to be a prophet in their own right. The efforts of Meacham and William Hunt were followed by others. Joseph Carrion, with John Moses, Jim Keys, Brigham Young, and Henry Minthorn, traveled to the Cheyenne and Arapaho reservation to visit the revered Sitting Bull and learn more about the Ghost Dance. They stayed two months and, following instructions, Carrion fasted four days. Then during a Ghost Dance he had a vision that his host, Sitting Bull, declared authentic.[69]

The Pawnees returned to their reservation and found people eager to hear what they had learned. Carrion announced that Frank White misled them, that he did not have the power to bless them, and that they had the right to experience visions whose authenticity did not have to be verified and interpreted by White.[70] Carrion's move to overcome White's control of the Ghost Dance was successful. Like other historic cults and religions, its leadership and practices broadened and changed. The addition of the hand game, with differing owners, procedures, songs, and paraphernalia, illustrated this in the following years.

On 26 January 1893 Frank White died. Neither Lesser nor Murie nor any other source found gives details of his death. No matter how controversial he became during the short period when he introduced and conducted the Ghost Dance, Frank White initiated a renewed Pawnee solidarity and resistance to government attempts to control their decision making as they confronted and challenged efforts to end the dance and their belief in it.

In 1894 an unnamed Pawnee visited Wovoka to bring a gift from the Pawnees. When he placed the gift of forty silver dollars at Wovoka's feet, however, it was refused. The *Elko Daily Independent* reported on 22 August that Wovoka refused to take it because he said it might be tainted and that he might die because of witchcraft. No details are given about why he believed this or refused the gift, if he actually did.[71] Earlier in 1892 he apparently tired of devotees' visits. According to an agency farmer who claimed to know him well, "There have been several delegations of Eastern tribes to interview the 'Messiah,' some are pleased and some are not. He is not pleased with their visits and does not advocate 'Ghost dances' here or among other tribes."[72] When the Kiowa Apiatan, visited him before this, he was less than welcoming and lay with a blanket over his head, "singing to himself and paying no attention to the visitor."[73] It was said that this lack of courtesy and respect, as the visitor saw it, attributed to the Kiowas' rejection of the religion.

In the last years of the century, the Pawnee Ghost Dance continued. For the most part the government had lost the war against it. On 24 January 1896 a territory newspaper reported that the four bands of the Pawnee tribe have "all left their farms and moved into tepees on Black Bear Creek, and have gone to ghost dancing and making medicine." In July 1897 the same paper reported that the Pawnees and about three hundred Osages were Ghost Dancing on Cole (Coal) Creek fourteen miles northwest of Blackburn.[74]

The twentieth century arrived, and despite government disapproval, the Ghost Dance and hand game persisted. In October 1900 an important visitor arrived at the Pawnee agency. It was Sitting Bull, along with his wife and child and Scabby Bull with his wife and child, who had received permission to visit. It is assumed they attended a Ghost Dance, but no report of that has been discovered.[75] It must have been a remarkable experience for the believers to have this man among them.

In May 1902, agent John Jensen received an Indian Office letter that he forwarded to the Pawnee Indian school superintendent, now in charge of the subagency's affairs. The letter stated that George A. Dorsey of the Field Columbian Museum had informed the commissioner that he had visited the Pawnees and that the Ghost Dance continued. The superintendent responded to the commissioner, not attempting to hide his annoyance that Dorsey had not come to him to talk about the situation. He then gave an informative description of the Pawnee Ghost Dance at the time:

I have the honor to state that the Pawnee Indians no longer believe, as at first, namely that this dancing will bring back the buffalo and cause the white man to depart. As at present practiced the method is for some one to invite the tribe to the dance, which usually lasts about five days, though sometimes less. This feast usually costs the Indian $60.00 or more. In most cases others contribute, making the expense for the dinner some $75. The dance begins in the morning, intermits for a time, then is taken up again from perhaps, 10 to 12, then is discontinued until one or two. After that the dance begins again, lasting from two to three hours when the daily feast is given. The dance begins about sun down and continues until sun rise. This is about the daily programme. At the conclusion of this entertainment given by this Indian, with perhaps a few days intermission, – some one else may give a dance, providing a feast as above. The interval is sometimes filled by other dances and by what is called "Hand Games."

All this time people may remain congregated in a common camp. It may continue for a week or two months. All of the Indians are not there all the time. They come and go. As to its prevalence it is not confined to any particular element among them. It is participated in, almost universally.[76]

He went on to explain that as the white man talked to God in prayer, the Indian claimed that in the Ghost Dance trance he saw and also talked to God. However, in the behavior of the dance the superintendent believed there was much moral harm. "The indiscriminate mingling [illegible] together . . . frequently causes separating in the family and other immoral results." These he did not describe. As a final comment on Dorsey, he said that he had found out that when Dorsey visited, there were no Ghost Dances in progress, and if he had come to the office he would have found out more than he seemed to know![77]

Wichita and Effie Blaine continued to participate in the Ghost Dance for many years. They took their daughter Viola, born in 1904, with them when she was about seven or eight years old. The dance took place at a big Ghost Dance camp in the country several miles southeast of town. The people danced all night and quit before sunrise. Viola saw people fall down and stay on the ground in a trance. While one woman lay on the ground, a man came running and called out that a team of horses was running loose in the camp and nobody had caught them. People had better take their children and get into their tipis. Viola watched the woman jump right up and run to find her children. Viola's mother later said she thought the woman was just pretending and not really in a trance at all.[78]

The Blaines attended Ghost Dances at several dance grounds. One was near the Cimarron River at the Wilson camp and another was on the Taylor place southeast of the agency. Effie Blaine attended those dances and was noted for being a good Ghost Dance singer.[79] She had several visions in which songs came to her. Two of her songs were about the crow, an important symbolic figure in the Ghost Dance and hand game. Effie belonged to the Crows, dancers who claimed to be associated with the crow and could see a crow moving inside the Ghost Dance circle. According to Effie, the crow could take the dancer to Mother Moon or to the Ghost Dance Messiah. One song she received during a trance said, "The crow, we see his likeness moving inside the circle of dancers."[80] Another of her songs said,

> The crow is calling. The crow is calling,
> Now I am active. Now I am active.
> In the place whence Mother Moon comes,
> In the place whence Mother Moon comes.[81]

This song refers to the importance of the crow as a messenger who comes from the heavens and tells the people on earth about their dead relatives in the land beyond. This concept, built on older beliefs about the crow, became a motivation for many Pawnees' participation and continued adherence to the Ghost Dance as more kin members died each year than were born in the new century's early years.

A significant change, partially attributable to the Ghost Dance, appeared after the turn of the century. Some young men showed less interest in learning the old tribal ceremonies. James Murie, writing to Alice Fletcher, who was studying and recording Pawnee ceremonies, said that the old leader of the Pipe Dance (Hako) had been trying to teach the "old religion," but his young apprentices "seem to have no interest in the ceremonies. They are given more to the Ghost Dance."[82] Even some members of the sacred societies, including Wichita Blaine, divided their participation between the old rituals and the new.

Proselytizing by Christian missionaries began to threaten the older religious practices as well as the Ghost Dance. In 1906 the Southern Baptist denomination built an Indian mission church, and Rev. J. G. Brendel became its first missionary. On 1 October 1908 he visited a Ghost Dance camp where he said he was invited to speak. The Ghost Dance encampment lasted four days, and he spoke each day. But he said he could not tell how much good he had done, because "they were so frantic and wild at times."[83] Sometime during this period, Effie Blaine decided to visit a missionary meeting. The Pawnees sat behind one another in rows. The missionary's Pawnee interpreter turned to the attentive listeners and explained that now was the time to turn to the Great Father in Heaven and believe in his son, Jesus. He then explained how beneficial this would be for the Pawnees. It would be like getting on a train and traveling to a wonderful place. "Now is the time to get on the train to Jeesuss," he proclaimed. "Follow us and get on the train to Jeesuss." He got behind the missionary, and they both began to move like a train, pumping their arms and calling out, "Choo-choo-choo" as they moved between the rows of startled Pawnees. "Brother, get on the train," they would urge. "Here, sister, won't you get on the train to Jeesuss?" One by one a few Pawnees who decided to go along with the action joined the "train" and shuffled after one other up and down the rows. Most of the Pawnees still sat listening to the train and watching the spectacle. To increase participation, the missionary and assistant increased the fervor of their actions and message. All of a sudden somebody choo-chooed too close to the wood-burning stove and let out a yell. There was silence, then one of the old Pawnee men said for all to hear, "I thought they said you won't get to that hot place they talk about if you get on the train to Jeesuss." Muffled snickering could be heard here and there. Effie lost her curiosity about the new "train" religion at that point and continued participating in the Ghost Dance and other traditional ceremonies.[84]

By 1915, the year of Garland Blaine's birth, James Murie claimed that the fervor of the Ghost Dance had diminished and that few trances were occurring, but songs were still created and valued.[85] He may not have been accurate in this statement about lessened fervor, for as a Skidi he did not always have information about the three south bands' ceremonies and activities, particularly when they became aware that he was "finding out things for the white people."[86]

In the 1920s when Garland Blaine was a boy, he attended Ghost Dances with his grandparents. At one he watched a Ghost Dance participant close his eyes and slowly begin to assume the manner, posture, and sounds of a certain animal.[87] As the animal sounds came, other men, usually older ones with a black handkerchief or feather in their hands, would go out toward him or others in similar emotional states. They stood before each one and waved the handkerchief or feather as the songs were sung. They stayed near them all during the ensuing trance state, which was astonishing to see. Even with their eyes closed, the spellbound dancers would move rapidly around the floor in the round house. They performed without falling over or running into the hot wood stoves or the walls. When the episode began to end, two or three people came from the audience to help those who sank to the floor. He marveled at the endurance they showed in the exhausting behavior of the trance. Most were old people, and they were very weak after it was over – limp and breathing rapidly. White Elk and Sherman Keller were two leaders who went out with a feather or handkerchief to "knock them down."[88]

One elderly Pawnee woman remembers Ghost Dances held in the south round house. One of the dancers was Stella Rouwalk Knifechief.

> She was very heavy. The round house had a sliding door. It was about a foot open. She had a trance during which she danced on her tiptoes. Suddenly she went right through the door, even though it was open just a foot. I saw it.
>
> Dolly Moore, Wilson Moore's mother, used to have all-night Ghost Dances at her place after the north round house was abandoned. They used the Mose Yellow Horse dance. Once it was cold and Ossie Norman, married to Walter, went into a trance. She kept trying to get out of the ring, but they held her in. They were afraid something might get her in the timber. My sister and I locked arms to keep her in. The last real trances I know about were in the 1930s at Dolly Moore's.[89]

As late as the mid-1930s, before World War II, the Pawnees were very active in the Ghost Dance. One day Garland Blaine drove to Pawnee and walked into a store where there were chairs near the door and old people, including Effie Blaine, usually sat and visited. She was not there that day, and two elderly women told him she was at the dance. "What dance, he asked?" They said it was the Ghost Dance and told him it was out at the old Norman place. "They are going to dance this afternoon and tonight," they added. He drove to the place, which was probably seven miles south of town. When he arrived there were quite a few people there – a hundred or so. That particular afternoon Jesse Peters was leading the songs. Jesse was probably in his sixties or a little older. Jim Little Sun, a younger man, probably in his forties, was helping Jesse with the singing. He was learning the songs from Jesse. There were other leaders at this time, including Henry Goodfox and Tom Morgan. The older leaders still wore a bunch of crow feathers tied in their hair. Wichita Blaine was dead, but Effie remained active. Not everyone who attended danced. Men like Bill Morgan and Lawrence Goodfox watched.[90]

So Garland sat there for a while enjoying himself. He respected the dance and totally believed in it. In his mind he was singing with the singers while his grandmother danced. He sat there maybe an hour before they stopped dancing. Then he went to see his grandmother.[91]

For a long time only Ghost Dance songs were sung at Pawnee hand games. They were sacred then, but now the games are just a social activity. Once in a while at a hand game, people will request Ghost Dance singing. Someone at the drum will sing two or three songs, and the people will get up and dance in a circle.[92] There are two types of songs associated with the Ghost Dance and the hand game. Ghost Dance prayer songs that were received in a trance or dream were performed only while doing the Ghost Dance. Other songs were sung only at hand games. One of the songs Wichita Blaine sang after he saw his little boys was a Ghost Dance prayer song. A hand game song that Effie Blaine composed said, "I hear the sound of a child crying, 'Is my mother coming?' / Here I walk around."[93]

During the following years, whenever called upon, Garland would join tribal members who remembered the Ghost Dance as children or adults and wanted to recall those times by singing and dancing. Now, he said, it had become a social dance with none of the deep emotional reactions of the past. Only a few people knew the songs well enough to lead the dancers. Garland danced for the last time in 1975 when the

Pawnee Heritage Club held a dance and feast at the Pawnee Reserve tribal campgrounds. This event commemorated the hundred years the Pawnees had lived in Oklahoma. He and Philip Jim led the dance and began the songs, and Garland shook the gourd rattle that marked the rhythm. About forty kinsmen and friends joined hands and, with the dance's quick side steps, moved clockwise in a circle. The songs still sounded like people crying if one listened closely.

FIVE

"They Were All around Us"

On and on the questions renew:
After so many bitter years, haven't we earned the good life.
Do we deserve it or not?

Yevgeny Yevtushenko, *The Collected Poems, 1952–1990*

The Indians, I think have been mistreated by all who have come in contact with them. They have been promised things for giving up their homes and have received nothing. All rights have been taken away from them and their worship has been made fun of. The white men do not understand the Indian.

Samuel Walker, Pawnee, 25 February 1938

Some white people are good, and some are devils. I know that.

A Pawnee, May 1992

Wichita and Effie Blaine were wary of white people, believing that you have to think about whether what they say to you is true. They tend not to do as they say. Their views paralleled other Pawnees' experiences with Indian agents, agency employees, and United States government officials in Washington DC that fostered a stereotype of whites as untrustworthy, greedy, and controlling. This opinion did not diminish in the 1890s when the Pawnees were forced to take individual land allotments and relinquish their reservation land that the government called surplus.

Suddenly the whites were all around the Pawnees when their land was first opened to white settlement. In camp in their tipi late at night, Effie and Wichita could hear wagons going by. Now and then they would hear someone call out softly in the dark, "John, hey, John," not as loud as though attempting to wake someone asleep. Wichita would take his .45-caliber revolver and go out, and Effie stood behind him with a rifle. Most of the night callers were honest and only wanted water, and the Blaines gave it to them if they could spare it. Others did not look right to them. They thought they would have taken their horses or something from their little camp if they had not stepped out and showed their guns. Other Pawnees did have things stolen by the newcomers.[1]

As time went by, more and more white settlers came in and crowded all around the Blaines and other Pawnees. At first the settlers were poor and lived in tents and dugouts with things stacked outside. Gradually, as they improved their lives, they built little houses and cut up the land with wire fences. One family never seemed to do any better. They lived in an old put-together place and had lots of children. The Pawnees called the man Farmer Tattered.[2]

The Pawnees channeled their resentment by making fun of the new-comers, calling them names and treating them disdainfully if they met.[3] They did not want them there and resented their living on Pawnee land. In the beginning the new settlers eyed the Pawnees with just as much suspicion. Nate Swalley said his wife was afraid of Indians, believing that they were mean and would attack them. Sadie Hughes remembered that she and her children were always afraid of the Pawnees. One evening while her husband was away she took the children for a walk on their new farm. At some distance from the house she saw a "large Indian man" going toward the house. She and her children ran as fast as they could and reached the door just as the man, who had not stopped, went around the corner of the house and disappeared among the trees. (The Pawnee may well have been following the route he had always taken across the fields before fences and the new farmhouse obstructed his path.) She told her husband about it when he came home, saying she was afraid he was going to steal the baby she had left sleeping in the house. He laughed at her, saying that the Indians had all the babies they could care for and didn't want any white ones.[4]

A few newcomers seemed to have positive attitudes. Lotta Harris Mosier held a lifelong interest in the Pawnees. She grew up near the old Pawnee village site in Republic County, Kansas, and used to play in the ruins as a child. When she came to Oklahoma Territory in the early years she taught school in a tent and took her students to attend Pawnee dances and other events so that they could learn about the people.[5]

Since the early days of European contact, fear of Native Americans had created scare stories often reported in the press, and in some places that continued until the early twentieth century. Some exaggerated reports described violent acts. John H. Conley said that his father made the run in 1889, settled with his family near Guthrie, Oklahoma Territory, and became a government game hunter in the area, shooting prairie chickens, quail, and wild turkeys. After preparing them by drying and salting, he took them to the railroad in Guthrie and shipped them to St. Louis.[6] One time, he said, "we were attacked by seven savage Pawnee Indians, and my elder son was badly wounded but recovered. Our barn was burned down, and three cows killed." The Indians attempted to burn the house but did not succeed. How he knew they were Pawnees he did not say, but he reported the incident to Pawnee county sheriff McCrea, who said there was not much he could do because the names of the accused were not known.[7] The Pawnee reservation lay many miles from Guthrie, so if the incident did occur, other Indians could have been involved.

As early as 1834 it became illegal to hunt on Indian land. If caught one faced forfeiture of "all traps, guns, ammunitions and peltries taken," as well as a fine.[8] During the years following allotment there was an increasing scarcity of game and loss of land where Indians could hunt for food. One non-Indian hunter reported that he invited a group of friends from Kansas to come down in 1890 before allotment for a "pleasure hunting trip. They had made a pretty good kill, when the Pawnee Indian Police came upon them, took their game, guns and everything away from them and made them get out."[9]

The Pawnees also had their scare stories of white hostility carried to an extreme. Passage of the 1890 Organic Act (51 Cong. 1 sess., chap. 182, 26 Stat. 81) that organized Oklahoma Territory established locations for future county seats. Individuals eager to begin a new life and make money (called seeking one's fortune) in the newly opened Indian land founded the small town of Pawnee as county seat for County Q, as it was then called. Near the present-day fairgrounds stood a sawmill that supplied lumber to build the new town's houses and commercial buildings. One elderly

Pawnee recalled that her mother had told her a Pawnee man whose name she could not remember liked to watch the mill's operation. One day the white men working there grabbed him and sawed him in half. And, she added, nothing was said or done about it. Probably the white people said he fell under the blade and was killed, she reasoned.[10] No known source reported such an incident.

Newspapers continued to contribute their share of stories that added to non-Indians' fears. The *New York Times,* using a source from Guthrie, Oklahoma, declared on 26 December 1901 that the Pawnees had a dance and believed that "great herds of buffalo" would return. Apparently this referred to the Ghost Dance. The article continued:

> The Pawnee Indians are on the war path. An immense buffalo bull was so injured in being transferred from the Santa Fe stockyards to Pawnee Bill's ranch south of town that he had to be killed. The meat was given by Major Lillie to Indians for a "buffalo dance." The Pawnees claimed the vast herds of buffalo are coming back to their country and many of them have notified the white lessees to vacate their ranches at once as they wish to lay the fences low so that the buffalo will have full sway of the country. The white people from the remote parts of the reservation are coming in to Pawnee to report that the Indians are acting in a threatening manner. Pawnee Bill has placed armed guards around his buffalo ranch as the red men are camping in the timber a little west of there and in sight of the herds. From their suspicious actions he thinks they intend to liberate [his] herd and perhaps kill them. The United States Indian agent at that point has been notified and has made a report to the Commissioner of Indian Affairs in Washington.[11]

This exaggerated tale cannot be substantiated and apparently grew out of the rumors of this sort that spread throughout the country from time to time.

Time and experience tempered the negativity Pawnees and whites felt toward each other, especially in the countryside. As the non-Indian newcomers began to settle on their new farms and leaseholds, they found they had Pawnee neighbors nearby. Several factors contributed to their concealing any antipathy they may have held. Showing antagonism might lead to retaliation. And good relations seemed wise if they wanted to lease

Pawnee lands from their owners and receive help in emergencies such as grass, house, or barn fires or in finding lost or straying cattle.

A positive attitude toward the Pawnees living around them is suggested in statements by several white farmers. One, Mrs. W. H. Custer, described the thoughtfulness of her Pawnee neighbors. She and her husband leased from John Box three eighty-acre tracts about eight miles north of Pawnee on Coal Creek. Her husband became very ill with "malaria-typhoid fever." He was delirious part of the time, and she was caring for him alone. The Custers' leasehold was near a place where the Skidis camped. One day when they came to camp, they found that Mr. Custer was very ill. They left so as not to disturb him. Once an Indian woman came with some herbs in her hands. She held them out for Mrs. Custer to take and tried to sympathize and console her. That night John Box came and sat by her husband all night. She said, "I tried to get him to lie down, but he wouldn't. He certainly was a good friend."

She continued that they often sold beef to their Indian neighbors. John Box told them never to sell to anyone unless he brought them – that if they did this, they would always get their money when Pawnee annuity payment time came. "And," she said, "we always did."[12] This view of John Box contradicts his step-granddaughter's opinion that he hated white people, which she formed when she used to sit and listen to his stories in the 1920s.[13] This dichotomy of views resulted from a long experience with whites. As chiefs of the Skidi band, he and his brother White Eagle had confronted agents, superintendents, land commissioners, and others for many years in Nebraska and Indian Territory. The diplomacy and goodwill shown in these meetings usually aimed to promote and save Pawnee tribal autonomy, land, and traditional ways. As was often true, they and other Pawnee leaders suffered rejection of their attempts.

Wichita Blaine had strong negative opinions about some whites, but he later acknowledged that his white neighbors near his allotment were mostly good people. When he and Effie found their sight increasingly impaired from trachoma about 1910, neighbors would sometimes chop wood and help in other ways.

Directly to the west of Effie Blaine's allotment lived the two old sisters Julia and Susie Wichita.[14] Susie was the older and used to sit in the house and happily talk to herself when visitors came. Wichita helped them with chores around the house when he could still see well before trachoma caused eventual blindness.[15] Sometimes they asked him to sing for them. They wore their skirts like the Wichita women, wrapped around and tucked in. They had a yard of about an acre, and they kept it clear. It was said that every blade of grass and stick was picked up and neatly stacked around the bases of the many trees. Twigs as small as two inches were picked up each day. When they needed kindling for the stove, they would go out and get it from around the trees.[16]

Julia's white neighbors were kind people and were good to her, even learning to speak some Pawnee. She would go out on her porch and shout across the road, *"Pi ru ski,"* young man, when something needed doing, such as cutting off a tree limb. They used to ask if she wanted to go to town to shop, and she would ride sitting up straight in the backseat of their touring car.[17]

It appears that around the turn of the century the farmers on their new homesteads and their Pawnee neighbors maintained cordial relationships, although this was not always true, especially when lease money the Pawnee family needed was not paid when it was due.[18] But even then certain white families earned respect and were talked about with favor. The Graham family owned a restaurant in Pawnee, and the Pawnees went there because they were well treated.[19] After Effie became blind from trachoma about 1910, Mrs. Graham, who was known as "Piety" by the Pawnees, would come over and warn her if the floor was wet from mopping, take her hand, and lead her to the table. Then she read her the menu in English. Effie had learned what the items were, especially "rows peep." She made her selection, and in the kitchen they cut her meat for her. They brought her coffee, and if they did not notice that she wanted more, she would strike her cup with her spoon and call out, "Piruski, coppee." Mrs. Graham was kind to all the old Indians. Effie would pat her on the arm and say, "Meesis Graham, good woman," in Pawnee.[20]

In the 1930s a white farm family received favorable comments. A Pawnee family had several children. When they wanted to go to a Peyote Church meeting, they would ask their white neighbors to keep the children overnight. The people wanted to do so, so there was no problem. As time passed, they would leave them for a weekend, when they wanted to go to a powwow. Eventually the children stayed two or three weeks at a time,[21] which was not considered an imposition among Indian people. It was being helpful, showed trust, and was an extension of the traditional obligations in an extended family system where relatives or neighbors cared for each other's children.

When another child was born and just beginning to walk, the parents took it to the white neighbors and told them that if they wanted the child, they could take it and raise it. The neighbors were happy to do so. After the birth of the next child, the same thing happened. Eventually these two children were adopted by the middle-aged couple. The Pawnees saw them when they brought the little children to town. They were well dressed and would hang onto the old man's legs. It was known that they would have advantages, and the couple was respected for what they were doing for the children.[22]

Although in many instances the Pawnees appeared to have attained trusting relationships with neighboring farmers, it became apparent that their experiences when they went to nearby towns to buy supplies and do other business often renewed their older suspicion and mistrust of whites.

On the reservation, and in Genoa and other towns near the Pawnees' Nebraska reservation, traders had brown sugar, hardtack, coffee, knives, kettles, cloth, and other articles for which the Pawnees exchanged buffalo hides and animal pelts or that they obtained on credit. The Pawnees favored one trader even though "he probably cheated the hell out of them," Garland Blaine said. The Pawnee women liked his wife, whom they called "Pumpkin" because her girth was similar to her height. Both the trader and his wife learned to speak Pawnee, and because they could communicate, the Pawnees trusted them more than others.

The licensed government Indian trader also served the Pawnees' needs in Indian Territory. Before allotment, one or two men were permitted to set up stores on the reservation, usually near the agency. Some of the first agency traders and assistants were Harry Pratt and William Bishop, who had worked for the trader Stacy Matlock in Nebraska. In Indian Territory Bishop became a silent partner in the trading post. Across from the present-day Indian Hospital stood another store owned by Nicholson and Oats. Charles E. Vandervoort worked there at first, but later he had his own trading post. In 1891 he claimed he had been a licensed trader since 1885.[23]

After allotment and the land run of 1893, the government trader position no longer existed, and Vandervoort and some agency employees took up their livelihoods in the new town of Pawnee. One of them was W. B. Webb, an agency clerk. His daughter, born in 1896 at the Pawnee agency, claimed her father went into the banking business and organized an early Pawnee bank.[24] James B. Davis, who came down from Nebraska with the Pawnees and "handled cattle and horses" at the agency, set up a meat market in the new town. Later he became president of the Pawnee National Bank. Hazel Walker's grandparents traded with the Indians and sometimes took moccasins, beadwork, and articles of clothing in trade.[25]

Thomas E. Berry, an Indian trader, left government service and went into business in town with a Mr. Loughton to open a meat market.[26] H. M. Thompson came to Pawnee in 1898 and began working for the two men, whose relationship became strained. Berry suggested to Thompson that he buy out Loughton's share and said he would lend him the money to do so. Thompson accepted the offer and recalled that "when I went in with Berry [and Loughton], their daily receipts run around $8 to $12 a day. In about four months after I went in with Berry, our receipts run around $150 a day."[27]

Thompson noted that the Pawnees received their annuity payment from the government twice a year. They bought meat and other necessities on credit during the intervening months. He had a special means of ensuring that his Indian customers paid their accounts. About two or three weeks before payment time, he traveled out of town to visit each of the four band chiefs. After talking a little while, he offered each one a beef on foot. This act, he claimed, guaranteed that all credit bills would be paid.

On annuity payment day, he and Berry placed a table by the door where the agency personnel handed out the annuity. Thompson said, "I would handle the bills and collect the money from the Pawnees on one side of the table, and Mr. Berry sat on the other side of the table with a big book." When a Pawnee paid, Thompson told Berry, who entered the amount in the ledger, subtracting it from the amount owed. The accuracy of the grocery prices entered or computations made as to the amount owed after annuity payment cannot be determined. The Pawnees often said they did "not know numbers." When they thought they had paid all that was due a merchant, they often found out they were still in debt. And they never knew if the price asked for goods was the amount the merchant wrote down in their account.

Apparently Thomas E. Berry had sufficient influence, or whatever it took, to succeed as well as he did. J. M. Herd declared that if a merchant stood well with the Indian agent, he had good business; if he did not, he had little.[28] There had long been rumors of profitable collusion between agents and traders, and from time to time government investigations confirmed or disproved wrongdoing.[29] T. J. Morgan, commissioner of Indian affairs, declared in 1890 that "the system of restricting trade with Indians on reservations to persons who hold a license issued by the Commissioner of Indian Affairs is a relic of the old system of considering an Indian as a ward, a reservation as a corral and a tradership as a golden opportunity for plunder and profit."[30]

Not all merchants in Pawnee flourished. David N. Hatfield said he had a succession of stores in the town but finally went broke. He said he had

> credited out so much that I couldn't get anything back. I traded with the Indians, and there were a lot of the Indians who owed me at the time of their death. There was a law at that time where you sell dead allotments.[31] The Indians who owed you at the time of their death, their debts could be collected by itemizing several bills that the Indian owed me. I sent the bills to the agent who was Mr. Nellis, and he put his approval on the bills and sent the bills to Washington. From the bills I got back from Washington, $1,800.20. That was the only time that I ever got paid. The rest of the bills that I sent to the agency to be collected were pigeon-holed, and so I lost about $14,000. That certainly broke me. I've been out of the business since then. I was in the meat and grocery market business eighteen years.[32]

By 1900, concern grew over the increasing indebtedness of Indians across the country. Commissioner W. A. Jones noted that Indians' money went to pay debts to the traders. Knowing that Indians would soon receive some money often led traders to "unscrupulously" encourage them to buy on credit, thus "obligating funds they hoped to receive far in the future." The routine could be continued until all funds were gone. The commissioner declared that at some agencies the state of affairs was scandalous.[33]

The government proclaimed that Indians must learn to handle their funds more wisely. On 1 April 1904 an Indian Office regulation declared that after that date the creditor must take full risk for any debts owed

by Indians, and the agency superintendent could not assist in debt collection. It was hoped that this would curtail the wholesale extension of
credit that kept the Indians in constant debt.[34] To further develop their
financial awareness and responsibility, in 1905 Commissioner F. E. Leupp
said that Indians' money should be placed in local banks, "in reasonably
small parcels so industries of the neighborhood will have use of it." The
Indians should have access to it and use a merchant "who will ask of
him a fair price."[35] How this was to be monitored is not said, but it
seems apparent that Indians' money seemed important to the economic
growth of the emerging town of Pawnee. The use of credit instead of cash
continued, however. For the most part Pawnees' income from the small
annual annuity of less than $50 and from leased land, if the individual
owned any, did not cover a year's expenses. A few Pawnees found work in
the local economy, but most had to use credit to obtain needed articles.

More money came into the hands of local merchants and banks as
a result of the 2 March 1907 act (34 Stat. L. 1221), which provided
that competent and creditworthy Indians could apply for their share of
the money held in trust by the United States Treasury. These funds had
accumulated from tribal land cession sales. An application had to be
approved by the secretary of the interior after the superintendent sent
in a form that answered several questions about the individual's capacity.
Each Pawnee would receive between $500 and $600. There was no great
rush to carry out the act's provisions so that the Pawnees and others could
receive their funds, as Wichita Blaine's application dated 12 May 1912
from the agent to the commissioner reads in part:

> I am forwarding herewith application of Wichita Blaine for appor-
> tionment and allotment under provisions of the Act of Congress of
> March 2, 1907 (34 Stat. L. 1221) of his pro rata share of the trust
> funds on deposit in the Treasury of the United States to the credit of
> the Pawnee tribe of Indians. His application is made under section 2,
> Incompetent Indians. Applicant is a man 51 years of age, married
> and has four children, whose ages are 24, 14, 9 and 7 years. . . . The
> man is helpless because of the fact that he is practically blind. He
> can see enough so that he can go around by himself but his eyes are
> in such condition that it is absolutely impossible for him to engage
> in farming. If he did so, the dust arising from the fields would make

him totally blind in a very short time. His wife is in practically the same condition so far as her eyes are concerned. Neither of them has any earning capacity whatever. They receive together in lease and annuity funds, $387.50 [annually] which is not sufficient in their condition to properly support them and their children. It is for the purpose of helping out in their absolutely necessary family expenses that this man wishes to draw his trust funds, the same to be placed to his credit under the supervision of the superintendent and expended as authorized.[36]

If Wichita Blaine had requested that his money be placed in his hands, he would have been refused. There were rules and regulations regarding blind, crippled, and other disabled individuals called incompetent. One regulation stated that the agent shall superivise the use and expenditure of the Indian's money, and "if the Indian objects to these conditions or shows any disposition to act otherwise than in good faith, he will not be allowed to have the money, and the warrant will be returned to this Office for Cancellation."[37]

To further control Indian expenditures, the Indian Office directed on 30 April 1909 that Indians must receive agency permission to charge articles they needed if they had sufficient funds in their accounts.[38] This meant that a person who wanted to purchase anything had to go to the agency, as Wichita Blaine had to do earlier to obtain house materials. Unless there was a purchase order, a merchant could not sell the articles required.

THE PAWNEES AND THE MERCHANTS

Pawnees left their allotments or camps and went into Pawnee by wagon or horse to obtain their supplies on account from the storekeepers. Their view of the trading system's inequities had not changed appreciably since reservation times. *Ki ri wi su* – deceiver, cheater, faker – was the name given to Pawnee merchants.[39] When Effie Blaine entered a store, she would say in Pawnee, "You are a cheater." When the storekeeper heard this he would laugh, knowing what it meant but not seriously concerned about the accusation.[40] Effie probably wanted him to know she was aware of his sharp practices yet knew that the accusation would probably produce no favorable results.

Pawnees learned how to prove their point that a merchant's goods often cost too much and were not all they said they were. Whenever Effie

Blaine went into a shop to buy cloth, the clerk brought several bolts of cloth and laid them on the counter. She would lift an entire bolt to her nose and sometimes say, "This smells like it will fade," or "This one smells like the colors will run when washed." She would not buy anything that did not smell right to her.[41]

High Eagle, an elderly Pawnee and former United States Army Pawnee Scout, also tested the yard goods. He once took an interpreter into the Katz store when he needed material for a shirt. Barney Weil waited on him and asked him what he wanted. The interpreter said High Eagle wanted to buy red material, the best he had. Mr. Weil looked on the shelf and found a bolt of red cloth and brought it over to the counter. High Eagle looked at it, held it close to his eyes, and smelled it. Then he told the interpreter to tell Mr. Weil he was lying. "This is the material the government used to give away to us," he said. "It is the cheapest kind. Tell him to bring me something good."[42]

Another elderly Pawnee also visited a local store to buy material. He too asked for the best the store had. The merchant brought out a bolt and unrolled some of it, saying it was $3 a yard – a fairly high price. The Pawnee looked at it, took the loose end of the bolt, then tore the cloth down the middle about seven or eight inches to see how strong it was. Then he reached down a yard or so, picked up a handful of material and stuck it in his mouth. He chewed on it awhile, then spit right in the middle of the counter. The saliva was red. He turned to his interpreter and said, "See, he is lying. He wants a fortune for this!" The younger man, said, "Grandpa, what you have done is very bad in the white man's way. It was bad enough that you tore it." The old man said, "He lied to me, and now he has suffered the consequences." And out he walked.[43]

Not all merchants were mistrusted. There was a man the Pawnees called Old Raggety Charlie. He sold knives, forks, thimbles, thread, and other small items from a pushcart on the square. His goods were not of high quality, but he seemed to like the Pawnees. They considered him fair and bought from him. Another itinerant trader the Pawnees trusted they called Ki-tut-pu-ku, meaning "His voice sounded like saliva reverberating with a hollow sound in his throat." Ki-tut-pu-ku had a long white beard and spoke both Pawnee and Wichita. His clothes were dirty and matted and looked as if he made them himself. Two mules pulled his wagon, from which he sold pots, pans, and other things. He would stay around in the winter and cut wood for Indian families. He got very old and stopped coming in the 1930s.[44]

When the opportunity came, the Pawnees took their business out of town. When they visited the Henry Shooter place south of town to camp and hold a dance, Old Man Mathews and St. Elmo Jim and others took their wagons and drove to Glencoe, a small town nearby. Here they bought shoes, clothes, and groceries, which were much cheaper than in Pawnee. Later they wore their shoes or other clothes to a Pawnee store, showed them to the merchant, and told him how much they had paid for them in Glencoe. They added, "They are much better than yours – and cheaper." Whether this early attempt to establish competitive prices succeeded has not been determined.[45]

The Pawnees' ambivalence toward the town's business community continued in the 1920s and 1930s. Ikie Katz, whose father owned the Katz clothing store, made friends with some of the Indian boys. Times were hard then, and Ikie sometimes said his parents had not made a sale all day. He asked his Pawnee friends to go into the store and buy something. So if any of them had any money he would buy a pair of socks or a handkerchief. Sometimes Ikie would ask if anyone could buy him a sandwich, and he offered a pair of socks in trade.[46]

Several other merchants in the town are not remembered favorably by all Pawnee shoppers. One was the owner of the Peter Drug Store, established in 1903. It was a beautiful place with "Tiffany" glass, a long mirror, and bottles of colored water that caught the morning light. Old Man Peter was tightfisted and had a reputation for being hard on Indians. One time a little Indian boy come in and asked for an ice cream cone. Peter gave him one, and the boy handed him his pennies. He needed one more. So Peter reached over, took the cone out of the boy's hand, put the ice cream and cone back, and told the boy, "When you get enough money, come back and you can have a cone." An Indian who was watching followed him outside, gave him a penny, and told him to buy his ice cream at another store.[47]

THE PAWNEES AND THE BANKERS

It was not long after the town of Pawnee became established that town bankers came to play a major role in the Pawnees' lives. Some of the early bankers, such as Charles E. Vandervoort and Thomas E. Berry, had been

Indian traders. Also, Dr. C. W. Dreisbach, agency clerk W. B. Webb, and Dr. George H. Phillips entered the banking business after their agency employment ended. Isaac King Berry began his career at the agency in 1875 as a cattle herder. In 1878 he applied for and received a trader's license and ran a trading post for two years. He left that position and became a cattle rancher on the Cimarron River at the mouth of Stillwater Creek, where he stayed until 1891. His fortune grew, and he helped establish the Pawnee County Bank, chartered 11 December 1900.[48]

Other men associated with the new banks began as merchants in the new community. One was S. B. Berry. People claimed that he arrived on 16 September 1893, the day of the land run, and set up a store in a tent, selling groceries and hardware. In April of the following year the Bank of Pawnee was organized by Berry and F. M. Thompson. Later, when the bank became the First National Bank of Pawnee, Berry eventually became its manager.[49] Charles E. Vandervoort started building the First National Bank building in 1893 and completed it in 1894. By 1897 the former Indian trader and F. M. Thompson of the Arkansas Valley Bank, established in 1895, served on the organization committee for the new Oklahoma Bankers' Association. By 1901 Vandervoort had accumulated enough resources to construct another building on the town square. It first served as a "racket," or general merchandise store, then later the Marx brothers rented it as a clothing store.

The older Pawnees knew and talked about the early bankers in Pawnee – rarely complimentarily. They recalled that if they had debts and had to borrow money, they sometimes had to get mortgages on their land. They had difficulty repaying the loans, and some lost their land. One Pawnee remembered that his father and other Pawnee men were welcomed at one of the banks. They would go down a hall to a back room where there was a large table and some benches. The banker would walk in carrying a bottle or two of whiskey. "Here boys, have a drink. Enjoy yourselves," he would say. He put the bottles on the table and left the room.[50]

Later he came back smiling and asked, "Is there anything I can do for you boys? Do you need money?" Someone would say he needed to pay off some bills, and the banker would ask how much. Sometimes it could be as much as $100. The man would be given the money, and the banker had him put his thumbprint on a piece of paper. Others got money that way too, there in that back room, then they would have to come back and borrow more. Each time they either signed or put their thumbprint on a piece of paper. As time went by, they continued to borrow and could not pay it back. At some point this banker would say, "Well, so and so, I need to have my money back now, will you pay it?" The man could not, and he said no. He had to sign a paper, and the banker got his land for the borrowed money. This happened more than once, and the Pawnees claimed that a lot of them lost land that way. One man's cousin lost all his good bottomland along Black Bear Creek. Some of the Pawnee interpreters were said to be in on the deals; the old men often did not understand English, and by going along with the banker, the interpreters made money as they explained and manipulated the transactions.[51]

In 1910 Roam Chief, or Roaming Chief, a great warrior in Nebraska, ceremonial leader and chief of his band, had amassed a large debt to the Arkansas Valley National Bank of Pawnee. A statement of his indebtedness shows the date of the loan, the amount, the interest, and the total. On 2 July 1904 he borrowed $756. The interest was $539.20, for a total of $1,285.20 owed. The amounts he borrowed after that varied from $25 (interest $15.50) to $1 (interest $0.59). He made two payments in 1904 of $152.10 and $9.24, including principal and interest. On 10 May 1910 his indebtedness stood at $1,584.22, of which $645.22 was interest before the two payments above were credited.[52]

Oppressive Indian indebtedness at the Pawnee agency called for investigation, and in 1914 the Commissioner's Office sent a special agent to Pawnee to scrutinize the situation. His report revealed the troubled relationship between the Pawnees and certain town businessmen and bankers.

> Every Indian on the reservation, I believe, has a millstone of debt hanging around his neck, and there seems to be a well-systemized plan in the town of Pawnee to keep him in debt and charging him interest.
>
> There is one man named Spinning who has a large number of Indians in his debt. I have tried my best to find out how he figures interest, but he never can tell me, or he will not, and the Indians absolutely cannot tell me how much money they have received when they show me how much money Spinning's bill shows that he owes.

The Pawnee National Bank, an institution carrying $60,000.00 of Indian money, loans to the Indians weekly sums of money, which means his payment of annuity money and his payment of lease money. They claim they charge the legal rate of interest, and I have been unable to dispute the fact, but this much is well known, that the Indians who are paid their lease money and their annuity money in this office, it is almost safe to say that 90% of them paid their check over to the Pawnee National Bank for money that had been loaned to them from time to time and then they had began a new loan for the next six months. Just how much money the Pawnee Indians owe to the Pawnee National Bank is not known, but it must be up in the thousands of dollars. There is no time of the day that you cannot find a number of Indians in there waiting to borrow money in the back room. I believe, although I cannot prove it, that these people are getting a large rate of interest. They take a note for three to six months, have it paid, and take another note for three or six months and have that paid, and charge full interest. They tell me that where the Indian is reliable, and they know that he will pay his debts, that he gets the money just the same as the white man, that may be true, but it does not look good to me, and it should not look good to the Department that a bank carrying $60,000.00 of Indians money should be loaning this money to other Indians and charging them three times as much interest on their own money as the Indian himself is receiving. I believe that if the bank was properly investigated by a thoroughly competent bank man together with a duly authorized official bank examiner that there would be a condition found there which would cause the department to withdraw the Indian deposits now in that bank, in the same way that they did the money on deposit in the Ralston bank.[53]

Except for the bank at Ralston, the special agent did not mention in his report the business dealings of the town's other banks with the Indians. Other Pawnees' liabilities, such as Roaming Chief's indebtedness to the Arkansas Valley National Bank, indicate the practices suggested by the special agent's report were not unique to the Pawnee National Bank.

It is apparent that when there were few or no ways to earn money and few funds in an individual's account at the agency, it became necessary to find other resources to supply family needs. With several children to feed and clothe, the Blaines gradually became indebted to town bankers and other moneylenders. On 16 November 1901, Wichita Blaine placed an X on a note that reads: "March 13, 1902 after date, without grace, we promise to pay to Sarah E. Spinning on order One hundred and Eighty Dollars for value received, negotiable and payable at Pawnee O.T. without defalcation or discount, with 12 percent interest per annum from maturity until fully paid. The interest if not paid when due, to become part of the principal and bear the same rate of interest."[54]

R. C. Spinning, a local businessman, witnessed the marks of Wichita Blaine and Anna Wichita Blaine. In 1905 G. W. Nellis, agency superintendent, received notification that the note had not been completely paid. Spinning stated that on 1 March 1902 Blaine paid $5, on 12 March $12, on 8 September $5, and on 25 September 1902, $25. No further payments had been made, and with interest the amount of $190.44 was due. At the bottom of the page appeared the statement. "I Wichita Blaine and Anna Wichita Blaine, his wife, each for themselves state that we gave Mr. Spinning the note for $180.00 as above stated, and it was for meat, and to take up another note he held against us. We are both willing that Mr. Spinning may be paid out of any money coming to us from the sale of an inherited indian allotment."[55]

His indebtedness increased. Between 15 December 1904 and 2 June 1905 Blaine had accumulated a debt of $163.65 to D. N. Hatfield. On 14 May 1905 he owed banker G. M. Berry $305.13. On 10 May 1910 the First National Bank of Pawnee claimed he owed $782.09. The initial loan on 29 October 1903 had been $473; interest on the unpaid balance added to the final amount owed. He incurred other debts as well. In 1920 Dr. J. L. Lehew, to whom the Blaines were indebted, purchased half of Wichita's allotment through the agency.[56] It is not known whether he sold the allotment to Lehew for debts owed or whether he sold it for money to pay other debts to local merchants and bankers. By now he was totally blind.

The Blaine financial distress continued. In August 1924 the agent responded to a letter to the Washington Indian Office written by Louis Bayhylle for Effie Blaine. She complained that she could not get her funds from the agency for her needs. The agency superintendent replied that she and her husband were blind and on a monthly allowance. "Their funds are very limited and their source of income is practically exhausted. It was necessary to sell a portion of Mrs. Blaine's land to secure revenue for them."[57]

THE LAND: LEASE AND SALE

Today older Pawnees who lived during those years agree that many persons in their families lost their land in order to pay their debts. According to the General Allotment Act of 1887 (26 Stat. 794, 51 Cong. 2 sess.), Indian allotment land could not be alienated, and the United States would hold it in trust status for twenty-five years. Many idealist reformers of the time, who advocated the allotment policy, stated that the Indians should have their own land and become self-supporting in the whites' image. But somehow the idealism of the few faded before the reality that many citizens continued to care less about the Indians' having farms and more about acquiring Indian land as their own piece of America.

After allotment, the reservation became divided into individual Pawnee and settler land parcels. The newcomers soon observed the possibility of gaining the use of more Indian land. It became apparent to them as they drove by Indian places, or talked to each other in town, that many Indians would not or could not farm their land. In response to widespread pressure requesting permission to rent underutilized allotment land in other areas, an amendment to the 1887 General Allotment Act had become law on 28 February 1891. It declared that any disabled Indian who could not farm his allotment could lease it for three years for farming or grazing.[58] The Pawnees found that after allotment was completed, they were approached almost immediately by non-Indians who wanted to lease their land.

During the 1890s other congressional acts were passed that modified the earlier act. In 1894 the term "inability" was added to the conditions of old age and physical disability. The length of leasing was changed from three to five years, much to the benefit of non-Indians, because these additions permitted a greater number of Indian land leases to be made for a longer time, since "inability" could be and was interpreted broadly.

As more and more Pawnees chose to lease their new allotments, it became apparent that these regulations were defeating the purpose of turning Indians into self-sufficient individuals, so in 1897 the term "inability" was dropped and the time of the lease changed back to three years. Even allotment advocates now realized that lease laws had reaped unexpected results. Each year more and more individuals chose to lease instead of taking up the plow.[59] In some cases it was necessary. The Blaines could not farm after blindness came; for disabled individuals, leasing supplemented a meager income. Other Pawnees had minimal interest in farming their allotments. They wanted to leave their solitary farms periodically, camp near one another, and find satisfaction in traditional ways. The Christmas camps are still talked about. The Skidis built little houses around their round house and lived in them for extended periods during the major ceremonies. Additionally, farming did not suit everyone's ambitions and dreams. As one Pawnee said to me, it was as if someone said to the Italians, "You all have to be cooks and work in restaurants!"

There was an growing awareness of the Indian point of view. In his 1896 annual report, the Pawnee agent J. P. Woolsey recognized that "some Indians, like some white men, will make good farmers, while others never will. . . . Young fellows come back fresh from school fitted for something else that suits them far better than tilling the soil. . . . It is not suited to them nor they to it."[60]

Five years later the Pawnee superintendent answered a letter of 28 December 1901 from the commissioner. "I find that the Indians of this tribe have, so far as all farming operations are concerned, gone backward continually since the opening of the reservation."[61] He did not say so, but leasing allowed many Pawnees to gather, camp, and take part in their ceremonies, including the Ghost Dance.

In 1908 Commissioner F. E. Leupp made efforts to reform the leasing system in order to reach the government's unrelenting goal of creating self-sufficient Indians. He said leasing applied only to those who were unable to farm for specific reasons. He discouraged the practice of allowing any able-bodied man to lease his land. As an incentive to "progressive" tribal members, Indians could lease their own land and collect the rent if they could prove they were *competent* to do so. The agent would determine if a person was capable or not. All other leases continued to be subject to approval by the secretary of the interior.[62]

Competency was defined by three categories into which the superintendent placed Pawnee tribal members owning land. The first group consisted of those who had the education and general intelligence to handle their own allotments and those of their children. The second group included those who by reason of general character, and in many cases the ability to speak and write English, should be allowed the privilege of handling their own allotments but not those of their children. Like those individuals in the first group, they should be able to receive the funds held in trust for them by the United States Treasury. The third group consisted of those who because of old age, mental or physical infirmity, and inability to speak English were incompetent to take care of their own business: "These individuals and their children, their allotments and their annuity money should remain under the care of the government."[63] The first group contained the name of John Box, but Wichita and Effie Blaine did not appear on any list.

By 1910 all landowning tribal members were officially classified as competent or noncompetent to manage their land. The former group could lease their land, and the latter had to have the agency lease it for them and receive payment that went into their agency-controlled account.

It was not long before non-Indians' aspirations to lease Indian land changed to a desire to own it. The General Allotment Act provided that at the end of the twenty-five-year trust period the allotment owner would be issued a patent in fee for his land. For the Pawnees, that would be in 1918. By this time it was believed the Indians would have become successful in managing their own affairs and the government would remove itself from its oversight and guardianship role.

The Burke Act of 8 May 1906 stipulated that only Indians capable of responsibly handling their own affairs and business should receive title to their lands free of government supervision.[64] An individual considered and certified as competent to handle his own affairs could be granted a fee patent by the secretary of the interior *before* the twenty-five-year trust period expired. Once an Indian had title to his land, theoretically he was free to sell it. Cynics claimed there was another motivation for passing the act – that eventually this law would separate the Indians and their land permanently – and it proved true. Abuses in promoting and allowing land sales became numerous. In some areas white farmers and speculators urged allottees to apply for competency status, promising to buy their land when they acquired title to it. Banks lent money and held mortgages on land, and non-Indian guardians controlled minor Indians' land and its sale.

Nevertheless, in 1913 Commissioner Cato Sells believed that the Indian problem, as it was now called, would be solved by continuing and widening the program of granting patents. He repeated the old argument that the Indians should learn to stand on their own feet, have title to their own land, and not be under the control of the government. Sells received support for his views from some sources eager to acquire land then held in trust.

As a result of the policy, many Indians received fee patents whether they applied for them or not, and even if they said they did not want them. Specially appointed commissioners traveled around the country interviewing Indians or their agents and deciding on Indian competency. Often they talked only to the agent or superintendent and not to the Indians they were supposed to interview. When the commissioners came to Pawnee, Rush Roberts told the commissioners that he did not speak, read, or write English and did not want to have title to his land; he wanted it to stay in trust. He and others received fee patents anyway.[65]

In 1908 it was found that over 60 percent of the individuals granted title to their land soon lost it, usually by sale.[66] Thousands of acres of Indian land removed from trust status became the property of whites during the following years. In 1910–11 the Pawnee agency issued twenty-seven fee patents, of which twenty were sold.[67] To a great extent, in a short time the former owners found themselves poorer than ever; 60 percent or more of the sale money was turned over to their creditors.

In 1923 in his annual narrative report to the commissioner of Indian affairs, the Pawnee superintendent said:

Present indications are that what now appears to have been a too rapid granting of fee patents, and too much latitude as to sales, has tended toward congregating in towns and the leasing of farms where good homes had been provided, with the result that there is less progress in farming than should have been expected. It is of course impracticable to compel these Indian to remain on farms if they prefer some other mode of living, but we can, and probably should, use every available means to encourage and assist those who are able and willing to live on their own land.[68]

The original Pawnee reservation had contained 283,019.98 acres; the allotted land totaled 112,710.14 acres. By 1923 more than half of the allotment acreage, 69,710 acres, had been sold or had left trust status, and there were 43,000 acres held in trust by the federal government with much of it leased to area farmers and ranchers.[69]

Problems between lessees and Indian owners became a part of Indian-white relations. In the 1920s and 1930s times were hard in Oklahoma. Many white farmers could not or would not pay their annual rent. Some agency superintendents assiduously sought payment and turned the delinquent lessees' names over to the local United States attorney for prosecution. Others did little, allowing the whites to continue to use the land without paying, sympathizing with their plight but not with that of their Indian wards.

Other situations arose in which lessees attempted to cheat by deception or take advantage of an Indian's ignorance. Garland Blaine and his brother each inherited half of the 160-acre allotment of Maggie Box, their mother. When Garland married, he lived on his half in a small three-room frame house. He leased the bulk of his 80 acres to a white man and let the man's helper, Blackie, a black man, and his wife live in a small three-room house nearby. Blackie's main job was to take care of the lessee's cattle that grazed on the Blaine pastures.

Garland Blaine found odd jobs here and there, and from his agency-controlled account he received small amounts of the remaining royalties from a shallow oil well that had stopped producing. Some other lease money helped the family scrape by, but there was not always enough money even then.

The white man leased the land for $300 a year, paying half to each brother. One day some "government men" came to talk to Garland and asked if any of the cattle there were his. "No," he said. "occasionally I will ask for a calf, and my leaser will give it to me." (Leaser is the term commonly used for lessee.) Sometimes he sold the calf or butchered it for food; he did not have one at the moment.

Not long after that, the sheriff came and said he had arrested the lessee because he "rustled" cattle and brought them to the Blaine allotment. He kept them there awhile, then took them away and sold them. Rustling was a serious offense, and Garland later heard that the man had "done time."

This ended that lease arrangement, and soon after another man approached Blaine and said he would like to lease the land. "I don't have a lot of money, and I'll only be able to pay you $100 a year for your eighty," he claimed.

Blaine told him he'd been getting $150 and wanted that much. The man said maybe the next year he could pay that but not now, so he went away. Before the next leasing time came around, he returned and Blaine told him he would have to have $200. Times were getting harder, and he would have to have that much. "Oh, now, Garland, I can't afford that," the potential lessee replied. Garland knew he could, and finally the man agreed.

Garland Blaine told his wife that if the man came around and tried to talk her down on the amount, she was not to accept it. Nevertheless, after he went back to school at Chilocco, the man came to the house and pressured her into signing the lease papers (which she could do) for $100. He said he would pay it in four installments of $25. When Garland came home and heard what happened, he "blew his top," he said. But it was too late. He went to see the man, who said, "Business is business, and when you do business with your friends you must keep your wits about you."

Next year when the man came by Garland Blaine informed him that since he had been taken advantage of, now he would not lease the land for anything less than $200. It was too early to get the lease papers from the agency, and Blaine had found work as a plasterer and had to go to Kansas.

The man waited until Garland was gone and came during a time when he knew money was scarce. He offered Garland's wife the same amount, $100, with the same sad story of how hard up he was, and again the woman signed the papers.

The next year he came by, and this time he smiled and said, "Well, I guess you want to lease it again for $100?" Garland Blaine replied, "No, you are wrong. This year I want $300 for the land, and I know I can get it." (Tex Wells, an old cowboy, had said he would offer that much.) The lessee thought and said, "Well, I guess you are right. I'll give you a check." "No, I want cash," Garland interrupted. So after thinking that over, the man pulled a small roll of bills out of his overalls pocket and handed over the $300, saying, "I'll go into town and change the date on the old lease papers, and that'll be fine."

The same day Wes Wells, Tex's son, came to the house and said, "Garland, come to town. I want you to hear something at the Pitch Parlor." They went into town, and Garland stood outside the place, where he could hear but couldn't be seen. Wes went into the hall and started to talk. "Well,

Berry, you didn't lease that Blaine place for $100 again did you?" The man laughed, "No, the boy's got a job now, but when he weren't working, you could wave $100 in front of them, and they'd jump at it like frogs." At this Garland said, "It was all I could do not to go in there and go after him."

Wes came out and said, "Did you hear that? Did you lease to him?" "Yes," said Garland, but he wants to use last year's lease papers. I haven't signed anything. He paid me." Wes said, "Well, as he always says, business is business. How much do you want to lease if for? $300?" Blaine agreed. "Well," said Wes, "let's go to the agency and make out the correct papers, and I'll pay you $300."

So they went to the agency and drew up new papers. Wes asked the agent if he could pay Garland directly and not go through the agency as was usual. The agent said, "Okay," and Tex handed Garland the money.

By that evening the story was all over town that old Berry had finally "got took." The next morning he came to the house before the sun rose. "Garland," he yelled outside, "did you lease your land to Wes?" Garland went out and said, "Yes I did." "Well then," said the man, "give me my money back." Garland looked surprised and said, "What money?" The other yelled, "I gave you $300!" "Why, you didn't give me a thing," Garland responded. "He blew his top and threatened to put the law on me," Garland recalled." He didn't do it, though."

Garland further recalled, "Not long after that the leaser's son came up to me and said, 'You did a bad thing to my father.' " Garland answered, "I did a bad thing once, but he's done a bad thing to me every time he's leased my land." Hoping to catch him, the son asked, "What bad thing did you do to him?" Garland looked right at him and said, "I turned him down on the lease this last time. And as your Dad always says, business is business."

This account illustrates the difficulties that existed for many Pawnee individuals. They had insufficient capital to buy equipment, seed, and stock to farm for themselves, or obtain employment in the surrounding depression-poor area, where they might be the last ones hired. So leasing their land became the only option for obtaining income. In leasing, the Blaines and others usually had to accept the amount offered. They usually had to stick with the same lessee because there was little chance to get another offer. When money was needed in the past and the present, many Indians went to their lessees and borrowed on next year's lease money.

This helped the lessee to maintain his lease, particularly if it happened during the last year of the lease period and the money could not be paid back. Since the individual was indebted, he was obligated to lease again to the lessee, even if he did not particularly like the man or his offer. This could go on for years.[70] Although some Pawnees have found their lessees honest and helpful, others claim that some lessors have ruined Indian land when they could get away with it. They have let the farm ponds erode, overgrazed the land, and let fences run down, even though their lease agreements state this was not allowed.[71]

GUARDIANSHIPS

It is apparent that many guardians were appointed without regard to their fitness and insolvent bondsmen accepted. It was not uncommon for lands of minor Indian children to be sold on appraisement influenced by prospective purchasers and for inadequate prices. Excessive compensation was many times allowed guardians and unreasonably large fees paid to attorneys. Under these conditions the property of Indian children was frequently so ravished that when final reports were called for they were not forthcoming, and estates were often found to have been dissipated and their bondsmen financially irresponsible. Altogether it developed a condition demanding speedy and radical reforms.

Cato Sells, Commissioner of Indian Affairs, September 21, 1913

Today very few Pawnees remember that their parents or grandparents or their peers had white guardians in the century's early years. The oldest living Pawnee, Myra Lone Chief Eppler, who was 102 years old on 15 July 1996, did remember the "gardeens" of her childhood. "But why did they have guardians?" asked an eighty-five-year-old relative seated nearby. "So and so had her parents. Austin had his grandparents. . . . Why did they have to have a guardian?"[72]

The General Allotment Act of 1887, section 6, stated that "upon the completion of said allotments and the patenting of the lands to said allottees, each and every member of the respective bands or tribes of Indians to whom allotments have been made shall have the benefit of and be subject to the laws, both civil and criminal, of the State or Territory in which they may reside."[73] The Organic Act of 1890 that established Oklahoma Territory provided that as soon as Indian reservations opened to settlement, their inhabitants should become citizens of the territory.[74]

After allotment and the breakup of the reservation, the former Pawnee reservation area became part of Oklahoma Territory, and of the state of Oklahoma in 1907.

Before the opening of the Cherokee Outlet, Grover Cleveland's presidential proclamation of 19 August 1893 provided for the establishment of various counties in the new territory. Some received temporary letter names; County Q later became Pawnee County.[75] Territorial courts had criminal jurisdiction over Indians in Oklahoma Territory, as they did in other territories where Indians lived. The first statutes of the new territory established a district court system under which Indians became subject to certain laws affecting marriage, death, inheritance, property, guardianship, and other matters.[76]

Important cultural changes occurred at this time and in 1907, when Oklahoma Territory and Indian Territory became the state of Oklahoma. Polygamy, a traditional marriage system among many tribal societies worldwide, was frowned upon as immoral by the larger society and was also illegal. According to the law the few Pawnee men who had more than one wife had to select one and put aside the others.[77] A Pawnee county court docket volume registered the names of a Pawnee husband, his wives, their ages, and the woman he chose to be his legal wife. It is aptly named the "Selection Docket." After statehood in 1907, marriage licenses and registration of legally attested vows had to be recorded in county records.[78] Although traditional marriage patterns continued for a while, with interfamily arrangements, gift exchanges, feasts, and ceremonies between kin groups, most couples later traveled to the courthouse to marry in the white man's way. Others, now members of Indian mission churches, made their vows before a Christian minister.

Pawnee traditional culture emphasized the importance and cohesiveness of the family. If one parent or both died, family members such as grandparents, uncles, and aunts took the children and provided for their well-being. There was no need for outsiders to become part of the process. However, after territorial law imposed itself upon customary ways, the Pawnees learned about the concept of legal guardianship as the white man defined it. As early as 1894, County Q (Pawnee County) probate court records indicate that many Pawnee children had guardians assigned to them. For the most part guardians were family members who would have acted as surrogate parents without legal intervention. Among the listed guardians were Harry Coons, James R. Murie, Alfred Murie, Fearing Bear Wilde, Joseph Howell, Emmett Pearson, Seeing Eagle, Alex Hand, Walter Sun Chief, Lone Chief, Running Scout, Thomas Morgan, Brave Chief, John Moses, Eagle Chief, Charles Chapman, Webster Fox, Belle Coons, Isabelle Evarts, Joseph Carrion, George Howell, and Henry Eagle Chief. The majority of these guardians were Skidis, as were the children.[79]

The extensive territorial guardianship laws, modeled after the *Statutes of Nebraska,* included the duties and responsibilities of the local Pawnee probate court in these matters.[80] On 26 February 1895, a court hearing designated Jerry Minor, a white man, guardian of Gertie Esau, age eleven. He claimed to be her stepfather. Her parents, Joseph and Nora Esau, were dead. Listed as relatives were her uncles, the Skidi chief Lone Chief and his brother Emmett Pierson; her half-sister, Mary Murie; and her half-aunt, Mrs. John Box. Nothing is known about her relatives' response to this legal action, if they even knew about it at the time.

Hearing witnesses were Dr. G. H. Phillips, A. A. Paterson, George Cotton, C. E. Vandervoort, and Robert Chasteen, deputy sheriff. Their names were to appear frequently as the years passed. Although Phillips, Vandervoort, and Chasteen were witnesses, it was not long before they themselves began to appear in the records as guardians, and Pawnee relatives were less frequently selected or were removed by the probate court and replaced by local non-Indians – entrepreneurs who saw guardianship as good business.

According to the *Statutes of Oklahoma* in 1890, the laws regarding guardianship provided, among other stipulations, that each guardian should manage the estate of the minor until that person came of age or married, or until the guardian was discharged. He was to "dispose of and manage the estate according to law and for the best interest of the ward."[81] All of a minor's debts were to be paid by the guardian from the minor's funds, and if they were insufficient, the guardian could sell the minor's real estate after obtaining an order from the court. A crucial statement allowing for misuse of the prerogative stated that "the guardian may join in and assent to a partition of the real estate of the ward, whenever such assent may be given by any person."[82] The guardian could also charge the minor's estate for "reasonable" expenses incurred in fulfilling his duties.[83] These regulations opened the way for well-practiced malfeasance.

Pawnee minors did not have great amounts of money. Their agency-controlled accounts held their annual annuity, amounting to less than $100 a year, as well an any income from their allotments or inherited land. Their wealth lay in their land. As a result of the high death rate of parents, grandparents, and other kin members, many children had inherited interests in a number of allotments, as did Garland Blaine and his brother. Early on this important fact caught the attention of certain local whites. Using the law to advance their financial status became a compelling reason for non-Indians to become involved in the "graft" of guardianship, as the historian Angie Debo described the practice in *And Still the Waters Run,* a story of this scandalous situation in the Creek Nation in Indian Territory.[84]

These guardianship laws allowed for control of minors' real estate and the income from it and for its sale. Few non-Indians would assume the duties of guardianship out of the goodness of their hearts, especially those who controlled the funds and lands of over thirty children (see appendix B). It became a business, allowing guardians to make money in various ways, as is demonstrated by a letter of 30 May 1904 from a Kansas City bondsman to the Pawnee superintendent.

> I have noticed by the papers of recent date, that there is going to be a payment of money to the Indians soon. In the settlement and payment of money there are Guardians appointed for minor children, and in that event, bond is required I suppose, the same as other places, is it not? I would like to know about the date, you expect this payment to be made and who the Probate Judge is of your place.
>
> I am anxious to get some of this business and any information you can give me on this, will be highly appreciated.[85]

Would-be guardians solicited the names of prospective wards from the Pawnee Indian Agency clerk-in-charge, W. B. Webb. He left agency employment and became a guardian himself in 1901 and 1902, acquiring. among his thirteen wards, Bessie Blaine, age six, and James G. Blaine, age fifteen, children of Wichita and Effie Blaine.[86] Like others', his fortune escalated, and he later became active in the management of a local bank.

Other former agency employees also entered the guardian business, including Joseph D. Turner, a former additional farmer with thirteen wards,

Dr. G. H. Phillips, with fourteen, and C. E. Vandervoort with eighteen. Court records show that one of Vandervoort's wards, Eugene Haymond, age three, had real estate valued at $10,000. The individual with the greatest known number of wards was Robert Chasteen, who between 1899 and 1901 acquired guardianship rights over thirty-three children. The oldest, Kate Walker, was seventeen years old, the youngest, Mary E. Carrion, was three. As the years passed, other guardians included local doctors, dentists, merchants, druggists, bankers, ranchers, and others (see appendix B).[87]

Agency superindentents and clerks worked closely with guardians. Besides submitting minors' names, they sent petitions for guardian appointments to the local probate judge. For example, Maud New Rider, Harry Fox, and Cora and Julia Jim were assigned to G. H. Phillips, and Dora Rutter to H. E. Thompson, on 16 April 1904.[88]

If a minor's expenses and his guardian's fees exceeded the amount in the minor's funds, then his land could be appraised and sold. Petitions for sale of a minor's land had to be signed by the guardian and returned to the agency.[89] Certain guardians sought appointment so as to place themselves in a position to purchase their wards' lands. A 1912 map of Pawnee County shows this is true. Many minors' heirship lands now carried the name of their guardians or others.[90]

Land speculators in Pawnee worked with guardians, and appraisers appointed by the court, to make a profit from Indian land sales. Court records reveal that some guardians appraised the land of other guardians' minors[91] – a cozy arrangement it seems. Other means existed for selling a minor's land. The child's guardian could persuade the parent to consent to the sale. It was legal, though the parent received less than the sale price because numerous court, attorney, and guardian fees were subtracted.[92]

The congressional act of 27 May 1902 was a great boon to guardians and others with profit motives. It stated that land inherited by minors from deceased allottees could be sold only by a court-appointed guardian. All such sales should be approved by the secretary of the interior with full title given to the purchaser upon this approval.[93] Study of the Pawnee guardian list in appendix B shows that the number of guardians expanded rapidly at that time.

Regardless of the desire or ability of parents or other relatives to care for a child, court dockets contain the following often erroneous entries in referring to Indian kinsmen: "Mother doesn't properly care for the person or property of said minor. Has no relatives capable of managing it." "His mother does not properly save his income for his benefit. No relative capable." "Nearest relative does not properly care for real estate of said minor and does not save for him any portion of the money belonging to said minor." The phrase "has no relatives capable or competent of managing estate" appears in case after case. For Garland Blaine's father, who was fifteen years old in 1902, a notation reads, "The said minor is possessed of valuable real estate which is not being properly cared for for his use and benefit."[94] At the time, however, his allotment was leased and the income helped support his family. Such false comments enabled the court to assign numerous non-Indian guardians.

Former agency employees who became guardians had previous access to Indian records, so they knew who owned land and what its value was. They probably also knew the minors' parents and relatives and in most situations understood that they were fully capable of caring for their children. Nevertheless, they did not hesitate to lie to gain guardianship rights for themselves and others. Many men they maligned were respected tribal leaders. Captain Jim was the Pitahawirata band chief, a former United States Army Pawnee Scout, and a respected ceremonial leader. His two children, Viola, five, and Cora, seven, became wards of the former agency clerk W. B. Webb on 1 October 1902. The notation in the court record refusing Jim's petition to remain his children's guardian reads: "Your petitioners Captain Jim, Lucy Smith, Hannah Jim and St. Elmo Jim, all Pawnee Indians and none of them are fit to be the guardians of the estates of said minors."[95]

Affronted and angry about the guardianship villainy among their people, Ponca tribal leaders took their protests to Washington DC. The tribe was under the same agency superintendent and jurisdiction as were the Pawnees, Otoes, Missourias, and Tonkawas. Horse Chief Eagle, the chief, stated that the Department of the Interior forced the appointment of white guardians over the property of the Ponca minor children. In addition, through this action they claimed that the "government is selling their land and allowing them but $10 per month to live upon. The Indians feel that they are being wronged in this, that they can rent their lands for more than $10 a per month, thus receiving more than is coming to them through the beneficent administration through the department of the interior and still have their lands left. They also object to white guardians for the property of their children, alleging that they are competent and that they will look after their children's affairs with more genuine interest in the welfare of their offspring than white men could possibly have."[96]

The irregularities of the Indian minors' guardian situation in Oklahoma Territory received official notice. In 1905 Colonel John Mosby, an attorney with the United States Department of Justice, arrived in Oklahoma to investigate the various charges. A newspaper in Oklahoma City reported that he came to investigate the condition of minor Indians' estates, "particularly in Pawnee County, the Osages, Payne and Lincoln Counties." It was said that the Indian children were systematically being robbed by their guardians and that Horace Speed, the United States attorney for Oklahoma Territory, had requested the investigation. The newspaper added that the colonel was a courtly elderly gentleman who ordered a pitcher of buttermilk upon his arrival at the Oklahoma City hotel.[97] Regardless of his temperate preference in liquid refreshment and his well-mannered demeanor, he knew his business and had previously worked in the Territory at Ardmore, where his investigation of school warrant frauds had led to indictments and convictions.

The arrival of a representative of the United States Department of Justice did not deter the territorial effort to add to guardians' powers and income. In the month after Mosby's arrival, the territorial legislature passed and Governor Ferguson signed bills that allowed Indians' guardians to lease oil and gas rights for royalties and to mortgage their wards' real estate.[98]

Mosby's investigation brought results. On 20 March 1906 Indian agents and superintendents received instructions to sign leases for minors and incompetents, including those with guardians assigned to them. No money from leasing could be turned over to guardians appointed by the probate courts. Judges of such courts were to inform guardians to close their accounts and turn their minors' funds over to Indian agency officers.[99]

In July 1906 Cassius R. Peck, an assistant United States attorney, received the authority to carry out the assignment to see that guardianship became each agency superintendent's responsibility.[100] On 20 September 1906 a ruling stated that "it is the desire of the Department [of the Interior] that Agents and Superintendents shall be appointed guardians for minor Indian children" and added that if the minor's parents were competent, they should be their child's guardians.[101]

In a ruling of 4 February 1907 agents and superintendents could sign leases "for and on behalf of all minor and incompetent Indian allottees without being appointed by the Probate Courts for that purpose."[102] In August 1907 the Pawnee superintendent, George Nellis, ordered C. H. Stewart to discharge all guardians and turn their wardships over to him as directed by law.[103]

The state rejected these rulings. In December 1907 the Oklahoma state attorney general's office declared that the county court had the power to appoint guardians for minor Indian children until otherwise provided for by Congress. The county court also had the power to approve Indian leases made by guardians. The opinion was based on section 13 of the Oklahoma Enabling Act, which stated that the state had jurisdiction over all matters that were not appealed to the United States circuit court.[104] From this interpretation, it was concluded that the state had jurisdiction over all probate matters involving Indian minors.[105]

The new state was not about to give up the bonanza derived from powers held by the court and its appointed guardians, or to relinquish any authority on issues it considered states' rights. Under the new state's laws, under "Guardian and Ward" sections, extensive rules detailed duties and responsibilities.[106] In February 1908 Congress declared that Indian minors of the Five Civilized Tribes must be placed under the jurisdiction of the state probate courts, like all other minors in the state. At the same time the law stated that a female reached majority at eighteen and a male at age twenty-one. This extended the period under which a guardian would control the Indian minor's funds and property. The laws did provide for prosecution of guardian malfeasance, however, and the secretary of the interior could reclaim lands gained by fraud.[107]

The 1903 *Oklahoma Territorial Statutes* stated that a minor, after reaching age fourteen, could nominate his own guardian. If he failed to choose, then the court could appoint one.[108] In the Pawnee court records, there are several instances of this. The minor was required to sign a form agreeing to the appointment of a named guardian. In the case of James G. Blaine, the signature was not his.[109] When Maggie Box reached age fourteen in 1906, C. E. Vandervoort became her guardian, and the record reads, "I join in above petition," but Maggie Box's signature appears to be in the same writing as is the rest of the record's entry.[110] Vandervoort was not discharged as her guardian until 15 January 1914, after her marriage. Ezra Tilden, father of Katie Tilden, age fourteen, approved, as did she, of Vandervoort's becoming her guardian on 23 January 1906. He retained guardianship until 1914, as he did for Warren Leader, age fourteen in 1906.[111] These and other Pawnees were in their twenties when guardians no longer controlled their funds and land. The incentive for Blaine and others to accede to guardianship control of their funds has not been discovered.

In the spring of 1994 Myra Eppler (M. E.), soon to be one hundred years old, and her eighty-five-year-old relative (M. C.) discussed guardianship with me (M. B.). Portions of the recorded conversation show the two elderly women's feelings and knowledge.

M.C. WHO was your guardian?

M.E. I didn't have any. I had my folks.

M.C. BUT Warren Leader and Walter Keys had their people, and Vandervoort was still their guardian! I don't understand that.

M.E. INSTEAD of going to the agency, they went to their gardeen to get their money.

M.C. AND that guardian took some of that money from them.

M.E. LIKE the Knife Chiefs and Sarah. They had a gardeen, and I would go with them on Saturdays, and they would get their money. I don't know how they kept records.

M.B. [SHOWS a photocopy of a courthouse record with a guardian's account charges listed.]

M.E. WELL they got paid.

M.C. THEY got paid more than they should have!

M.E. I know Vandervoort got a lot of them [minors]. He was with the First National Bank, on the north side of the square near the jewelry store. Then they moved them across the street. And that First National Bank is on the corner and we called it the Chawi

Bank. They did all their business there, and Vandervoort was with the National Bank, and he worked with the Skidis. When I grew up the superintendent was my gardeen, even though my folks were living. My money was in there, but my parents could go over there, like my mother wanted to get my money, so she told the agent, you give me her money, and I'll give her ten acres of my land. So they did. I was about ten.

M.C. JIM Murie had some.[112]

M.E. YOU know how James R. Murie was. He was smart, and you have to be smart to be a crook.

M.C. YES, he was too smart.

M.E. MY uncle Knife Chief passed away and his children had to go under guardianship . . . where they had lands you know. They had to have somebody to look after them. The gardeens kept the children's money, and they used to go there on town days [from school]. There would be a whole line of them lined up ready to get some money – same gardeen. Some of them gardeens were in real estate.

M.C. [LOOKING at the document copy] There is Eugene Haymond with property worth $10,000. His guardian was Vandervoort, and that is how he got his money.

M.B. [TELLS about Wichita Blaine's debts to Spinning.]

M.E. HE was one of them that worked against the Indians.

M.B. How did he do that?

M.E. THEY'D borrow money from him, and all at once he'd foreclose. They would say one thing, and then they'd tell you something else. You know they had to have interpreters. And a lot of them interpreters were just as crooked.

M.C. JUST as crooked, they got something, naturally.

M.E. YES. Lehew was pretty good, but I don't know, my folks did not deal with them [guardians]. But Vandervoort, I don't know how he did it. But those gardeens did get a lot when those children who had oil . . . when the oil came in.[113]

In the early 1900s oil and gas discoveries in Oklahoma Territory and Indian Territory caught the attention of speculators and "oil men" from all over the country. Many Pawnee allotments were leased for possible oil and gas exploration. In 1914 the Eastern Oil Company of Buffalo, New York, leased White Horse's allotment. By 21 June 1918, agency records indicate that it had been sold to a local banker, Frank Hudson.[114] His heirs retained no mineral rights. According to agency correspondence with Frank Hudson, Lagoon Oil and Gas held a lease to Maggie Box Blaine's allotment. She petitioned to sell half of it but died in 1916 before the sale could be completed. She left two minor heirs who were almost destitute except for the property that descended to them through their parents. The agency recommended that the oil and gas lease be continued.[115] Many Pawnees sold their land to pay debts to men interested in the possibility of profitable oil discoveries. They had found yet another way to become wealthy from Indian land.

In summary, the words of Angie Debo are appropriate:

> Historians have been inclined to pussyfoot in this field of Indian exploitation. . . . The [Oklahoma] Indian allotments added together formed an area about the size of Indiana, rich in farmland, coal, and timber, and richer in oil production than any other state of the Union. This was a prize worth seizing. Rival combinations of guardians and attorneys fought each other to control the courts; public sentiment supporting the business was strong enough to dominate the legislature; and, with a few honorable exceptions, the press was purchased and the church was silenced by the profits of the unholy traffic.[116]

The Pawnees found this to be true. Although there were individuals they trusted and admired, for the most part they discovered that the whites had appeared again and found new ways to profit from them in matters concerning their land, their business dealings, their banking, and their children.

Part Two

BECOMING PAWNEE

SIX

Becoming Pawnee

"They told me it was a nice sunny day when I was born, March 25, 1915," Garland Blaine recalled. "My mother, Maggie Box Blaine, who had been staying with my paternal grandparents, traveled to her brother's, Ernest Box's, home near the town of Pawnee, so that Dr. J. L. Lehew could attend the birth." She would have stayed at her maternal home, but her mother was deceased and about this time her father, John Box, had remarried and gone to live with a new wife.

> My mother and her brothers were members of the Skidi band, and I think they did not follow all of the old ways such as having an Indian doctor attend the birth. The Pitahawirata band, to which my father belonged, tended to be more conservative and to follow the traditional methods of childbirth.[1] But it was not unusual for Dr. Lehew to attend Indian births, and he told the Pawnees who believed in white doctors that whenever a child was to be born [they should] come after him. A midwife came first, usually staying a few days with the family. When the time came, she would tell someone to get the doctor. Many Indians lived out in the country, and sometimes the child would be born before the doctor arrived in his horse and buggy. I think that Dr. Lehew arrived in time for my birth, because years later in Pawnee, he would say to me, "You are my boy. I attended your mother." He thought a lot of me.[2]
>
> My father was named after the prominent politician James G. Blaine. He was not present at my birth, and later I was told that

he had been away playing baseball with one of the traveling teams, possibly the Nebraska Indians, Triple I League.

My mother named me Garland James. The James was for my father; I do not know where she got the name Garland. Addie said she picked it out herself before I was born. Mother said it had a beautiful sound and a good rhythm to it. She had attended Haskell Indian School in Kansas and may have read it in a book. If I had been a girl my name would have been Elaine, my father's brother, Elmer, once told me.

If my mother had stayed with my Pitahawirata grandparents, my birth might have occurred in the traditional way. In those days the attendant or midwife could be an older lady, perhaps a relative such as a woman's mother, great-aunt, or grandmother. No younger person, such as a child, could be present, and usually, unless it was a doctor, a man was never allowed to be present because women should not expose themselves to any man except their husbands. If it was seen that the delivery was going to be difficult, a Pawnee doctor was called who had had a sacred vision in which he received the prayers, songs, and names of herbs, roots, and other things to use as medicines during the birthing process.

At one time Garland's grandmother Effie explained to him about the birth of one of his uncles. Her labor had been long, and she could not give birth. John Ruwalk was the closest doctor at the time, and he came with Rena, his wife, Eagle Chief's sister. Eagle Chief was then the head chief of the Pitahawirata band. Effie and Rena were cousins, but in the Indian way she called Rena Mother. When they got there Effie was sitting in the position to give birth. Large pillows had been placed behind her back to support her. Old Pawnee women in Nebraska and Oklahoma used to tell the young women to sit up for birthing. They said, "Those white people lay down. Don't go to them for giving birth. Go to our old women who know about such things."

John Ruwalk sat on her right side. Rena sat at her feet. My grandfather, Wichita Blaine, faced John on the left side. When John sang the special song, Grandfather, who was also a doctor, sang with him. Then the midwife sat beside Rena. Grandmother said she was in great pain and she could hardly breathe. The doctor talked to her, "I want you to know that there is only one place to look to for help.

That's the only place where we all look, and that is to Tirawahat [the supreme being].[3] He will feel sorry for us [bless us]. God felt sorry for me and I have this knowledge that was passed to me by his grace." That meant that through his sacred vision, John had gained knowledge that enabled him to assist in childbirth. He continued, "Now we are both looking to Tirawahat, and when I doctor you, I have sincere faith that He will bless you, and that you may see yourself again [have your child], and that you will live. So we must think now as one, and put our thoughts in his hands, or give our thoughts to Him."

My grandmother said that he took tobacco and medicine from his Sacred Bundle. Then he put medicine on hot coals nearby, and smoke rose in the room. She smelled it, and it drifted over her body. Then he started procedures that included talking and putting his hands on vital spots so as to cause childbirth to come about. She said she felt strangely consoled and fear left her. "My mind was made up to do whatever he told me. Even with all those people around me, a strange calmness came over me." The pain was there, but the fear left her and she wanted to do what was asked of her. When John started to sing his song, the pain became intense, and she felt she would become unconscious. It seemed like she would choke and stop breathing. "As he started his song, I put my faith in him. When he sang the part that says, 'When everything is well, now that I see myself again,' that is when delivery came. Tirawahat let me have my child. That night I saw magic."

Customarily, the doctor who was called would observe the mother and talk to her. Then he would know what animal, bird, or plant spirit she favored. Garland said his mother was said to be a flower because she was bright and alert in the morning and began to droop or fade in the afternoon. If the doctor could not help a woman because he did not have the ability or knowledge to relate to her particular spirit, he would recommend another doctor who did have it to come and treat her. But if the woman was having a very difficult time or there was not enough time to summon another doctor, he would do what he could do to assist in the birth. In most cases the woman's spirit was known and the doctor who could treat her was present.

After the birth, the midwife wrapped the umbilical cord around her index finger, with the heel of her hand touching the child's stomach. Or she would hold the cord and measure it a hand's width from the navel. This gave sufficient length to make the separation. The cord was doubled back and tied next to the stomach with sinew, then the sinew was wrapped around this fold four times and the cord and sinew were cut below the tie. Buffalo sinew was best, and in Nebraska they hardly ever used any other kind. After the people came to live in Indian Territory in the 1870s, however, it was necessary to use sinew from cows or other animals because buffalo sinew became hard to get. Preferably, the wrapped cord was kept greased with buffalo tallow. In time the healed cord would separate from the body. The Pawnees thought that white doctors left too much cord and cut it too far from the infant's body.

It was customary for the afterbirth to be buried outside the dwelling toward the east. The father usually did this, and it was thought to be important because a new day and life begin in the east. Garland remembered seeing this done after family births until he was ten or twelve, when his cousin was born.

Garland Blaine believed that Pawnee doctoring utilized psychological techniques. "In the case of childbirth," he said,

> it was important to get the confidence of the woman. The burning smell of the medicine and the use of hands on the forehead and other places were important. Prayers and lectures given would bring a united group response of deep thought. It was all earnestness. Confidence came. In the case of my grandmother, there may have been something in her mind concerning her and preventing birth. In such times it may leave under these circumstances, and the birth process would go naturally.
>
> I was born a male child. At that time the sex of the baby made some difference. The Pawnees valued a female child highly. They would come to see it and hold it, and say how wonderful it was to have a girl baby. They rejoiced with the family over her birth. However, a baby boy did not receive such adulation. Although the family was happy and pleased to see the little boy, they would often pick it up and say, Oh, you will see hard times. And sometimes they would cry for it. It was always better to have a girl. This was because

women were associated with life and its production. This belief was also interwoven with the importance of Mother Corn and Mother Earth in our religious beliefs.

Effie Blaine told Garland that the boy is lost to the family when he marries and must work to support the girl's family. Females were valued because their husbands brought wealth in the form of a bride gift at the time of marriage. When Effie married, she told her grandson that her family received several horses and many other items from her new husband's family.

The number of babies born was also important. Some tribes, such as the Poncas, were afraid of twins, but the Pawnee Pitahawirata are not. They think there is something mystical about them. They can do things that are unaccountable by reasoning. It is said that you must always be kind to them and let them have their way. If one dies, it is still with the other. Treat them carefully. They have magical powers. Be extra gentle with them because Tirawahat made them twice.[4]

I don't know how my Skidi mother was treated after my birth, but among the Pitahawirata, after giving birth, a wide band was wrapped snugly around the mother's stomach, and she spent several days lying down. Women were told to lie mostly on their stomach. My grandmother explained that the purpose of this was to keep the stomach from "folding out," and if this is done, then everything will go back in place. When my aunt had her children she did this, and grandmother made her stay in bed two weeks. But Grandmother said that when the tribe had traveled on the hunt it was not possible for women giving birth to have such a confinement.

Soon after a baby's birth, an adult in the family would warm his hands and begin to shape the baby's nose. With two fingers on either side of the bridge, the person would press gently down the sides to the base. This was done while holding the baby or while it was on its cradle board. A wetted thumb would be placed in the mouth and pressed against the roof to straighten the tooth ridge and open nasal passages. This was done so that a child would not grow up sniffling. That may sound strange, but if a child sniffed and snorted, the people would say, "Well he must have been born an orphan. He had no one to take care of him when he was born."

When a child is born, people visit the family and bring gifts to the family and the newborn. The infant's family and the gift bearers meet at the door, and each prays aloud for the other's family. For instance, my being head chief, I am expected to visit the family that has a new baby. For some reason I may be a month late. When I get to the house and the door is opened, I may say, "I hear a young lady or boy came here." Usually the grandparents or older relatives that may be present come forward and greet me. Then I will smile and say, "I am so sorry that I am late." Then I say he or she is probably eating well and is a young grown person by now, so I have brought some food. The family all come forward, and I shake and hold hands with each of them, and we all pray aloud for each other and the new baby.

During my first year of life, from March through May, I probably spent time at Uncle Ernest's for a while, then went to my Blaine grandparents' place. Later we visited Birdie Mannington and Addie Yellow Calf, our Skidi relatives. Birdie lived near Masham. I was told we visited Grandpa John Box and Mother's other brother, Henry Box. During the summer months of June, July, and August we returned to my Blaine grandparents' home. My father came home after the baseball season was over, and then we probably alternated between Grandma Addie's and Grandma Blaine's. We kept some clothes in both places.

My father was a professional baseball player. He had gone to Carlisle and had played with Jim Thorpe on the teams there. Father was gone a lot, and my mother did not want to stay by herself with a new baby; and the relatives would not have allowed that. That is why she took turns visiting both the Skidi and Pitahawirata sides of the family while my father was away.

The first winter was spent in town, but the year ended in tragedy. His father was killed in December 1915. When Garland was young he was told that his father had drowned, but the truth was that he died or was killed in the local Pawnee city jail. The story is told that he had just received a contract from the Chicago White Sox to play baseball for the next season and was celebrating with his friends. He drank too much, it was claimed, and was arrested and taken to the Pawnee jail. During the night, it was said, he was smoking, the bedding caught fire, and he was burned so badly that he died. An elderly Pawnee, who knew a man who had worked at the jail at that time, said that Garland's father was beaten to death by a jailer, then the fire was set to cover the crime. Maggie Box Blaine had the incident investigated, but the town's doctors who were selected to do the autopsy said he died of burns. Other elderly Pawnees have said Jim Blaine was killed in that jail.[5]

At this time Garland was nine months old and knew nothing of this tragedy. His mother was expecting another baby. He said, "I do not know if I was still nursing at this time or not. The old Pitahawiratas believed it was correct to wean a child before it was a year old. At about eight months a baby would be given a piece of gristle, just small enough for him to grasp, but too big for him to swallow. He could hold this in his hand and suck on it. At ten months the weaning process began, often aided by a bitter substance applied to the breast." Effie Blaine stated that all her children had been weaned before the first year. She said that if a child was still nursing at two, then his mother, whoever she was, was an old lady and still nursing, and that her child was walking around and still nursing.

> There were other ideas about nursing and weaning held by our old people when I was young. They said that if a baby's parents lived nearby, right after, or soon after, a grandchild is born, the grandparents should have the mother bring the baby to the grandparents, or they should go get the child and take it home with them. Then before he gets too hungry and it is time to nurse, they should take him back to his mother. They should have him stay with them off and on, so that he gets used to them. He will love them and trust them because he knows that when he gets hungry they will effect his being fed by taking him to his mother. When it's time for weaning, they will continue to keep him during the day and feed him soup rather than taking him to his mother.

Some babies fussed a little, but others accepted the new food, apparently without noticing the change. This relationship between grandparents and grandchildren was considered sacred. It was said that grandchildren are from God and have power by their presence to keep a person active and thus living.[6]

Certain old ladies were baby doctors. When a baby or a young child who was not yet talking got ill, depressed, or out of sorts, it would be taken to the old lady, who would observe it. She could talk with the baby and understand what it said. She would take it to bed with her, and late at night you could hear baby sounds and the old lady talking.

When morning came the old lady would say to the parents, "The baby told me last night what you are doing, and this is what you must do for this child to be made well." The parent would take the child and follow the baby doctor's directions, and usually the baby would recover.

But sometimes babies did not recover. Garland said a baby knows many things. It knows if it is not wanted, and it will leave (die) when it has a chance. This is what the old people say about a baby who dies when its paternity has been denied. A baby knows and understands many things. It forgets these things when it grows into learning. Therefore you should love a baby and hold it and be careful what you say and do – because it really knows more than you think it does.

In cases of establishing paternity or legitimacy, if a young unmarried woman became pregnant, definite steps were taken.

> In our band, if the girl was forced and raped, one of her uncles had the right to kill the man. However, if she had been observed luring him, then it was considered her fault. The girl would usually tell her family who the father was, but sometimes the man would deny it. My grandmother told me that in Nebraska the father could go to the boy's or man's home and "slash him," and the assembled relatives would not lift a hand to help him because the father was thought be fully justified.[7] Sometimes the man did not want to marry her or was already married, or it could happen that the girl's family would not want that particular man as part of their family. In any case, as her pregnancy became apparent, the expression "she is pregnant, but not married," would be heard among the people. If the baby was illegitimate and died soon after birth, the old people would repeat, "A baby knows many things. It knows if it is not wanted and will leave when it has a chance."

If the family of an unmarried boy or man was decent and of good standing, the pregnant girl's father or uncle went to the man's mudlodge or house when all members of his family were present. In a nice way the father or uncle told the gathered family that he knew "things happen." He told the boy not to be afraid and invited him to come to his dwelling and talk to the girl. He added that, if they liked each other enough to consider marriage, it would be agreeable with her family. He concluded that he hoped the boy's relatives would agree. But if the boy had caught the girl alone and forced her, and if he did not come to her father and tell him what he had done or talk to the girl within three days, then when the father or uncle faced the boy and his family he would say, "If I see you anywhere, you are dead." If the boy had been seeing the girl secretly and wanted to be with her, however, he usually would come to talk to her father within three days. If the girl's family wanted marriage but the boy's family refused, her family could make life hard for him. Men would run him through the village, and all would whip him three or four times, Garland said. Confrontation continued in Indian Territory and Oklahoma. Cases are known when an uncle or other close male relative accosted a man believed to have made an unmarried girl pregnant. It was accepted that he could question, threaten, and sometimes injure the man, particularly one who was already married.

Garland recalled that in May of either 1924 or 1927, there were several illegitimate births in the tribe. Before the time of the next big tribal summer camp, each band's chiefs went around to each family in the band and said, "We wish to keep such disgraceful things from happening, so watch your children." The Pawnees did not believe in unrestricted sexual license that led to unwanted pregnancy and the denial of paternity.

In the normal circumstances of marriage, there were certain beliefs about pregnancy and the welfare of the fetus. Effie Blaine was very strict with her daughter. She told her she should not look at anything out of the ordinary, such as the "freaks" in the visiting carnival. Nor could she observe a calf or colt being born lest it bring on premature labor. Observing or handling freshly killed or bloody things was also forbidden. There was a fear of the umbilical cord being wrapped around the baby's neck, and there were certain beliefs about how to keep this from happening. And it was very important to avoid sexual intercourse during pregnancy or nursing, since the male odors would make the unborn or nursing baby sick.

Garland was born during the time when many of these traditional beliefs and practices were still current among older Pawnees, even though many young people in Indian schools had been exposed to lessons that deprecated their culture in an effort to teach them a "better way" of living.

He remembered many of his childhood experiences in learning how to be a Pawnee, and he related the means used to ensure proper behavior. He explained the ways a male child became socialized as he recalled what happened to him and what he learned from others. This began with the infant's experiences and continued through boyhood.

Sometimes during my early years I was the rebellious inhabitant of a cradle board or baby board. Aunt Viola used to put me on the board and take me downtown because it wasn't proper for her to go by herself. She often stopped at a store and had things to carry. Damn, I used to hate that board. I was all tied and wrapped up. If you ever saw a baby on a cradle board, it looks like a cocoon. If my arms were loose it was OK, but if they tied my arms in, I hated that, and I would yell my head off. Now I think they put me on the board when I was slightly beyond my infant years.

The baby boards in our Pitahawirata band were burned out of flat timber. The charred part was scraped off with a rock or knife. They made the wrapping of soft deerskin with the hair removed. In the winter, solid pieces of skin were used. My grandmother Blaine washed the cover skin of her children's cradle board in the creek by scrubbing it with sand or hitting it against a rock. Then while it dried she stretched it now and then to keep it soft. Sand was used to clean many things, including dishes, when the Pawnees lived in camps near streams.

There was a small pillow and a thin mattress. A little roll of skin or cloth one to two inches thick was placed under the knees. It was almost as wide as the board. The infant's feet were kept together with toes pointed up while the baby was wrapped. The pillow under the head was about eight to ten inches long and two inches thick and four to five inches wide. My grandmother made my board, and because she was blind she couldn't decorate it, so it was plain, with no beadwork, painted stripes, or brass nails placed on it in designs. All four of my children were on baby boards. Their mother, a Ponca, had that tradition in her tribe.

An elderly Skidi Pawnee woman, born in 1910, said she and everyone she knew was placed on a cradle board at birth. They were used to keep the baby's legs and back straight. She said the boards got plainer, and the hoop over the top had a cloth or netting to keep off the flies, which were very bad in those days as the number of cattle, horses, and hogs on the farms increased. In the 1930s many babies continued to be placed on cradle boards and carried to dances and other gatherings. Some old women continued to carry their grandchildren on their backs in a shawl even after that. Cora Levier Pratt used to do that.[8]

"Children were welcomed, and in many families there was a favorite child," Garland stated. It was expected that there would be one child who held this position, and the others should not resent it. They were taught not be jealous because, as the people said, jealousy kills. This respect for the position of one chosen sibling may have helped in passing authority and responsibility from one generation to the next if death or some other disruption damaged the family structure. The chosen child must have had certain attributes that caused the parents to assign this position.

Apparently other tribes also had this custom or knew that the Pawnees had it. In Oklahoma, the Cheyennes tried to retrieve the sacred arrows that the Pawnees had captured from them in a battle when they lived in Nebraska.[9] They came several times – five, it was said – and they brought food and appealed to the favorite child in the Skidi family holding the arrows, who was the one who could grant their request. But this child, now an elderly woman, refused.[10]

The Pawnees practiced interfamilial child adoptions. The custom provided for the well-being of children as well as the adopting tribal members. For instance, an older couple with no one to care for them would sometimes ask kinsmen with several children to let them adopt one. They explained that they were old and could not do some of the necessary heavy work. They promised to care for the child as its parents did. At other times, the parent or parents would take the initiative if they saw that some incapacitated person or couple needed someone with them. They would take one of their children to that home and offer the child for adoption. Poor parents with several children sometimes offered a child to ensure its welfare and improve their own.

> In any case, the child was always told who he was to live with and the reason for his going. His parents told him, "We are your parents and love you, and you can come to see and visit us whenever you want to. We will be happy to see you." Children grew up seeing this happen,

and if it should happen to them it was not traumatic. Another form of adoption took place in Oklahoma after there were so many deaths in the tribe. Any relative who could would adopt the orphans. My brother and I are examples of that.

Another problem that resulted from a high tribal death rate was what could be translated from Pawnee as "momism." Evolving in Nebraska even before the Pawnees came to Indian Territory, it was seen as a problem during the nineteenth century, when warfare and disease killed many people, including men with families. Many women were left with only one child, and if it were a son, grandfathers or uncles would step in if they saw that the mother was indulging and overprotecting the child. They would try to persuade her to treat the child differently, but sometimes it did no good.

At meals the Pawnees seated a young problem child away from his mother. He sat beside his father or between his father and someone else whom he was not accustomed to manipulating. The mother sat two places beyond the child on the father's other side. This was often requested by an older person of authority if the mother overindulged the child. She could not protest.

I was scared of Sam Horse Chief. He was in our band, related to my grandmother, and was Geneva Sun Eagle's father.[11] He would come around and frown at me, and when I was very little I would run and hide. In later years when he came I would stand my ground, and as he saw me standing there, he would call out, "I'm thirsty." I would go and get the water bucket, take it outside, and dump it. Then I'd go to the well and pump a bucket of fresh water, stagger with it back to the house, get a cup, and approach him, saying politely, "Here, good sir, is your water." He would then stick out his tongue. "Bless my tongue," he'd say. And I would go through the motions with my hands. Then I heard, "Wet my tongue," and I'd sprinkle water on his tongue, not knowing what was coming next. His wife, Mary, would feel sorry for me and say, "Come sit here beside me," which I certainly would be glad to do by this time. She'd say, "Listen to all the things you hear. You will grow up to be a strong, good man." Later I realized that Sam knew what his role behavior should be toward me, who lived with blind grandparents who could not see what I was doing. So he did what was expected in putting me through the paces of submitting to authority and taking directions.

Another yet that I recall was White Elk, or A-ka-ra-rus, which meant Hairy Mouth. He was about as old as my grandfather. There were three other old men that all the children were afraid of; Sam Horse Chief, High Eagle, whom we lived with for a while, and Spotted Horse, who died when I was young. The little children in the band were really afraid of him. He was always gruff and ordered them to do things. When children acted badly, their parents would threaten to tell old man Spotted Horse, who had been a great warrior in Nebraska. My grandfather would threaten me, and I'd say, "Oh no, Grandfather, I'll be good."

Although the children were afraid, they respected all these old men, and when our young men reached a certain age, during a Pawnee gathering, an old man would call a young man forward. He then turned and talked about him to the people. He'd say that he'd seen him grow up and he would praise him for certain things he'd seen him do. Then he would talk to him quietly, bless him and give him a blanket, and say to him for all to hear, "You are a young man now. *Ra wa*." It was our public ritual for acknowledging a young man's assumption of manhood.

Up to age four, boys stayed mostly around their mothers. After that they were encouraged to stay around older males such as their fathers and uncles. If a young boy hurt himself and ran crying to his mother, she would pick him up and comfort him until he stopped crying. As soon as he did this, she would tell him to go to his father or uncle, informing them that he was coming and what had happened. They would sit down and talk to him, hear what had happened, and involve him in some male activity, thus beginning the transition to a male-oriented role. After the 1870s, when there were so many adult deaths, this learning and normalization of male behavior became difficult.

When you are about six, you begin to look at men. They are straight and tall, and you wish to be like them. You are encouraged to go and ask to "extend hands," which means in English that you ask to "lend a hand." You watch men do things. If they are doing something you ask, "Can I help you?" If they are butchering, they'll say, "Keep the dogs away," or "Get a branch and keep the flies away," or "Go tell so and so to do or bring something." They ask you to repeat what they have said, and if you can't remember it exactly, they'll say, "You go play. Next time you remember what you have heard." My grandparents were pleased when told I was not sent to play.

But I was sent to play for other reasons when my grandparents went to visit. We often drove the wagon to see St. Elmo and Susie Jim, our relatives. My grandparents always kept me close to them and allowed me little freedom of movement. Grandma Susie would tell me to go out to play, then turn to my grandfather and say, "I sent him out to play." If someone speaks up for a child, as was the case here, the parents never argued unless it was a matter of health. They then would wait until the child was not there and explain.

Susie Bear Chief Jim told the author that she always felt sorry for Garland when he was a little boy because he had to do everything for his grandparents and guide them around and never had time to play like other children. Sometimes she found him new clothes because his grandmother could not see how worn his clothes became. Garland remembered that the patches his grandmother made on his clothes were always lumpy and made with cloth that did not match the original garment's color.

In Nebraska especially, grandparents were often responsible for children from the age that they were toddlers up until puberty. Sometimes it would be a great-uncle or the oldest man in the household. Whoever he was, in the early morning he would awaken the little boys and say, "Do you want to go scout? Come on, be a man." And they would get up and follow him out some distance and *kat su* or *pi us* away from the dwelling. While they were out, the man would tell them what he had done as a scout or hunter, or whatever he thought was important for them to know. He told the little boys what was expected of them. Then he'd take them back to the mudlodge or tipi. If the father was away, or dead, the grandfather or uncle became responsible for the children of the household.

By the age of ten boys completely left their sisters' sphere of activity. They just wanted to be with boys and men, but they didn't play with big boys, who usually didn't want them around. When I was growing up, there was an exception. The older boys watched over us while we swam in Black Bear Creek. Little boys constantly tried to get their attention. I remember once when I was older, some little boys at Pawnee came running to where we big boys were. "Hey, we saw something up there on the hill!" they cried. "What is it?" we asked. "We don't know, we think it is a BIG *tankaroof* [kangaroo]." "Yes, a BIG *tankaroof*," echoed another. We knew they hadn't see anything, they just wanted attention.

As the boys in the family approached puberty, the father exerted authority and became the predominant figure in their lives. When it was still dark in the morning, he would wake the boys and say something like, "If you want to be a man, there is no better training than to get on a horse and go out and scout. Let's go. To be a man is to survive." Then he went with his sons down to the creek to wash. After that those who were thirteen or fourteen years were told to go and check on the horses. The older ones got on their horses and rode out to observe and stayed until the sun came up. Then they came back. The "horse checkers" came back then from the fields or corrals too to eat the morning meal.[12]

If anyone hesitated to get up promptly, he was dragged out of bed onto the floor. I saw my grandfather pull his son, my uncle Elmer, out of his bed and stand him on his feet and say, "Look at you – look at you. You are not a man," when he would not get up as early as Grandfather wished. A boy who did not have an older man to teach him, or who would not listen, was called a poor man all his life.

In the Nebraska village people watched to see who got up early. One family group might constantly be up before others. People would say, "See that family over there, they are always up and out before we are. They are men." This gave that household status, so others would try to chum around with the early risers. Sometimes one of the early riser families would be invited to eat a meal with your family. The father would say of the invited man, "Here is a man. Bring him a pillow." He'd praise him, and always his sons would listen and be told to be like this man, their neighbor.

If some family was always last in stirring around, the father of an early riser family would say, "Who are you?" if one of the boy members of a continuously lazy family should come into the mudlodge. "I have not seen you. Do you get up in the morning and scout?" Then he would tell the boy visitor what his family did and ask if the boy's family did this. If the boy would say yes, they did, the father would say, "Well, we never see you. Maybe you are out when we are eating." Then he'd add, "Well, it's good to have some one out scouting then," which was sarcasm.

Public opinion exerted strong social control in this and other instances, teaching the young that people observed and censured actions that did not meet village expectations. In Nebraska it was essential to teach consistent responsibility for sharing the obligation of protecting the family and village against enemy attack. Most Pawnee enemies were said to attack a village at daybreak – hence the emphasis on early rising and teaching the young men to go out to scout. Even in Indian Territory, when threat of enemy attack disappeared, insistence on early rising continued as a method for instilling self-discipline in a man, as the example of Elmer and Wichita Blaine illustrated. Uncle Elmer, born in 1902, became caught between the traditional world of his parents, Wichita and Effie, and the non-Indian world of the government school. There he was taught that his Indian ways were no longer important or functional and that he should try to be like a white man. The internal conflict continued when he ran away from school and when he later began to drink alcohol to excess. Some other young Pawnee men of his generation, living between the demands of traditional life and the pull of modern ways, also developed a "drinking problem."

There were other methods for shaping the child's character so that, it was hoped, he would know, accept, and follow the rules of his family and village. Discipline could be quite strict. There is an expression that means "you will be forcibly dipped in water." If a child continued to cry and complain after everything possible had been done for it, then a "grandparent," not a close relative, would take it to the river or spring and put it in, bring it out, wash it off, put it under again, bring it out, and dry it off, talking to it all the while. This was done two or three times until the child controlled itself and stopped crying. It did not like this. Afterward when it cried for no reason, the parents would say, "You will be dipped in water" and threaten to tell so and so. The child would immediately stop whining or misbehaving. It was afraid of that person who had submerged it in cold water. All this may sound drastic, but in the old days when there were enemies around, or game to hunt, a crying child caught their attention.

Occasionally an individual would overdiscipline a child using physical abuse. At that time an old person would go up to the abuser and say, "Have pity for me. I was never treated like this. You were never treated like this." The old person talked with compassion and a pleading tone. "Tirawahat is looking at you." He would place his hands on the person's head and shoulders in a blessing motion and say, "God didn't send you this child to abuse."

In other instances a great warrior came up to an abuser and shouted for all to hear, "Stop that! Here you are a man and you are doing a despicable thing. If what the child did makes you that angry, say so, but in good ways. Boys will be boys!" He would stand there until the man told the child to leave. Then the warrior would change his voice and in a good way tell the man how he punished his children in a different and acceptable way.

Children had their own defense against punishment. They learned that if they were about to be switched, they could run up to an old person, and their parents would not touch them. If the parent jerked the child away, he was considered contemptible and would have scorn heaped on him by the old person. People would shun such a person and would not trust him. If, however, he told the old person in a quiet way what the child had done, it might then be released, but it could not be switched.

Women disciplined both boys and girls. Men punished only boys. Men would go to women to tell them about a girl child's unacceptable behavior, then the woman punished the girl. If a man switched a girl, an older person who heard about it would strongly admonish him, saying that only a woman could do that, and he should tell a woman relative what the child had done.

After the Pawnees came to Oklahoma from Nebraska, problems began with intergenerational communication. The young people who went to Indian school had to learn English and were discouraged from speaking Pawnee and even punished for it. Many older people could not speak English or could not speak it well, so bilingual communication often led to much confusion as the years went by. The adults were often thinking in Pawnee with the concepts of their time and trying to translate what they wanted to say into English – as much as they knew of it. What they said was sometimes quite different from what they meant in talking with children and grandchildren who spoke and understood less and less Pawnee.

An example of this occurred when Garland's brother was very young and was learning to play checkers with his "father," the man who had adopted him. The young boy made frequent mistakes, and finally he heard, "Ben, you just can't think; you do not have any sense." The man stopped playing with him and left the table.[13] Garland said this had a profound effect on his brother in that he believed he could not think, that he was stupid. He told him years later that he had always believed what his father said from that day. What the man really thought was, "Ben you are too young yet to understand how to do this." But as he tried to say it in English, it came out the way it did.[14] Misunderstandings became frequent when older people with limited English tried to transfer concepts and values to their children, who were often away at school for months at a time where they were not allowed to speak Pawnee, and who gradually lost comprehension of their own language.

CHILD-REARING ATTITUDES AND BEHAVIORS

At one time Garland Blaine discussed some Pawnee precepts for child rearing:

1. Food was always important in the relationships of adults and children. If children asked for something to eat when a woman was cooking, they were never refused food. Even if it was only a little, the children would be happy; if you refused, they might think you did not love them. The Pawnees say, "Refusal runs deep in the child's mind."

2. If children said or did something they should not do when interacting with other people, they were told, "You must go and apologize or make right what you have done wrong." Adults would add, "Look around. Where can you go? You can't lift up a corner of the sky and hide under it," meaning one cannot escape the consequences of wrong behavior.

3. *U ri kah hah ri wis.*[15] Older people said this to a youngster who was listening to their conversation, or eavesdropping. It means that when you face someone you are listening, but that when you turn your head sideways you are "ear crosswise," or eavesdropping, but trying to appear that you are not. The expression was a rebuke.

4. Another expression said, "Do not the eye make long [time]." Children were told this when they stared – it meant not to gawk, which was

impolite because somebody might have a physical defect. Parents said this automatically, but they would check to see what the child was staring at. It might be danger. Because of enemy attacks in Nebraska, children were told that if you stare too long at one thing you might miss something you should see, something dangerous. Adults explained that it is good to look, but you should look *everywhere* – at your feet, halfway to the horizon, at the horizon, from you to the horizon, in all four directions.

5. "Death comes." A child was prepared for change in the family structure. After European contact, recurrent warfare and disease increased for most plains Indian tribes. The Pawnee population declined from an estimated 12,000 in the 1830s to fewer than 3,000 in the 1870s and fewer than 700 in 1900. As one response to the loss of many family members, children learned that "a young person is to be good to people. Death comes. God makes it that way." A mother or father may die. If the mother should die, the father would say, "I must find another woman to take care of you and the others." So speaking of a particular woman, it was said, "You must be good to her because she will take care of you. You want her to like you because she may help you to live." Garland added, "since my grandparents were old and incapacitated, they were very serious in teaching me that 'death comes.' They were old, and I had no mother or father, and I understood."

6. Teasing will happen to you. Children were instructed to be polite to people, even if an older person should come and tease you. Accept it. Tease back just enough to give others the opportunity to tease you even harder, so that they can "score on you." Teasing served several purposes. It taught children to keep their temper and react in a nonviolent or nonemotional way, even when angered. Two Otoe women used to tease Garland when he was young.[16]

First, they would shake my grandmother's hand if we met in town. Then we'd all sit down on the courthouse lawn to visit, and both of them would put their arms around me and pull me either way. Each one would say, "Are you going to be my husband?" I would be mad, but I sat there, looked straight ahead, and tried not to make a face. (I was very adept at sticking out my lower lip when angry, and someone had told Grandmother, who had talked to me about not doing that.) Later, after they got up and went on, Grandma would say, "Don't be

mad. Don't say anything. They are just having fun. It is their way."
This taught me to control my feelings and that different tribes had
different ways, and we must keep open-minded about it, especially
since we all lived so close together.[17]

"When Pawnee women teased you or patted you as a youth, you were
told not to mind, that was what women did, paid physical attention to
men. You were told that when you grew up, a boy will be a man and a
girl will be a woman." It was implied that no same-sex physical attraction
should exist.[18]

Girls were not teased at this age, but boys were teased by both men
and women of their band in this manner. A man could ask a young
boy approaching adolescence, "Do you have a girl friend? Have you
ever rubbed your hand on her leg?" And they would ask you this and
that, and some of us young boys had never heard of such things. Now
and then an elderly lady would come and sit beside me and put my
hand on her leg and ask, "Are you going to marry me?" I would be
so embarrassed I could have died. But I stayed there, smiled, didn't
pull my leg away, and didn't get up and walk away. I knew I was being
teased.

Later you would ask your folks, do men rub women's legs? What
for? They would talk to you in a serious way. Yes, that's what they do.
This is the way God made it. You have seen horses bite each other's
necks? God made it that way, and they would go on to explain that
this and other acts we had seen in nature were the way it was with
people. They talked about sexual activities in a quiet way, bringing
in God who had made us and this act sacred. It was not "dirty" or
embarrassing to us to learn about these things.

They talked then about your wife-to-be. When you have a wife, my
people told me, if you do these things with other women, then you
have nothing for your wife. When you get older and see a woman you
want for your wife, you tell your folks who she is and we will discuss
it, because this is very serious. It concerns God. My people, who were
of the Kawarakis part of the Pitahawirata band, viewed many things
as sacred.[19]

7. Take care of your sister. Wichita Blaine said that when he was young
and the Pawnees went on the hunt in Nebraska as a band and tribe, the

little boys would catch birds along the way. To do this they took sticks or small branches about one to two inches in diameter and cut off their smaller branches, leaving prongs about three to four inches long along the length. The father made the first bird flail for his son, but later he learned to make them for himself. Well-to-do families would sometimes have small bows and arrows made for their sons, or if they had time, the fathers and uncles would make them. Everyone, rich and poor alike, could have a staff.

The boys went to places where the blackbirds and other birds ate seeds from horse droppings near the village or in the corrals near the mudlodges. If they lay very quietly they could hit the birds with the flail or shoot them with their bows and arrows. Then, after killing a few, they brought the birds home for the evening meal. Women of the household cut them open and cleaned them. They put them on the coals, and the feathers burned off as they were turned. Little boys were sure to get the heads; they put them in their mouths and pulled off the bills. They ate all the rest – every part. Grandmother Blaine said it would sound like Cracker Jack as they chewed bones and all.

There was a lesson in all this. The mother told the boys, "See, you are taking care of your sister, and you will all your life. See, your grandmother is eating. Your mother is eating. Your sister is eating." When the men in the household came in, the mother turned to them and said, "See, he has brought food. He will be a good hunter." This attention made the little boy feel needed and established in his mind that males helped provide food for the family.

While the little boys ate the heads, their sisters got pieces of the carcass, as did their older brothers if there was enough. The little girls learned to turn the birds on the fire. The mothers would say, "Don't let the head burn, your brother is going to eat it. You will always prepare food for him when he comes to visit you." Brothers and sisters grew up caring for one another's welfare. At this point, in the 1850s to 1860s, some aspects remained of a more detailed matriarchy that had existed before large population losses and other factors changed the social structure in the last part of the nineteenth century. In Indian Territory before the turn of the century, this pattern could not be maintained as changes occurred in family structure and residence patterns. Brothers and sisters were often sent or compelled to attend Indian schools when they were quite young. Here they were separated from one another, living in boys' or girls' dormitories. Separate classes emphasized the domestic arts for girls, and boys were taught agriculture or other non-Indian male occupations such as carpentry, cobbling, or masonry. This separation and institutionalized role change lessened the need for the older pattern of sibling interdependence.

A few remnants of this matrifocal pattern exist. Whenever Garland Blaine visited a female relative that he called a sister in Pawnee kinship terms, he took meat and bread to her family. She would ask if he could stay to eat. If he could, she would prepare a meal using the meat he brought. Garland Blaine concluded by saying, "My grandparents knew the old ways, and they wanted me to learn and follow them in order to be a good Pawnee man. These things I have told you about are what I remember hearing and learning in my own childhood and youth."[20]

SEVEN

Childhood in Pawnee

Garland Blaine continued with the account of his childhood.

After my father died, my mother and I moved back to Addie Yellow Calf's, and on July 16, 1916, my brother, named after my father, was born. That summer the annual Baptist church association took place at the Pawnee fairground. It was big – like a powwow with many camps. All the church members would go. Those who didn't camp came during the day and listened to the preaching. There were mostly white people and church officials there. Preachers were assigned to their new churches.

My mother's relatives were not avid churchgoers, but if they were in town and it was good weather, they would go to these summer meetings. And it was during this summer that I have the only memory of my mother. That's when I remember seeing her, but I do not remember her face. I remember Birdie Mannington holding me in her arms with my mother a few feet away. Birdie was trying to have me indicate that I wanted my mother. I can remember nothing about her features, but I knew that it was my mother there.

In September of 1916 Mother and I became ill with diphtheria. On October 1, Mother died. I was very sick during October, November, and December. I stayed part of the time in the Pawnee Indian School clinic in the Girls' Building. At the time Mother died, the Indian agency did not know what to do with me or my brother, who was a few months old. I was expected to die any time. My mother's cousin,

Mary Weeks, came and adopted my brother Jim. I stayed at the Indian school with Mr. and Mrs. Sarver, employees, looking after me. Miss Long, another employee, also took care of me. I was told later, she wanted to adopt me, but she was not married, and therefore she could not do so. I was very emaciated, they say, and Aunt May Lockley, who I think worked at the school then, fed me with an eyedropper. Finally she and Old Lady Dog Chief, both Skidi relatives, wanted to take me out of the clinic. They said, "If he is to die, he might as well be with us. We don't want him dying by himself. So we will take him." My grandparents Blaine said the same thing. They came to take me home when they heard that I was to die. Effie Blaine said, "I can't see well, Wichita Blaine can't see well. Old Lady Dog Chief has good eyes. She can take care of him better." So she and Aunt May took me away.[1]

One day my Skidi cousins and Aunt May and I were in the courthouse yard. The Pawnees used to go there to sit on the ground and visit. It was enjoyable because most of them lived out in the country and could not see each other often. My young cousins were eating crackers or something, but I couldn't because I was ill and too young. They had laid me down, and my father's brother, my uncle Elmer Blaine, came by. Thinking I was not getting any food and the cousins were, he said, "You bad Skidis, you won't take care of him." He reached down and picked me up and carried me over to where his parents, Effie and Wichita, were sitting. Elmer was about fourteen or fifteen and had just run away from school, probably Chilocco, and did not know of my illness. My grandparents and Aunt Viola, Elmer's sister, were getting ready to go home in the their wagon. He came carrying me and said, "Look, they are not taking care of him." They said I was very thin and black and blue.[2] Aunt May came over and said, "Elmer is young; he doesn't understand." They discussed it and decided I would go with my father's family. May told Viola how to feed me so I would not choke. They took me home, and I lived with my Pitahawirata grandparents from then on.

In the spring of 1917 I began getting well. We were staying at Colonel Mitchell's place at this time with two old ladies, Tstaruriwa and possibly her sister. She was Colonel Moore's aunt and the sister of Colonel Mitchell. One day Tstaruriwa carried me outside on the little porch or stoop and put me down and went back inside. I was just learning to crawl and moved over to the screen door and sat there looking around. In a little while she came out and apparently did not look down to see me. When she opened the door, it pushed me over the edge. I fell on an empty peach can, and its open lid edge cut my cheek. I still have the scar.[3]

That spring I had a little white fur coat with black dots or spots on it. Possibly Grandma Addie bought it. There were pictures of me in it. My other memory of that time came in the summer. I was still crawling, and in the yard red ants got all over me. Uncle Elmer heard my screams and came out, knocking them off with his hat. I couldn't seem to remember my experience and went to that spot several times with the same results. I probably remember this so well because Uncle Elmer probably had a thing or two to say after the second or third time.

That summer, now into my third year, I was beginning to walk, but I was still small and thin. At this time we moved and lived in a tipi at the Roan Chief place, some seven or eight miles south of town.[4] There was a mudlodge there, and other relatives were camping nearby. You probably remember hearing about Roan Chief. He was over seven feet tall and had to stoop when he entered a room through a normal door. He was part Pitahawirata and part Chawi and head chief of the Pawnees at this time. My grandmother called him Father in the Pawnee way because his mother and her father were brother and sister. His deceased wife, Eva Fields, was a Skidi related to my mother.

In the fall Elmer went off to Haskell Indian School in Kansas, and Viola went to the Pawnee Indian Boarding School. Grandpa and Grandma and I moved into the mudlodge when it turned cold. We stayed there the winter of 1917–18.[5] During that time there was a Bear Dance and a Buffalo Dance in the mudlodge, and I "danced" for the first time. My grandfather belonged to those dances. I would stand by him, hold his hand, and just bend my knees and bob up and down, more or less in time to the drum. I saw Roan Chief dance the Bear Dance at that time.

In the spring of 1918 we moved up to Roan Chief's large two-story white frame house. Upstairs was a big room contoured to the hip-gabled roof. Downstairs there were two bedrooms, one large sitting room, a large kitchen, and a pantry. They invited us to stay, I think, because it was difficult for my grandparents to manage with such a small child, now that Elmer and Viola were away at school. Also, Roan Chief was not well and my grandmother wanted to help the best she could.[6] We slept upstairs. I remember the huge upholstered rocker that had been specially made for him because he was such a large man. Sometimes he would hold me and talk to me. Everyone held me. They told me this later and said they felt sorry for me because I was an orphan and my grandparents were blind or nearly so. When other little boys like Harrison Barker, William's son, came to visit with his folks, Roan Chief would sit in his chair, rock back and forth, clap his hands, and sing his scout songs from Nebraska where he was a warrior. We little boys would jump up and down around him trying to dance, and the others would laugh and clap for us.

Either late in that summer or in the fall of 1918, Roan Chief died. At this time the Chawis were having a Doctor Dance. Art Fields and Earl Adams were sent over to tell them. I remember that they got on horses and rode off fast. Years later they said Roan Chief probably had diabetes and did not know it. He got very heavy and had trouble with his leg and got gangrene. All I can remember about the funeral was the size of the big black casket and that it was in a big room with lots of people there. He was buried on his farm, and a marker placed there.

After Roan Chief died, we stayed in the house a little longer. I remember opening the door to the stairway and crawling upstairs to my pallet. I'd hear the "oooo ooooooo" sound of the wind. To me it was Roan Chief out there crying, and I thought he was feeling sorry for me. I knew he was dead because I'd seen him in his casket, but I knew that he was *out there*. There was no fear in me, no fear of the dead. I wanted to tell my grandma and grandpa, but I couldn't talk well enough. They'd pick me up and I would babble, but they couldn't understand and would laugh. I made all sorts of sounds. I wanted to tell them Roan Chief was out there crying.

When his son and his wife and family came to live in the house, we moved back into the nearby mudlodge. I slept on the north side of the lodge. There were just we three in it. There are few memories of the interior. There were a few old crates piled to make a cupboard where Grandma kept the food and dishes. I think we slept on the floor on pallets.

We needed water every day, and it was cold to go out and get it. Grandpa would pick me up and carry me down toward the spring some two hundred yards south of the mudlodge. We'd walk down there, and he'd put me down on the top of the rise and tell me to stay in that one place. He'd feel his way down to the spring, get the water, call out to me to get the direction, and when I would make a sound, he would feel his way up the hill, pick me up, and return carrying me and the bucket. Inwardly I knew he couldn't see well, but I couldn't verbalize it. He probably asked me questions about the way back, but I don't remember, although I did as I got older. He'd take me with him when he went to get wood for the fire, too. He was teaching me to be his eyes. When we needed staples, there would always be someone that would like a ride to town and would drive for my grandfather. Our team was a sorrel and a gray.

I was not always mindful of restrictions placed on me. There were praying mantises at Roan Chief's house. When it was warm, I would crawl to the south side of the house. The window screens were full of the insects. Someone would come and pick me up and warn me not to go there. They were afraid of them. But when no one was paying attention, I would crawl back around the house to see what the praying mantises were doing. My curiosity apparently overcame their admonitions. When we lived in a tipi at Roan Chief's, I remember crawling out under the flap and heading to Henry Shooter's mother's and sisters' tipi that stood some sixty yards south and west of the mudlodge. I'd move as fast as I could, before someone caught me and brought me back. If I made it over there, the old lady would give me cookies. I never gave up trying, but I remember more times being picked up and carried back "home" than success in getting cookies. Because of my illness my early physical development seems to have been retarded, so that I was still crawling when perhaps I should have been walking. At this time my name was Little Spotted Bear [Kuruks awaki].

The people camped there near the mudlodge for the dances and ceremonies, but after they were over they would take down their tipis, leave, and go to their own places. Then we were the only ones there. When we lived in the mudlodge in the winter, we did not take the tipi down. It was easier for my grandparents to leave it standing.

Sometime during that fall or early winter, we moved to the Henry Shooter place and camped there. Sometimes we would be asked to stay in the house, and sometimes Old Man Shooter would put up a tipi and we stayed in it. The reason for this, I was told, was that in his house there were only two stoves and there were too many people to crowd around them to keep warm. The tipi would have straw stuffed around the outside and inside at the bottom to keep the cold out. Grandmother was related to Bertha Shooter; that's why we stayed there.

One event that occurred during a very cold winter, the child did not forget. There was a bitterly cold spell and the snow became very deep. His grandparents decided a trip must be made to the little town of Glencoe for food. They prayed and cried over it because the trip took two to three hours and a blizzard had continued all night and all day. Garland would have to go along to help his grandfather "see" the road, but they feared the trip for his sake. They needed food, but there was no money. Outside the tipi his grandfather had stacked some cordwood to exchange for groceries. He loaded this in the wagon, then placed a large tin tub filled with earth and smoldering embers under the seat where Garland was to sit. The boy was carefully wrapped in canvas, and sacks were placed around his hands and legs so he would not freeze. Then the trip began, with the nearly blind grandfather driving the team.

When they got to the store in Glencoe, some men ran out to help them. They unhitched the snow-covered team and took care of the animals. They found the little boy all wrapped up with just his eyes showing. They lifted him off the wagon seat and carried him inside to get him warm. Garland remembered that they gave him hardtack, which he stuffed down as fast as he could. In exchange for the wood, they got some beef and other necessities. After they were warm, they were all bundled up again and got in the wagon to start home. The white men led the horses to the edge of town, and Garland and his grandfather began their journey back through the driving snow. When they arrived at the tipi, his grandmother came out to welcome them. They cried and prayed together over the safe return. Then they carried the food into the tipi.

Years later Garland Blaine, now a man, went back to the still small town of Glencoe, stopped at the store, and talked to some people sitting on the porch. In the course of the conversation he mentioned the trip he and his grandfather had made years ago. One old man got up and asked, "Were you that little boy?" Garland said he was. The old man told him, "I was one of the men who helped carry you into the store. After you made that ride in the blizzard with that old man, I always knew you'd grow up to be a real man." Garland continued:

Sometime after our stay at the Shooter place we moved into the town of Pawnee. We lived in the south part of town on the last street bordering Pawnee Bill's buffalo pasture.[7] Inside the house there was a big living room, to the left a bedroom, a hall, another bedroom, then another room. There was a kitchen, and upstairs there was one big room. Viola was there, and I think Elmer was there then, but he may have gone to Haskell Indian School.

That house was the first house I truly remember living in. I had several adventures there. Once I found a cigarette sack with loose tobacco in it. I decided to blow into the sack for some reason, with the result that the tobacco came out into my face and eyes. Viola heard my cries and immediately took me to the sink and washed out my eyes. Then, seeing there were still flecks of tobacco in my eyes, she got me down, lay on top of me so that I could not move, and with a needle removed the other tiny particles. I can still feel that tobacco when I remember that. Years later she said she could not recall doing this.

I remember being cold in that house. There was a cookstove in the kitchen, and I used to crawl between it and the wall and sit there to get warm. "Don't get behind there, or you will burn yourself," they'd say. But I would do it anyway to get warm. The hotter it was, the better I liked it. The kitchen's pantry was another place I spent some time in. It was under the stairs. I don't remember going down into a basement, but when I was in the pantry I could look down through the floor and see people downstairs. I'd think they were Chinese, and I'd try to get the big people in the house to look in the pantry by pointing, but they'd say, "There's nothing in there." The reason I thought that was once Aunt Viola and Martha Rice took me to a picture show and there was a slant-eyed Chinese in it, and he had two umbrellas and was walking on a tightwire. I saw his eyes, and they looked like the people in the basement. Maybe there were people playing cards down there, and looking at them from above they looked slant-eyed to me.

When we moved to Pawnee, the First World War was going on, and my folks knew all about it. My grandparents, coming from tipi and mudlodge life with occasional stays in houses, received advice about living in a house in town. There was one thing that stuck with me. People said, "Leave your key in your door on the inside because there are German spies around and they will stick some poison in the keyhole." Grandpa laughed about this and said there are lots of ways to get poison in a house – they could slide it under the door, for instance.

The Pawnees embraced the war effort with enthusiasm. Pawnees volunteered and were inducted into the armed services. Being a warrior and defending the tribe was a proud and traditional act. On the home front Pawnee agency personnel were directed to urge the Pawnees to support war costs by buying liberty bonds. In spite of the poverty of many families, including the Blaines, Pawnee funds were used to buy these bonds. The government held and dispersed funds only with the agents' recommendation and approval from the office of the commissioner of Indian affairs. By 10 October 1918 the Pawnees had bought liberty bonds worth $114,000 and in one way or other raised over $500 for the Red Cross.[8] A receipt dated 10 October 1918 stated that Garland J. Blaine purchased Liberty Loan bonds for $660.[9] It is not known if the agency superintendent sought his grandparents' approval for this purchase. It seems that impoverished people could have found better uses for the money.

Two months later, in December 1918, the Pawnee agent sent a request to the commissioner's office in Washington that $100 be taken from the child's funds. It said it was "needed for Support and Clothing. This child is an orphan, being cared for by his grandparents who are blind. They are in poor circumstances and haven't income enough to nearly support themselves. I request that I be allowed to pay out for the support of this child the same as though he was of school age, and the hundred dollars allowed is needed."[10] The amount of money in his account was $673.36, funds derived from the agency's leasing his deceased parents' allotments and from the annual annuity payment to Pawnee individuals.[11]

At age three Garland did not know that he was so generously supporting the United States government in its military efforts. He did remember when the boys came back to Pawnee after the armistice. He and his grandparents walked down to the train station with other townspeople to welcome their soldier relatives home. The men came marching in step up the street. After they were dismissed from ranks, the people ran to welcome them home. Garland said that some of them, like Frank Young Eagle and Harry Richards, looked for Wichita Blaine. They embraced and he blessed them, saying he was glad that Tirawahat had brought them safely home. He added, "You saw a hard time. It was lots worse than I ever saw." He said this thinking of his experiences as a United States Army Scout in action in Nebraska and other places. "After we walked home," Garland recalled, "Grandma and I helped rub Grandfather's legs that ached from the long walk." After the war, the Pawnee Indian agency listed the names of Pawnee servicemen with comments.

PAWNEE MEN IN WORLD WAR I SERVICE

Herbert Morris, Jacob Leader (over the top), John Spotted Horse Chief, Delbert Spotted Horse Chief (gassed) Walter Keys (went over the top), Grant White, Henry White (Co. A 131 Mach Gun Battalion [*sic*]. Died of wounds in hospital in France), Warren Leader (went over the top), Alex Eagle, Joe Ameelyonee? (Not Pawnee, but married a Pawnee), Harry Richards (Slightly wounded), Elmo Matlock (gassed), Frank Young Eagle (over top), Walter Norman, James Moses, James Sun Eagle (went over the top), Paul Little Eagle, Jobie Taylor, Thomas Hand, Ben Gover, Alex Adams, Burress Curly Chief, Arthur Coons, Jonathan New Rider (Bugler), Edgar Moore (79th Inf.), Henry Chapman, Harold Curly Chief, Louis Bayhylle, Lawrence Murie, Wallace Murie, Elmer Echo Hawk, James Mannington, Charley Wilson, Frank Riding In, Moses Yellow Horse and George EchoHawk (both started the day the armistice was signed and got as far as Guthrie [Okla.]), Emmett Carrion, Will Justice, Dick Smith, Henry Murie? Charley Riding Up, Sam Osborne, Ernest Wichita, George Roberts, Joe Esau.[12]

When the soldiers came home, the musicologist Frances Densmore was in Pawnee, recording Pawnee songs sung by Effie and Wichita Blaine, Dog Chief, John Luwalk, Horse Chief, Fannie Chapman, Mrs. Good Eagle, Mary Murie, and others. She recorded her observations of events following the Pawnee soldiers' arrival. She noticed that several soldiers were members of the Rainbow Division, and at one time during the conflict four of the men had stepped forward and volunteered for dangerous duty. One man brought back a German helmet, which his mother carried on top of a pole during a victory dance in the traditional way. A captured German knife was fastened on the helmet as a second trophy.[13] According to Garland Blaine and others, in addition to the helmet and knife some men brought strands of German hair taken from battlefield casualties.

Two dances were held, on 6 and 7 June 1919. The first was in the Skidi round house, a large wooden structure north of town. Densmore described it as six sided with an earth floor and an entrance to the east. About two hundred Pawnees attended, and those who could not get in crowded around the windows and doors. There was jubilation, with prayers of thanks for their men's safe return. "There were dances and one time forty-five women danced in a circle . . . it was a time of general rejoicing with sometimes three persons being on their feet at the same time, narrating some incident or giving a gift."[14]

Densmore noted particularly that she heard old warrior songs, and in *Pawnee Music* she included one sung by Wichita Blaine, called "A Woman Welcomes the Warriors." She noted that new songs, composed for the occasion, referred to submarines and airplanes, with the words sung to an older song's music.[15] She did not mention a song about the German Kaiser that proclaimed that the Pawnees went overseas to defeat him and did so.

The next day, 7 June, both Pawnees and white townspeople attended the second celebration. It began with Pawnee leaders solemnly smoking the sacred pipe. The soldiers received gifts, including two white horses led in by a woman.[16] The honored men danced, some dressed as Pawnee warriors and others, like Lawrence Murie, wearing their khaki uniforms. Densmore added that a young man who led the dancing carried a sword that had belonged to one of his ancestors. The parents of a man who died overseas stood before the assemblage, and a chief and others blessed them and talked to them quietly.[17]

After living in town about two years, Garland remembers, they left there and moved to High Eagle's place.

It was about ten to eleven miles directly south of Pawnee, off the main road near a woods, about a quarter mile from present Highway 18. My Grandmother called him Grandfather in the Pawnee way, I think he was Kitkahahki, but maybe Pitahawirata.[18] They may have been cousins, but I am not sure. He was old and lived alone, and he probably invited my grandparents to come and stay with him. I was about four or five at this time and became very interested in horses. I don't remember how it happened, but one of the horses on the place kicked me so severely that it required emergency treatment. Grandfather put wet rags on the wound on my stomach, hitched the team, and somehow the two men got me to town to Dr. Lehew's place, where he stitched me up.

High Eagle and my grandfather were United States Pawnee Scouts in Nebraska. They were Buffalo Society doctors. He was much older than Grandpa and wore braids, and in winter a black overcoat and cap.[19] He never wore a belt, but a handwoven four-inch-wide sash through his belt loops.

Sometimes he would take me with him when he needed to find roots for his medicines. He could not see very well and wanted me to help him. We would go into the woods, find the roots, and every now and then he would sit down to rest. Sometimes he would paint my mouth, chin, and lower face dark with mud from the creek. This is how he looked in the Buffalo Dance, he said. We would sit by the creek in the shade, and he would talk to me about many things. When we came back and got to the yard, he'd say, "*Ruwa,* dance." And I would be jumping up and down, and he'd sing his songs and clap. Hearing the singing, Grandma would come on the porch, and would really be mad at me for going off in the woods to get medicines. She didn't say anything at that moment because it was said that he was one of those doctors that had a name for using strong medicine for revenge. It was claimed that people would go to him, and he'd give them medicine to use to get even with people. He denied this.[20]

At other times, Grandmother would scold me and he would say, "Don't get after him. He is smart and he wants to learn things." But to make her feel better, he'd say to me, "When someone is talking, they are not talking for nothing, so you listen." So when he and Grandpa would sit and talk, I would listen to remember.

Once he went with two friends on the train that ran near the reservation to Columbus, Nebraska.[21] They went to trade their furs for food and other things. When they arrived they noticed a tent, and inside were buffalo robes and bearskins with heads that would fit over a man. A man there saw them and asked if they would like to do something for him. What, they asked? Would you dance? No, they would not. They had to go trade, then go back to their village. He talked to them some more, offering them money to dance. Just one time, said High Eagle, who being the oldest was the spokesman. More than that, the man dickered. In any event, one drummed and sang, and High Eagle and the other man danced. High Eagle said, "I knew it wasn't right, but I thought it was just a short time, and no one would know."

By now a crowd had gathered as a result of the man's stepping outside the tent and ballyhooing the event. As they danced the crowd moved in closer to see. High Eagle said they would reach out at the people, who would lean backward, scared. After they finished the man gave them some money and said if they danced again he would pay them some more. They repeated that they had to leave, trade, and go home. Besides if they stayed someone might steal their furs. No, said the man, come here, and they went around to the back of the tent, where he showed them a large wagon with a place to lock things in. I'll lock it, he said, and nobody can steal your furs. They agreed and stayed to dance again with lots of people watching. Suddenly they heard a commotion and were told that the Sioux had killed all the Pawnees. They did not know what to think or do. One of them said he did not believe it could be true. They decided to go home to their village as soon as possible. They got on the train, climbed to the top, and returned home. When they got there the village was mourning. Wailing was heard everywhere.

High Eagle said in later years that it was his punishment. The first time he danced in Columbus, his father's brother was killed. The second time his brother's wife, and the third time his cousins were all killed by the Sioux while on the hunt at the place they now call Massacre Canyon, in August 1873.[22]

High Eagle never really accepted reservation life under the government. He also wanted to defy aging. Once he decided to dye his long white braided hair black [see fig. 1]. He did, and it turned purple. It looked awful. He would even try to gallop on his horse with the young men and go have a drink with them in town. He lived longer than my grandfather and died when he was over one hundred years old, they say.

Even now I remember what he told me when I was a child. Once, years later, I went back to the creek where we gathered medicines, and he painted my face with mud and sang his buffalo doctor songs. He was teaching me to remember. This is one song I sang by the creek in his memory:

> As I stand. There I stood.
> Buffalo I stand as. As I stand
> As I stand. There I stood
> Buffalo I stand as. As I stand.
> It is as a buffalo I stand here.
> I refer to that place where I stood as a buffalo.
> To halt at that special revered ground.[23]

EIGHT

The Old and the New

Wichita Blaine said that before Garland was born he could farm for himself and do many things he could not do after he became blind. In the spring of 1906 he decided to have a house built on the allotment and live there with his family, and plow the fields and raise corn and other things. He went to the agent and told him what he wanted to do. And because the government continued to want the Indians to live and work on their allotments, in April the agent sent a letter to Washington requesting that $500 be taken from his money kept by the government. At that time he had a credit of $1,702.83.[1] Indian funds held in trust by the government came from leasing of allotments, treaty annuity payments, and tribal land cession sales. The commissioner's office had to approve the expenditure of Indians' funds, even for a pair of shoes. If they wanted their money for anything, they had to go to the agent. Then they didn't get the money in their own hands; when the store found they had permission to buy certain things, it sent the bill to the agency.

The frame house that the agent approved was to have three rooms. In June Wichita Blaine had to go to the agent again and ask if he could have a well drilled for water. This was approved by the commissioner's office, and it cost $100. In July he went to town again and asked for a barn–chicken house and a privy. This request cost $210 for the former and $25 for the outhouse.[2] At the same time, he requested money to buy furniture. He said he made so many trips because he was afraid if he asked for everything at once he would not get it. When the approval came, it and all the authorizations ended with the words, "You will see that the money is used for the purposes specified and to the best interests of the Indian."

For $120.50, the Blaines bought the following: six chairs and one rocker for $9.50; one child's chair for $1.50; one table and one cupboard for $12; one bedstead, springs, and mattress for $20; one cookstove for $24; seven curtains for $3.50; and a sewing machine for $35.[3] They were going to live in the white man's way in a house on a farm away from everybody. Garland said, "Grandpa had a team, and he said he plowed his fields and planted them and kept down the weeds. How many acres he cultivated, I do not know. Sometime early in the next year, vandals came and maliciously damaged his new house.[4] Nobody seemed to know who did it, and I was never told why Grandpa thought it was done." The commissioner's office approved funds to have the damage repaired.

At this time, in 1906, the serious eye disease trachoma had not yet afflicted them, so Wichita could farm and Effie could carry on her household and garden tasks and care for her children. By the time of Garland's birth in 1915, the disease had advanced to the point that Effie said she could not care for him after his mother died. When Elmer picked him up in the courtyard and carried him to his parents, however, thinking the child suffered neglect, they took him home in the wagon and began to take care of him.

Sixteen-year-old Elmer avoided returning to school in the fall of 1918. On 10 October he was charged with truancy and forced to appear before the Pawnee city justice of the peace, where he had to pay a fine and court costs of $5. This act had the desired effect, because by 26 October he was reported to be in school.[5] His reluctance to leave his parents may be explained by a Pawnee agency request to the commissioner on 4 June 1918 stating, "The parents of Elmer are both partially blind and in destitute circumstance. They receive very little rental from their land, as it is only fair land and does not bring a large rental. The funds received from this source are not sufficient to support the parents of Elmer and the rest of the family. It is the desire of the parents that he be granted his trust funds at this time in order that he may have funds in this office for his uses. The parents are old and dependent."[6] Elmer knew that with the little child to care for, he was needed at home.

Now there was little help with the farmwork as Wichita's eyesight failed and Effie became less and less able to see. Bessie had been taken off to Chilocco Indian School, and Viola attended Pawnee Indian Boarding School in town. In a year or so, Elmer married Kate Howell and moved away from home. Garland began the life he led for many years. He became the eyes and often the hands for his grandparents when no one else was there.[7]

It was a very difficult life for such a small child, but he never remembered those times with bitterness or gave the impression that it was an overwhelming and unfair responsibility. In recounting memories of his early life, he said:

The winters then seem to have been much colder than they are now. When we lived on the allotment there was a woodpile about as far as our mailbox from here, about one hundred feet it seemed to me. I was about three or four, and I had to go and get wood for the stove we had. I couldn't carry much or move very fast with my load. I remember that my fingers felt frozen when I got to the house. That went on all winter.

When the pile got low I would tell Grandpa, and he would say, "Well, I guess we'd better go to the barn and hitch up the horses and wagon and go to the creek." I would take his hand and lead him to the barn. He knew all about horses and could hitch up the horses after I would put his hand on the gear. I helped him as much as I could, and when we got the horses harnessed to the wagon, he'd lift me up on the seat and we'd start off to the creek, less than a half mile away. There were fallen limbs in the woods that skirted the creek. I'd watch the horses' breath in the cold air and listen to the sound of the wheels crunching the snow and dry weeds as we crossed the fields toward the creek. That was the first time I became aware of air and breathing. Grandpa told me that the air we took into our bodies was Tirawahat's air, and that we used it to talk, pray, and sing. It should never be used in bad ways when we spoke.

When we got to the creek, an offshoot of Camp Creek, we would get off the wagon and Grandfather would lift out his ax. Then he would ask me to look around and show him where there were fallen limbs of firewood size. He would feel the limbs or logs and would fix his position so he could swing the ax and strike the wood. Before he started he always told me where to stand and not to move. He could tell from the sound and feeling the cut how he was doing. Sometimes I was set to gathering kindling at a safe distance. Sometimes he took long limbs and loaded them in the wagon to cut up at the house. When he figured we had enough wood, he would help me up on the seat, climb up himself, and with the leather harness creaking as the horses turned the wagon, we would go home. It was on these trips that I learned to tell Grandpa what I saw ahead so he could guide the horses. In time I learned all the turns on the dirt roads between home and Pawnee. I had a little red knitted cap I wore, and there is a picture of me in it somewhere.

Grandpa was very careful with our wagon. He would ask me to check the whiffletree and the tongue. He'd say, "Look close, see if everything is all right." I'd look them over and tell him what I saw. He would walk up to the wheel, shake it hard, and sometimes he'd say, "We are going to have to grease this." Sometimes the leather collar would need to be replaced. Although he could not see and I was about five, we would work on it. Sometimes I'd be told to look the brake over and see if all the parts were right.

When we unhitched the horses, we'd put the whiffletree under the tongue so it was up off the ground. Then we would hang the harnesses over the tongue. Some people hung the harness over the back wheels, but Grandpa didn't like to do that. He'd say that's where the horses were tied, and where they were fed. He always said, "Do things the hard way, even if it takes longer. It's better. Don't do things the easy way."

I learned that the sound or lack of sound of your wagon was important. People took pride in having a wagon that didn't squeak. Arriving at a gathering as silently as possible was the ideal. A squeaking wagon meant lack of pride and attention to your vehicle. I think if Grandpa had lived long enough to have a car he probably would have had it checked constantly to see that it was kept up.

Sometimes Grandpa and I would have to walk somewhere on the dirt road that ran along in front of our place. Sometimes I held his hand, and sometimes I would be skipping along in front of him, while he would be trudging along behind me. Once in a while he stumbled and fell, and I heard him say, "Fate what is this? Why are you doing this to me? God, you took my eyes away. You took my sons away, and you left me with a little boy. What is his fate? Are you causing me to fall? Do you want this boy to hear me, to see me? And maybe in later life for him to be a good man by his feeling sorry for me now?"

I heard the Pawnee expression for fate and asked him what that was. He explained that Tirawahat made fate. It had a lot to do with what happened to a person. It was something beyond man's control. Grandpa explained it by saying, "I did not mean to become blind, but fate decided that it would happen." When Grandpa and I attended a ceremony, he would pray. He would say in Pawnee, "I hope I am sitting here again, and fate will see me through by your [Tirawahat's] doing." He also said that when warriors were not killed in battle with the enemy, they would say, "Fate came close to me, I received a gift, and lived through danger." Thinking about the mysterious force called fate, created by Tirawahat, I became very puzzled, but I grew to understand it as the years went by.

Once in a while Grandpa and I would have to go to the woods to cut down a living tree. Before going to do this or any similar endeavor, he would stand before our sacred bundle and say, "You are still watching. I still have these ways. I still have you, and you are still looking over me. We are going down to disturb Tirawahat's trees, but they are to do us good." Then when we came to the tree, he would explain to me that when we cut down a living tree we prayed and told the tree that we had to cut it down because it was going to help us in some way, and that we were thankful to Tirawahat and hoped that the tree's spirit would understand. He lifted his hands to the sky when he prayed, and I stood beside him and did the same.

One of the things we used green wood for was to build a sweat lodge in our yard. The trimmed branches or saplings were bent over and fastened into an inverted bowl-shaped basket framework. It was five feet tall at the center. We didn't have any skins to cover it, so they used old flour sacks or canvas tarps. Several rocks were placed in a little dug-out place in the center so you could build a fire under them. We gathered a sagelike plant to cover the dirt floor. My grandparents and I would go in there about once a week or more. Water poured over the hot rocks danced and sputtered, and steam came up in a cloud and filled the space. You could take two or three regular baths

8. Maggie Box Blaine, mother of Garland J. Blaine and James G. Blaine. She was a member of the Skidi band and attended Haskell Institute. (Author's collection)

9. James G. Blaine, father of Garland J. Blaine, wearing the Blaine bear claw necklace. (Author's collection)

10. James G. Blaine played baseball at Carlisle
School and later with the Nebraska Indians
team, about 1914 or 1915. (Author's
collection)

11. Ted Eagle Chief and soldiers of the 179th
Infantry, Company B, 17 June 1923, Fort Sill,
Oklahoma. (Courtesy of Oklahoma Historical
Society, Archives and Manuscripts Division)

X 6

EAGLE CHIEF

6/17/23

12. Garland J. Blaine (second from left) as a member of the American Indian mounted troop at the New York World's Fair, 1938. (Author's collection).

13. Prairie View School, which Garland Blaine attended for one year. Listed on the photograph are Bob Cather, Lewis Chadwick, Clement Wadlow, Otis Miller, Clair Talbert, Rowena McCracken, Geneva Gentry, Louella McCracken, Hollis Hedges, Mauverine Talbert, Lucille Talbert, Stella Miller, Hugh Talbert, Julia Pasley, and the teacher, Ollie Schooler. Apparently the written list is not in order, and it does not contain the number of students the photograph shows. (Courtesy of Pawnee County Historical Society)

14. Garland J. Blaine, Kuruks awaki, at a Pawnee Buffalo Dance at the John Ruwalk mudlodge west of Pawnee, Oklahoma. (Author's collection)

15. Garland J. Blaine's drawing of his childhood vision of the sacred buffalo in the mudlodge. (Author's collection)

16. Garland J. Blaine wearing a bear claw
necklace. Taken by the author, 1964.

and still not get the dirt off as well as in a sweat lodge sweat. The first time you poured the water, just the scalp sweats, and then the dirt and water descends the body as the period lengthens and more water is poured. I went in with them until I got older, when just men go in together.

Grandma believed in the effectiveness of the sweat in keeping clean. She had a way of letting a person know if he hadn't been in there often enough. Although she couldn't see much, she could smell odors. I remember one man who came under her scrutiny. Grandma would know this man was visiting us, and she would say, "Oh, my boy here is always hanging around those Osages with their tattoos. Oh, look, you have all those marks under your chin. You must be tattooed." Then she would get up close and peer at him and say, "Oh, no, it's just a dirty neck. You just *never* wash." Willie would never say a thing. About three o'clock in the afternoon he would tell his boys to go down to the creek and bring some wood to heat the rocks. If he could see we had plenty of wood, he'd use ours. Then in the evening Grandpa, Willie, the boys, and I would go in the sweat lodge and stay until Willie got really clean. He knew Grandma was waiting outside.

Besides carrying wood for the stove that served as a cookstove and as a heating stove when the wood door was left open, I had other jobs, one of which was unraveling flour sack seams. Flour sacks were very useful. Towels and shirts could be made on the sewing machine, that somehow Grandma was able to use. To help I learned to thread the needle. She also used flour sacks to make patches that she sewed on our clothes. Patches were on top of patches, and our relatives, that could see better than Grandma, said my clothes had all sizes of patches and nothing matched when I was little.

One of the hardest things for Grandma was cooking, because the stove was hot and she burned herself a lot. When I got tall enough I could help her move the kettle, or climb up on a chair and stir whatever was cooking. That was of continual interest to me because I was always hungry.

We didn't have much furniture. I remember there were some trunks around the walls and a chest of drawers. There was only one bed. Children slept on pallets on the floor. I slept on one in the bedroom where my grandparents slept. At bedtime all the doors were closed and the screenless windows shut and tightly covered, preferably with World War I blankets that either had been issued to the Pawnees or that someone had brought home from the war, I'm not sure. We slept like that because Grandpa and Grandma had grown up in the windowless earthlodges and tipis in Nebraska. I think they believed that the night air could cause sickness. There had been so much sickness in the tribe that it was thought that it had to come through the air, or from witching by someone who wanted to get even for something or was jealous.

My grandparents kept me close to them, not only because they needed me to lead them around, but because I was little and they needed to protect me from harm. They were very apprehensive because they could not see me. But when I was older they would let me run up on the hill near our house if I would yell back now and then to let them know I was all right. This hill belonged to me, I said to myself. From the top I could see for miles and see the sun reflected off the white tombstones in the Skidi cemetery where my mother and father were buried. Sometimes I would lie down in the warm sun on a large flat rock that is about six feet long. Nearby it stood a large gray square rock with green and yellow lichens painting its rough surface. In the center was a low place that after a rain filled with water. I used to put my head down and drink, pretending that this rock was my table. When I faced east, I could see a long ridge where coyotes lived and began to howl just at sunset. I could not be up there then by myself, so in the daytime I called them little brothers and would howl across the distance to them to see if they would answer me. They never did, and Grandpa said they only howled at night because they were waiting all day to talk to Mother Moon. Now and then I go back, park my car on the road and walk up my hill and sit on the rock, and look down to the place where the house used to be. Coyotes still howl from the distant ridge.

Perhaps as I got older my grandpa and grandma realized that I had to have freedom to learn to take care of myself, because when I was about seven or eight, they would let me go to the creek when it was mostly dried up in the summer. It wasn't so far that I could not hear Grandpa shout when he wanted me to come home. After they gave me warnings about this and that, I would pick up the small bow and arrows that Grandfather made for me and tell them that I was going to visit the eagles. They had a nest in the top of a very tall dead tree.[8] They flew over to the Arkansas River to hunt, Grandpa said, and we could hear them call when they soared. I would creep very quietly across the field, like Grandpa taught me he did when he was a scout. I tried to get near the woods without their knowing it, but they always saw me coming. I would finally reach the base of a nearby tree, sit down with my back pressed against it, and keep very still. After a while they seemed to forget that I was there and would settle down and finally go to sleep. Then they made the darndest noise. That was what I was waiting for. They were snoring, *real* snores, but I liked to pretend they were talking to me, and I hoped that they would drop a feather where I could find it. I knew eagles were important and that men wore their feathers in their hair during our dances. Grandpa told me about the time when he was a warrior and fighting the Cheyennes at Powder River. During the battle he was up in the hills scouting, and three Cheyennes all with guns suddenly came around some rocks and saw him. He knew he would be shot, so he fell to the ground, rolled over and jumped up yelling with his hands full of dirt, threw it in their faces, dodged, and eluded them in the rocks.

Later, when he went to Pawnee war dances, it was the custom if someone dropped a feather they wore, it would be picked up by the person dancing who saw it and took it to a former warrior. He would then hold up the feather, stand, and tell of his exploits in battle. Then he would return the feather to its owner. He would be given a gift for doing this. Sometimes he would pray instead of telling an exploit. I heard Grandpa tell about the Cheyennes when a feather was brought to him. I wanted to have a feather to wear when I got big. Later, when I grew to be a man and it was time to change my name, my grandmother had a dream. In her dream she saw two eagles. She believed that her dream told her what my name would be, so I was named From the Heavens Two Eagles Come Flying (Tirawahat retakats wesitawa) in a naming ceremony before the people.

Besides watching the eagles, there were other things to do down by the creek. Grandpa told me about making little clay horses, and when I went down there I would find a little wet place where there was some clay. I would dig some out and shape horses and little men. I would squat there with the cicadas shrilling in rising and falling cadences in the native pecan trees around me and pretend I was a great warrior like my grandpas and Roan Chief and High Eagle. Sometimes a leg would break off, and then all you had to do was spit on it and smooth it back on. Then you put them where they would dry. After they were dry the next day or so, you licked them with your tongue, and this made them look rough like the hide of a horse. The clay tasted good, and I wonder if a lot of little boys who made horses consumed a lot of clay like me.

Grandma had a garden. Usually women did all the gardening, but it took both my grandparents to make ours. I can't remember planting any seeds. That part was sacred, and a woman must do it. But I did help weed because I could see what was a weed and what was corn or squash, melons, beans, or pumpkins. They had muskmelons, but they were not the size you see now. I would carry three at one time, and it was my job, early on a summer's morning when the meadowlarks called to welcome the day, to go out and bring the melons into the kitchen while they were still cool. Grandma loved melons. When the watermelons were ready, I would lead Grandpa to the part of the garden where they were and show him one that I hoped was ripe. If he decided it was, he thanked the plant, cut off the melon, and carried it into the house. When more were ripe than we could eat at one time, Grandma carried them into the bedroom and put them under the bed. Even when she was very old and lived with my Aunt Viola in town and had to buy watermelons, she managed to keep one or two under her bed. Even if she had none and I brought her one when I came to visit, she would say, "Tanka you," in English, smile, and put it under her bed.

As I grew older I knew other children. Sometimes they came to the house with their parents, and sometimes we visited them. I learned how to play games and how to talk with them and think of grownups as people in a different world. I spent so much time alone with my grandparents, and although I loved them dearly, they could not play with me. Life was mostly a serious affair, and I often felt lonely. I knew I had a little brother, but he lived with the Skidis and we rarely saw each other. I had three little Skidi girl cousins whose mother was my mother's cousin. Occasionally I would be taken to visit them for a few days, if there was someone who could stay with my grandparents. I took a little carpetbag with a few clothes in it. I liked to go there because there was someone to play with, and there was always enough food. My cousins, Ruth, Rosanna, and Dorothy, called me little brother. Their mother, Addie Troth Yellow Calf, would sometimes buy me clothes. I remember the little fur coat she bought, and a scooter. I took it home and spent hours playing with it. In later years my cousins said they always wanted their mother to adopt me so I could live with them all the time.

Girl cousins were fine, but boys were even better to play with Garland discovered.

I met little boys when we went to visit such people as the Jims or Roan Chief, or when we attended the ceremonies or Christmas camps. Here, when the grownups attended to their business and Grandma and Grandpa were with friends or relatives who could help them when they needed it, I was allowed to play. Those were wonderful times. I discovered there were others who could make clay men and horses and pretend the Pawnees attacked their enemies.

Other times we would sing or try to sing like the men did. We didn't know all the words, so we would make them up and sing as loud as we could, and sometimes they came out funny, and we'd laugh, fall down and roll around on the ground and wrestle.

Sometimes the men talked of old times, and we little boys gathered around them. They might begin to sing, and when they saw that we were attentive, they would ask us if we wanted to dance. They told us to sing and trot around in a little circle if it was outside under the trees. If inside the house or mudlodge, they would sit on the floor against the wall and we would sing and trot in front of them. Roan Chief would sit and swing one arm back and forth, and the men would sing along. Sometimes, at a certain place in the song, they'd say, "Holler!" and we'd all holler. Afterward they'd give us some change, and we'd divide it.

When I was about six, or maybe a little older, Grandma and Grandpa attended one of the church association camp meetings near town. There were other Pawnee people there, and we could visit with them and listen to the different kind of singing that the white people did. Besides that, the best part was the food served on long tables under the trees. And there was a big horse trough filled with ice blocks and water with cups attached to wires that hung from the trough's edge.

One day Bennie Burns came to our tent and asked my grandparents if he could take me to play with the other children. Grandma said yes, I could go, but I remember I didn't want to go. But Bennie took me off anyway. There was a big tent and a lot of little white children walking in a circle and singing. There were mostly girls, a few boys, and *they* didn't look too happy. I was put in the circle between two girls, took their hands, and started walking around in this circle. I couldn't sing because I did not know English. I felt foolish and kept glancing toward Bennie, hoping he would see how ridiculous this whole thing was and take me out of there. He didn't, and when it finally stopped, they herded us toward the benches under the tent where we were to hear the white preacher speak. Bennie gave me some change and told me that when the "bread" plate came by to put my money in it. I kept waiting for that plate to come by. When it did, I could see that there was no bread in it, just money. That meant all the bread was gone, so I didn't put my money in it. The whole thing was a big disappointment. Bennie took me back to the tent, and as we walked, I thought that going in circles with girls wasn't playing. Playing was running around with boys, climbing, making little horses – not this. I never said a word, though.

Grandma's cousin, Bob Hopkins, who had gotten religion, came by once where we were sitting at the long tables eating. He started telling people to come and fill up the seats in the tent to hear the word of Jesus Christ, son of our Father. Suddenly he stopped. He saw some beets in a dish on the table. I had been eyeing them during the whole meal. I had never seen them before, and they certainly looked good, but it was bad manners to ask for anything if you were little. You had to wait for an older person to offer you food and serve you. Since my grandparents could not see well, if at all, at this time, I had to hope that someone else would ask me about the beets. Bob looked again and stopped yelling his announcement and reached over and with two fingers carefully lifted a beet from the bowl and put it in his mouth. I looked up at him as he began chewing. He made a terrible face and looked right at me and said, THAT TASTES AWFUL! He coughed, spat, and coughed again, and sounded strangled the rest of the evening. So I never got any beets, and for a long time I never wanted any, even though I had never tasted them. Finally, when I was older, I ate some and liked them. The old people would say if you added vinegar to beets it would make you skinny. Then they would look at me and say, "But you are already skinny, so don't eat any beets." So beets have never played a major role in my life.

Most of the time when we were alone on the farm, away from tribal gatherings, I went on playing by myself. Somewhere we found an old tire. Not many people had cars, so where it came from I don't know. An old tire was one of the best things, if you could get one. What you couldn't do with a tire! You could roll it and run, and roll it and run! You could holler and roll it and run. You could take it up my hill, let go, and try to run down as fast as it rolled. It was wonderful fun.

Sometimes you could make playthings out of the plants and leaves around the place. If you hold a redbud leaf just right over the circle formed by your thumb and index finger, you can hit it with the flat of your hand and it makes a wonderful pop. Then there is a plant, a grass that is about four feet tall with a jointed stem. It has long thin, narrow gray-green leaves that droop. Little boys used to pick them, strip off the leaves and use them as spears or javelins. They would really smart if you got hit with one well thrown. We used to have mock battles and pretend we were fighting the Sioux. Nobody wanted to be a Sioux, but we had to take turns.

Another plant was *Pakus ku ru ri ki* [as written by Garland]. This was the name for a gourdlike plant. Only boys played with them, and this was in Nebraska. They could be found ripe in July about the time of the ceremonies and about the first of August when the corn was getting ripe. Grandpa said when he was a little boy, they used to find the plants when they were dry, break off the sections with the little "gourds," and shake them and imitate their fathers who used real gourds in dancing. I kept looking for them in the fields around the allotment, but I guess they didn't grow there.

"Uncle" is what the Pawnees call the whirlwind or dust devil, as it is sometimes called in Oklahoma. It is a manifestation of Uncle Wind, and the Pawnees have stories about him. Garland remembered that in the hot summer when the plowed fields got dry, and Uncle was blowing hard, "We little boys would watch for a column of swirling dust rising in a nearby field. We would run as hard as we could and get right in the middle of it, and run around and around with it, yelling and waving our arms all the time. The dry weeds and dirt would get in our hair, mouth, and eyes, but we kept at it until Uncle rose up in a swirl of gritty dust and dried grass and disappeared in the sky. Then we returned slowly back to the house, comparing this Uncle with other Uncles of summers past. We crept slowly because when we got home, we knew that Grandma or Aunt or Mother was going to be scowling, scolding, and leading us to the pump to be washed off, and saying, "Don't you do that again. What have I told you. Don't you do that again."[9]

Garland Blaine grew up with his Pitahawirata grandparents on the "south side," as the Skidis termed the south bands area on the other side of Black Bear Creek. He had fewer memories of his Skidi kinsmen, but those he had were vivid and important to the child.

Back in the twenties, when I was growing up, at one time the Skidis were having a Pipe Dance near the north [Skidi] round house.[10] During a part of this ceremony, as a chief, my grandfather Box got up and gave a short talk honoring the visiting band on behalf of the Skidis. Then he sang his warrior song. The drums began, and my grandfather started dancing. I can see him as he danced forward toward the singers seated around the drum in the middle of the floor. As he danced forward he put his left hand against his chest, and his right hand extended up toward the zenith, and then he brought his right hand to his chest and extended his left arm. He repeated these motions as he would dance forward a few steps, then backward a few steps. He repeated this until the end of his song. This was symbolic of worshiping.

Both John Box and White Eagle died in the 1920s. John Box was thought to be about ninety years old at the time of his death, on 8 November 1925. His brother had died on 25 July 1923. When Garland heard the news, he ran out of the allotment house near Maramec, went up to the top of the hill, and stayed there and cried all day. He said he had looked forward to dancing the Deer Dance for the first time with his grandfather White Eagle, who had taught him just what to do, and now they would never be able to do it.

There were many times when we would drive over in the wagon to his place and stay there two or three nights. In the evenings, my grandfathers Box and Blaine would sing the songs after my great-uncle White Eagle would start them off. While my two grandfathers sang, White Eagle told me where to be in relation to where he was standing during the dance. Then we would start out. He would say, when I get on one knee, you jump up and stand just immediately to my right, behind me. When I stand up and move forward, you come right along with me. You get right to my side, and just sort of bump my leg a little bit. I was performing like a little deer. He was a grown deer. When he died, I never got to dance or be with him again. It was one of the saddest times of my childhood. White Eagle's name in his later years was Some One to Have Respect and Love For. Another name he had was Leader Sitting Down.

Garland Blaine learned his grandfather Box's warrior song and White Eagle's Deer Dance songs when he was young. The first one here is Grandfather Box's song:

> Mother there she stands.
> Mother there she stands.
> Mother there she stands.
> Mother there she stands.
> In this way I rely on Mother Moon
> Mother there stands.

White Eagle's Deer Dance songs:

FIRST SONG
> As I come, As I come.
> I fear the forest.
> This eerie noise coming from this great dark forest.

SECOND SONG

As I become afraid of the dark forest,
Sun shines only atop the forest,
As I come. As I come.

In Pawnee songs there is always a story and meaning that cannot be determined by just hearing the words. One has to know the story to understand the meaning. In White Eagle's songs, his ancestor experienced this episode: When he went to sleep near the forest, he had a sacred vision. He saw a stag, and Tirawahat blessed him through this stag. The stag made the eerie noise in the forest, and when the man awoke he knew these songs. The stag taught him the songs and other things known to him.[11]

In traditional societies, songs and storytelling teach tribal, family, and personal history, which was important in cultures where reading and writing did not exist. Old men told of their youth and young men listened, as Garland did when he went with High Eagle to the creek and learned the buffalo songs and heard about other events in the old man's life. It was part of the technique of teaching values, right behavior, and history, and it also served to pass the time, as young Garland remembered.

Sometimes in bad weather, when it was cold and wet or snowy, Grandpa, Grandma, and I sat around the stove in the kitchen. I asked Grandpa to tell me about the places he had seen beyond the reservation. He had seen a lot of places before he married Grandma. Before then he worked in a coal mine in the Choctaw country, and he described the little lamp he wore on his head. He also worked for a year in a sawmill making shingles in southeastern Indian Territory or Arkansas – down there someplace. He wasn't sure of the exact place. When he went to Anadarko, where the Wichita agency was, he worked as a freighter carrying government goods. He said he learned to speak Comanche, which was then the language of trade. He taught me a few words, but they are forgotten.

To me the most exciting things to hear about were the times when he was growing up in Nebraska. When Grandpa could hear the coyotes howling on the hills across the valley from our allotment, it would remind him of wolves in Nebraska. He told me that they followed a solitary hunter if he had a horse loaded with meat. They would keep their distance but gradually close in. Then you threw a piece of meat to them to see if they were serious.

Once in the winter when there was snow on the ground, Grandpa killed a buffalo, cut it up and loaded it on his horse, and started back to the camp. He said, "I thought, 'There are wolves watching somewhere.' I had to take bones, hides, everything to camp, and it was five miles away. The horse was laden and I had to walk leading him. Pretty soon there was a wolf, then two, one on each side, trailing at a distance. The horse sensed them. I got my bow and arrows ready. I might have to turn the horse loose I thought, so they would follow it and I could escape. But I didn't want to do that because we needed food. So I stopped and threw off the backbone. They silently trotted up and began to eat that. They finished that and pretty soon they came on and there were seven of them. One came nearer and nearer. I shot at him but missed. They got closer and I stopped and threw off the head. They got that. Later I threw off the ribs, but it didn't stop them. They kept on following. I threw off the shanks, hooves and all. Then I stopped and hollered real loud and listened. Someone hollered back. I gave short yells that meant danger. This other man hollered a long yell in response. I kept going on the horse now. Soon a man and another man came over the ridge. They had no game. Then the wolves began to drop back and stopped following us. The man rode with me back to camp, and I gave him one leg. He was grateful." I sat there in our kitchen and shivered, seeing the wolves following Grandpa in the snow and getting closer and closer.

Grandpa had other exciting times when he was in the Wild West shows. When they pulled into a town on flatcars, all the white people waited and wanted to see the Indians from the Wild West. The people would holler WHAY, WHAY WHAY BIG INDIANS!! (This cry was later interpreted to be Hooray!) Grandpa said he went to Colorado with Buffalo Bill Cody, and "We showed there, in Omaha, Kansas City, St. Louis, Chicago, Columbus, Philadelphia, Washington City, and New York."

He laughed remembering what the white man told them to do when people came to watch them at mealtimes. They were told to act wild and eat "like animals." Their meat and soup was cooked in

a big kettle, and when it came time to eat it, they were supposed to
make noises like hungry bears, grab the meat, and devour it. They
put a big piece in their mouths, then jerked some off with their teeth.
It had soup on it, and that would fly all over the nearby people. The
women would squeal, and Grandpa would make a noise like a lot of
squeaking mice to show how they sounded. He would laugh and say,
"We were just young men, and we didn't care if we acted ridiculous,
but the older Indian men would go back behind to get something to
eat and talk normally, not wanting to be a part of such a spectacle." I
never remember hearing Grandpa say anything bad about the shows,
maybe because I was young, but other Indians had bad experiences
that I heard about later.[12]

At another time he joined some other Pawnees and went with
the Buffalo Bill and Pawnee Bill show. He said he saw Annie Oakley
shoot her rifle. Buffalo Bill would come riding in on his horse and
would stop and doff his hat, and the people would cheer. Grandpa
said he was a little man with reddish yellow hair. He would throw
a handkerchief on the ground, then ride around on his horse with
his head down and pick it up. He also could slide out of the saddle,
and holding the surcingle, go completely around the horse's belly,
then up into the saddle. Grandpa said, "We didn't think that was so
great; we did things like that all the time when we fought the enemy
or chased buffalo. But we didn't say anything. We were glad to earn
a little money and be off the reservation."

When our turn came we got on horses, rode around the wagons,
whooped and hollered, looked fierce, and got chased out by the
cowboys and soldiers. The people cheered. We had our thoughts
about that. We became friendly with other tribes. It wasn't hard. We
all had the same experiences with the white man. We Pawnees and
Sioux would talk about the old battles. We learned who certain brave
men were and what they had done. Later, when we came home we
told our folks the stories. Some of the older men didn't like to hear
that we made friends with the Cut Throats, as they still called the
Sioux in Pawnee.

Sometimes when we traveled with the shows we would talk about
the real United States soldiers we had seen when we were Army
Scouts. The Pawnees noticed that whenever a white trooper was

wounded and fell, he would always cry, "Wah tuh, wah tuh, wah tuh." He would sit up on the ground, brace himself with his arms back, and put his head back and say this. We thought this was strange. When you are wounded, you should crawl to cover, get out of sight, not just sit there in plain sight, and say, "Wah tuh, wah tuh, wah tuh." He said they all did this, and we Indian scouts thought it was mighty peculiar.

Grandpa died before I could tell him of my adventure in a Wild West show. In 1938 the World's Fair took place in New York. The people in charge decided that they wanted a mounted all-Indian honor guard. So they sent out a notice to agents and school superintendents across the country that they needed twenty-six young men who had to be of good character, not less than 5' 11" tall, able to express themselves well and ride a horse adeptly. Capt. James W. Lansing was in charge.

Dana Knight, Ponca, I, and some other boys from Oklahoma went to Haskell School to train. Soon we found ourselves in New York, riding in formation, doing maneuvers, and escorting important visitors at the fair. I met Queen Elizabeth and King George of England. They reviewed our troop, and as I stood erect, eyes forward, the queen stopped in front of me. She asked me a few questions about my family, and I answered. She wished me well in the future and moved on. A New York newspaper said I was the only one she stopped to talk to.

Our troopers became acquainted with the Indians who took part in the North Circus that played at the fair. One of the events had pioneer wagons, soldiers, cowboys, and Indians riding around the arena, with the Indians trying to attack the wagons and the soldiers and cowboys fighting them off. Sometimes we ate with the show Indians, and I noticed that one of the cowboys, a big fellow, a bully, liked to make fun of one of the Indians. One of them told me that during the show, the soldiers and cowboys fought with the Indians, who were killed or driven away. This particular white man liked to overdo the fighting part and really hit the Indians harder than he needed to.

One day this Indian got sick and asked me if I would fill in for him. I agreed, and he sent me to Mr. North, who told me exactly what to do. I was to run around yelling, wear a breechcloth and feathers, be painted, and carry bow and arrows. At a certain time a cowboy would come running up and fight with me. I was told to not fight too hard and let him get me down where he could finish me off. I agreed. When that scene came, and the wagons were circling, the soldiers shooting, and the cowboys chasing the Indians, I did my part. I whooped and hollered and ran around with the rest of the attacking Indians. Soon the cowboy from the restaurant came up and started to fight with me. He tried to get me to fall down, but I wouldn't fall. "Fall down, dammit," he swore. Instead I wrestled with him and finally knocked him down and sat on him. This unexpected struggle caught the audience's attention, and they began to cheer as I got the better of him. As he lay there, I said, "If you ever pick on any of us again, I'm going to find you and beat the tar out of you" – or words to that effect. Mr. North fired me.

Garland went on with his reminiscences of his childhood:

After Grandpa settled down with Grandma, his roving days were over. He now had a growing family, and he applied to join the agency Indian police. His family needed the extra money and rations in those hard times. At that time in the early 1890s, Grandpa still had a little warrior's braid on the back of his head. The agent wanted the police to have short hair, and you couldn't be hired unless your hair was short. The agent wanted Grandpa because he was a United States Pawnee Scout. Baptiste Bayhylle worked around the agency as an interpreter, and Grandpa talked to him about this. He told him he just couldn't cut his braid off. Baptiste thought awhile, then told Grandpa to tuck his braid inside his hat when the agent ordered them all to meet so he could talk to them and tell them what to do that day. Grandpa came in and forgot and took his hat off, and his braid fell down. The agent looked at him and said angrily, "Taka, your hair sure grew fast."[13] Grandpa had to cut it off that day.

As Kuruks awaki, Little Spotted Bear, grew older, Wichita Blaine and Effie Blaine realized that their grandson spoke little English. They knew he would have to go to school and learn to speak it, since they could not. Elmer, too, agreed that it was necessary. So one day the child heard his grandmother say, "Let's go to town and I will buy you some shoes." He had worn shoes before, mostly in the winter, but sometimes not then, if he had none. Effie knew the Pawnee Indian School, where he would go, gave shoes to the children, but she had heard they did not always fit, so she wanted him to have shoes he could wear.

Then something happened and the school informed them that he could not attend that year. Garland said:

It didn't make any difference to me. I wanted to go, but if I didn't, well, all right, I'd go next year. Then my uncle Elmer came out to the house and said, "Well, how about his school?" Grandma said, "They are not going to send him this year." Elmer declared, "He needs to go to school. He is almost eight years old now, so I think I'll take him out to this country school and enroll and start him there." Grandma asked me, "Do you want to got out there to that country school?" And I said, "Yes, I'll go out there." It was called Prairie View and was about two miles from the allotment.[14]

One morning soon after, my uncle and I started walking down the road. When we arrived, he knocked at the door. The teacher came and opened it. He said, "My name is Elmer Blaine, and this is my nephew and I want to enroll him in school." The teacher said, "Well, what grade is he in?" He answered, "He has never gone to school. The fact is he speaks very little English." She looked at me and said, "We will be glad to have him." I recognized her. Her brother's name was Schuler or Schooler. That was their last name. He drove a taxi in Pawnee. And that was his sister.

So we went in and he gave her my full name, and when I was born, and whatever else they had to know. Then he said, "Miss Schooler, sometimes this boy is a little headstrong, and if you have to take the switch to him, take it to him. And tell me about it, because he will get the same thing when he gets home. I believe in strict discipline, and he knows it. So if you feel that he's at a disadvantage, don't let him take advantage of that, but put him through the paces."

She said, "Oh, I'm sure we will get along just fine." So we went down the aisle and she made one boy move, and I sat in there, but I was too big. Pretty soon I was almost at the back of the room. There were four rows of seats, and two people could sit at one desk. There could have been about twenty children in the room. I noticed that I was the only Indian there.

She stood by my desk and asked if I had a pencil. I knew that word, so I reached in my pocket and pulled one out. Then she said, "Do you have any paper?" She pointed to a tablet on the desk next to me. My grandmother had bought me one of those Big Chief writing tablets, the kind when you mark on it, you don't erase it because it gets black all over. Well, I understood that and pulled it out all folded up. So she said, "It would be best if you did not fold your paper. Do you know what I mean?" So to let her know I understood, I put my hands on it and gave it a quick press. I understood English some, but I couldn't talk. I could say words, but I didn't know what they meant most of the time. I was a good imitator.

By now I felt everybody was looking at me, which I guess they were. I felt that everybody was going to laugh at me. I felt that way because I knew that I was different. I spoke a different language, I was a different color, and we ate different food. I knew this because whenever we stopped at any of the neighbors' homes, and if they asked us in to eat, there was a lot of these vegetables and salads that were foreign to me. I never saw some of these foods on our table. About the only things they had that we had were radishes. We would buy pickles, onions, but anything like lettuce, we didn't. We didn't drink milk. We didn't have cheese or butter.[15]

But back to school. This teacher kind of left me alone, you might say. So I thought, I'm going to buy another tablet. I'll just leave this one at home, and I'll just draw on it. I'll buy another tablet and I won't wrinkle it up. I'll buy some more pencils, and I'll use that pencil sharpener over there. And I'll make them real nice and smooth. Uncle had sharpened my pencil with a knife. It didn't look like the others. So the next time we went to town they bought me a real thick tablet and some more pencils.

The next day at school, we went out for recess, and when I came back my pencils were gone. Several of the boys around me had seen my pencils. I had maybe four or five – all different colors. So I looked and saw one of the boys get up and go to the teacher. She said, "Oh, that is a beautiful pencil, and you have just put your initials on there." Of course, I didn't know what initials meant. So when he came back and sat down, I looked over on his desk and he had my pencils.

I was about eight at the time, and he was about thirteen. I got up and went to the teacher, and in the best way, in my best English, I think I said, "Teacher, he got my pencils." I don't know, I might have said as I pointed at him, "Pencils mine he got."

Anyway, I let her know that he stole my pencils. She called him up there to her desk and he denied it. He said they were not my pencils. So I pointed at several boys, and I indicated that they knew they *were* my pencils because they saw me with them when I brought them into the school that morning. So she called these boys, but they didn't want to say anything. So they sat down, and she said to me, "Well he has his initials on them, so they are his pencils." So I knocked Otis down. Right there, I knocked him down.

What happened then? The teacher grabbed my arm, shook me a little bit and told me not to do that. She hustled me back to my seat. And Otis hollered, "Wait till school is out," which didn't mean anything to me. But that's just the thought I had, "Just wait till school is out."

So we went on ahead and stayed the day in school. When we had recess, I went out to the pump and got a drink of water. When dinnertime came we went outside to eat. I had some dry meat that Grandma fixed, and that was my food. Everybody went and sat by themselves. Some of the older boys sat together, and some of the older girls, but the little kids, we just sat anywhere. I guess we didn't have as much to talk about as the bigger boys.

When school was out, I could sense that something was taking place. I could see the boys get together, whisper, and look at me. But I didn't care. All I wanted to do was get to Otis. I waited till everybody left the room, and I walked outside. I had one little pencil, I guess somebody gave it to me. I had my papers. There was a little porch there, and all the boys gathered around there and they wouldn't let me leave. And I couldn't see Otis. It wasn't that I wanted to leave to get away from school. I wanted to leave and find Otis and get my pencils. But these boys wouldn't let me off the porch. Some of them were fifteen- and eighteen-year-old boys. Somebody came running around the edge of the school and said, "Teacher's gone." Then two of the boys grabbed my arms and said, "You want to fight Otis?" They took me around to the coal shed, and he was in there waiting. We went at it. Some of the boys must not have liked Otis, because I got some encouragement from them. Besides that, I think they wanted to see what I could do. So I got Otis down and pounded on him, and we got up and pushed each other around until the fight ended.

Well, when I got home, my uncle asked me where my pencils were. I said, "One boy stole them." He said, "Did you get them back?" and I said no. He told me that when I went to school, I was going to have to learn to protect myself. "There's a lot of things that are going to come up that you are not going to understand, but you are going to have to learn how to make your best way. So if you can get your pencils back, get them back."

The next day I went back to school. I could sense that the teacher acted different toward me. Well, she didn't give me any more time than she absolutely had to. And the boys would get together and make up their minds who they wanted to fight me. So from then, as soon as recess or lunchtime came, we would go out to the coal shed and have it out. It got to the point where they took up for the other boy more than me when I got him down. They would say, "Do you want to fight or do you want to wrestle?" It didn't make any difference to me. So every day I had to fight.

I felt let down. I knew the teacher must know what was going on, but she wasn't doing anything about it. I did not want to go to her for anything. I just did not feel good toward her. I began to feel she did not like me because I was an Indian. This was my first experience with feeling prejudice. I do not know whether she felt that way or not. Maybe she was doing her best; I don't know. But she was always brief with any correction on my paper or anything. If I didn't understand and would try to ask her, she would say, "I have already told you that." Maybe she did, but I didn't know enough English to know she had. With the others, she would stand there and go over and over it with them. So pretty soon whenever anything came up that I did not understand, I would think, "Well, I'll listen. Maybe somebody else made the same mistake. When she tells them, I'll hear it." Because I know she wouldn't tell me. And that's the way I did. So I learned by listening to her correct other people and trying to understand what she was saying. She didn't spend time with me; I guess she thought it was a waste of time. So I never went to her hardly for anything.

Sometimes we went out as a group at recess or noontime and played blindman's bluff or drop the handkerchief, or those games. Sometimes the teacher would come by, and all the kids would run up to her and want her to play. By God, I never did run up to her and want her to play. I knew if she joined the game I was going to get out. I just didn't feel like . . . I didn't want to make the situation any worse than what it was. I was afraid that anything I might do would agitate her feelings against me. I felt that she disliked me. She might not have, you know. But still, the way a small child feels toward a grownup, or the reaction he has toward a grownup, he is not ever very wrong.

I didn't go to school every day. I would go maybe a week, and then my folks would go visit somewhere, and I would have to go along. There would be nobody home. So maybe I would miss two weeks. Now, that is bad on Indian children. But maybe if somebody stayed home, then I could stay home and go to school.

Once in a while my uncle Elmer would come to school. The teacher would run to the door, bring him in, and tell him how well everything was with me. She'd come up and put her hand on my shoulder and pat it and say, "We are getting along just fine." She made me hate her. I did not want to tell my uncle how things really were because I knew how he was. If I told him, he might say something to her about it, and that would make it worse for me when he was not there. So I did not want to tell him anything. I let her think that she was hoodwinking him and she was hoodwinking me.

Once in a while it would be very cold weather. The school was out at four o'clock. On bitter days, about three o'clock, my Grandpa would come to get me on his horse. This old horse, Jim, would bring Grandpa to the school and walk right up to the gate. The teacher would go outside, and maybe Grandpa would already have the horse tied. She would take him by the arm, and bring him in and set him down. My Grandpa would ask, "Teacher me smoke?" And she would say, "Yes, Mr. Blaine, you go ahead and smoke." He knew all the children were probably watching him walleyed, since most of them were afraid of Indians. He would get that big long pipe out and put the tobacco in there, light it, and start smoking. The teacher was very nice to him, and he never knew what I went through there.

This teacher cut pictures out of magazines, like apples, saltshakers, flowers, rocks, anything, and she'd put these pictures up along the blackboard. Then she would write on the board how to spell these things. So I got to the place where I could read and write pretty good, but I still did not want to talk, because a lot of the words I could not say distinctly, and when I tried the others laughed, and I did not want anybody to laugh at me. It made me feel . . . it stopped me, you know. But when I got off to myself, I guess I sounded like a broken record saying those words over and over again.[16]

Did the teacher ever stop them from laughing at me? I don't think she ever pointed out to them to stop laughing at me. I think she hit the table with a little switch and said, "Everybody be quiet." I don't ever remember her telling me that I had to practice to speak distinctly, and that I wouldn't be able to say the words until I practiced them. All I remember her saying was, "Now everybody be quiet," and telling me, "Now you may proceed." That was her favorite word. So I would proceed hearing muffled snickers all around.

I had been taught not to make fun of anybody. So I would sit there and think to myself, "I wonder if their mothers and their grandmothers tell *them* not to make fun of anybody?" But as far as being hurt by it, [although] I did not like to hear it, I don't think I felt hurt by it because I knew that I was learning. But I knew that I couldn't talk well enough to make anybody understand. Whenever I was called on to say something, I would just sit there. I would not say anything. Then the teacher would say, "Garland, if you don't stand up and say something I am going to give you an F." "Go ahead and give it to me," I'd think. But whenever they would say, "Write this," usually I would get A's and B's on anything I handed in. I just did not want to talk. Whenever there was more than one word to spell or pronounce, we had to go to the front of the room to give or explain an answer. At first I would go up and try, but after a while I stopped that because I knew they were going to laugh at me, and I just did not want anybody to laugh. I really stopped talking after that.[17]

So finally that year of the first grade was over. I failed it. They gave out report cards that were different colors. If you made an F you got a yellow report card. If you made a D you got a green one. A C got you a red one. If you got a B you got a blue one, and an A, a white one. There was always one yellow one in there, and I always knew it was mine. When they would bring the report cards in, I could hear the children say, "Well that yellow one belongs to the Indian."

When my folks wanted me to go back in the fall, I refused. They questioned me, and finally I told them what that year had been like – about the fights, and the laughing, and the teacher, day after day. They understood and did not make me go, and I did not go to school again until I went to the Pawnee Indian school some years later.

Here again Garland confronted unsympathetic authority figures. He needed shoes badly. His were worn out and did not fit his feet any more, so he went into a shoe store on the square and told the man he needed to buy a pair of shoes. The man looked at him and told him he couldn't sell him any shoes unless he had credit and authorization from the agent. "I have money in the agency," Garland said. "You will be paid." But the man would not sell him any shoes. For the first time he confronted the system that controlled his money and how and when and where it was spent. He left the store and walked to the Pawnee agency, waited, and told the school superintendent he needed shoes. He could not wear the ones he had, he said, sticking his feet out so the man could see them. The man said he would authorize a purchase when he had time, but not then. Garland said:

I left the office angry. I went barefooted. One day I was in town; I still had no shoes. I walked down the alley and noticed the shoe store's open backdoor that led into the storeroom. I went in there and removed several pairs of children's shoes. Then I returned to school, went to the corncrib, and hid the shoes under the corn. I knew several other students that needed shoes badly. I took them to the corncrib to see if any of the shoes fitted. If they did, they wore the shoes. That was my first rebellion against the system. I thought I was getting even with the agent and the store man for the way I was treated.

Before I started to school at Prairie View, my grandparents talked to me and said that our old world was best, but that I must learn how to get along in the new world of the white man. My first experiences in that new world had been mostly a bitter disappointment. I think at that early age I decided I would never forget the old world of my grandparents and would hold it close to me all my life.

NINE

The Truths

During the great darkness, when our people were in their primordial noncon-
sciousness, they were awakened by a flash of lightning and the voice of Tirawahat,
God, speaking in the thunder. At that time he gave us life and we became
conscious.

Garland J. Blaine

I always wanted to know what God's mother looked like, and all the time you see
her in the flowers.

Pawnee song

Early in his life with his grandparents, Garland became aware of the
religious devotion around him. In the early morning he watched from
his pallet as his grandfather arose, put on his hat that he kept by his bed,
opened the east-facing front door, and stepped outside. There he looked
toward the sky and began his prayers aloud. In all matters of importance
he addressed his sacred bundle, including times when the family left
the house for a visit. He would say that he hoped it would watch over
them as they traveled and guide them safely home. At planting time he
took his pipe, walked into the field, knelt, touched Mother Earth and
thanked her for life, lighted the pipe, and in its smoke sent his prayers to
Tirawahat. After the seeds sprouted, he thanked the plants for helping
to sustain their lives. The last thing Garland remembered at night was his
grandfather thanking God for the day and acknowledging the trees that
supplied the boards that protected him and his family. The materials in

the house had absorbed and held the spirits of the formerly living trees. The spirit of Tirawahat was everywhere. So the child became aware of the sacredness of life around him.

In 1979, shortly before his death, Garland Blaine began writing the following story of his quest for knowledge about his tribal origins. It was not finished and was copied from his handwritten draft.

Pawnee – Pari – Ratahah kuki

Atiput, I said, in Pawnee, meaning grandfather, there is something I want to say. He turned his face in my direction and said solemnly, sit down here by me, for he must have sensed a profound question. I sat down to his right.

My grandfather, about seventy years of age, blind, sat for a moment, legs crossed, leaning slightly forward with each forearm resting on each knee. What do you want to say, he asked. Grandfather, I want to say, how did we, our people begin our lives?

Grandfather straightened his legs forward and with his fingers took the tautness out of his white muslin leggings. Then he rearranged his muslin wrap around his waist and midsection. He crossed his legs again and in a quiet voice began to pray.

When Grandfather finished his prayer, he leaned toward me and said in a strong whisper, listen closely and well. This is the way of our people. This is the way. Our Father, who made all things, did this for us. This, our story is very sacred to our people. God gave us our sacred life and consciousness.

In the beginning, it is said that suddenly the people became aware, and it was dark, it was night . . .

The talks continued as Garland grew older until he knew that the God was Tirawahat Atius, or Heaven Father Who Is Above, or Father Everywhere Above. In his grandfather's explanation, he said that in the beginning there was the force, and out of it he, the force, created everything. Tirawahat was everything. He is an unseen power with monotheistic attributes. His extension includes creation, the universe, and all that is beyond man to infinity. Tirawahat is everywhere, and in everything seen in nature. His intermediaries, such as the stars, constellations, winds, plants, and animals, could act in transmitting certain sacred knowledge and power to man when they appeared in dreams and visions.

All things were considered blessed by Tirawahat. But we did not pray to them as idols; we considered them extensions of Tirawahat, who could communicate through them with us in our visions and dreams. Grandmother Blaine used to sing this song. It reflects some of the Pawnees' beliefs.

> My only belief is in the Heaven.
> My only belief is in the Heaven.
> There is only one thing where my belief lies.
> Atius [Tirawahat] is the expanse of the Heavens.

Garland next explained the meaning of Tirawahat. "*Ti hut* means it is up there, that is, the moon, a star, in its own place. It means something moving – a moving thing in the universe. *Ra wa* is plural. So *Ti ra wa hat* means all those things or bodies suspended and moving in the universe. The entire heavens. Since Tirawahat made all things, we give him the human aspect of a father and call him Atius, our word for father. In Pawnee the complete term is Father Who Is Everywhere Above."[1]

Wichita Blaine had a sacred bundle, as did some others in the tribe. They played a vital role in Pawnee religious life. In Pawnee legends they are said to have been inspired and first created by Tirawahat and the sacred spirits themselves – so long ago that no one can tell how many generations revered them for their divine origins and the great powers they contained. Although scholars have described their presence among numerous American Indian cultures, Clark Wissler said that the most extensive use appeared to be among the Pawnees. He said, "The whole tribal organization is expressed in bundle rituals and their relations to each other . . . there was a hierarchy of bundles extending from the tribe down to the family groups."[2]

Sacred bundles described in Pawnee origin myths could originate as supernatural creations. They could also be created through human visions or dreams in which appeared the morning star, the evening star, and other heavenly bodies or events, or Tirawahat's animal creatures, such as the bear, beaver, eagle, and owl spirits that instructed the blessed individual in how to make his bundle, what objects it should contain, and what their meaning and power were. The individual would be taught certain songs and rituals to be performed at specified times. Any person thus blessed gained power and became respected by his fellow tribesmen. However, not everyone who sought a vision received it.

Sacred bundles were an important part of any Pawnee sacred society ritual. Each ritual leader or Pawnee doctor, like Wichita Blaine, possessed a bundle. Through the power found within it, depending on its purpose, the individual so empowered could cure the sick, determine the time for starting and carrying on the tribal hunt, accomplish marvelous feats of legerdemain during certain ceremonies, or have protection from the enemy, among other functions.

The Pawnees had an annual cycle of ceremonies in which specific sacred bundles played a major role. The ritual, if performed in accordance with ancient formalities, reassured the Pawnees their world remained in balance. These ceremonies reinforced their conviction that Tirawahat and other supernatural beings had given them life and the directions for sustaining it. This relationship was maintained by a respectful affiliation through the medium of the sacred bundle and the ceremonies or functions it commanded.[3]

It is not known how many Pawnee sacred bundles came to Indian Territory in the 1870s after the Pawnees' removal from their Nebraska homeland. The owners of those bundles and the men who performed the rituals using them were the last generation of Pawnees who received empowerment in their native country's sacred places. After death, many bundles were buried with their owners, who carried the ceremonial knowledge with them. When people died from the contagious diseases that decimated the tribe, the government ordered their belongings burned, including their sacred bundles. Many bundles found their way onto museum shelves when family economic stress caused them to be sold along with other traditional items such as clothing, utensils, and weapons. The introduction of the Native American Church and the twentieth-century advancement of Christianity decreased their importance. Today the complete ceremonies associated with them are no longer known to the Pawnees, but the respect and awe for those that remain in the tribe continues.[4]

During the years of drastic population decline, it became increasingly difficult for each band to perform the ceremonies and the activities that accompanied them owing to the loss of leaders and their sacred bundles. From necessity ceremonial leaders from the different bands consulted with one another. It was decided to combine their dances of the same type and in that way fill the ritual seats. Thus in any given ceremony, there could be members from all three South Bands, and later from the North Band. Each took his place, praying, singing, dancing, and performing his role according to traditional procedures in order to maintain the connection between the tribe and the sacred spirits.

Accompanying his grandparents, Garland observed, took part in, and remembered the ceremonies they attended. He said that one important purpose of the sacred society ceremonies during the early years in Indian Territory was to try to allay sickness and death in the tribe and to petition Tirawahat and Mother Earth for enough food and healthful surroundings. It never occurred to the Pawnees to cease their ceremonial efforts. Had they done so, their people's lives would become even more difficult than they were. As devout as the participants were in performing their ceremonies, it seemed impossible not to observe that an increasingly tenuous connection existed between them and their Nebraska spiritual origins. But their efforts continued.

To maintain the necessary number of participants in the sacred societies, the principal ceremonial figures had apprentices or protégés. Among Wichita Blaine's young men were Clyde Roaming Chief, Louis Matlock, and later his grandson, called "Little Shaking Ears" by the old men because he pricked up his ears to listen and learn like an alert little animal. He was instructed to remember the songs for each ritual and to sing or perform only when his grandfather told him to do so.

To be selected as an apprentice, a young man made his purpose known by carrying firewood and water, helping cook food for the ceremony, and running errands for an older man, who would keep an eye on him. If they were related, the younger man would call him "Father," and if unrelated, "Grandfather." To make his purpose clear, he could say, "Heru, Atias, I want you to look at me and feel compassion for me. I want pity to touch your heart with caring. I want to be taken into your dance. It makes me feel good to worship Tirawahat this way." Usually the older man had known the young man all his life, and he did not refuse the petition. Occasionally he did refuse, however, if he doubted his commitment and ability.

If the older man acquiesced, the young man took his position as an apprentice or novice for some period. This interval allowed the man and other members to judge his sincerity, character, and stability. The period could last a few years while the novice assumed more responsibility and gathered knowledge. He must learn rituals and songs by rote. He must begin to gather the paraphernalia and the different items of clothing that distinguished members. From time to time he would be asked if he had acquired this or that article. He had to ask permission to seek some items, such as tufts of buffalo wool and certain feathers. His amount of initiative was monitored. After time passed, they instructed him to bring his "equipment," sit with his mentor, and participate as directed. If he met the members' final approval, he was accepted. His parents went to each of the society's members and thanked them for blessing their son in this way. As he became established in the hierarchy, other younger men followed in his footsteps.

In Indian Territory, however, the process had to be shortened in order to maintain the ceremonies and compensate for the many members' deaths. Then a young man interested in becoming a member of a sacred society consistently attended the ceremonies and dances. His family encouraged him. In due time he would address the headman and tell him that being there made him feel good and that he would feel blessed if he could sit with them and learn. He would ask permission to become a member, and it would usually be granted.

All apprentices knew the story of one young man like themselves. It was called "Remember the Little Clay Horses":

> There was an outstanding young man in Nebraska who had started on his career to become a doctor. In his first year, he had surpassed all the other young men in his abilities. In fact the whole village talked about him. He had been able to perform better in the ways that first-year trainees were required to do. Now it seemed that it was a definite process, with one moving from one year to the next in his ability and training under the tutelage of an older doctor. When the second year came along he had acquired quite a reputation for his prowess in the mudlodges where the ceremonies took place. At this particular ceremony he was aware of his reputation. But he became aware that there was another young man there who was performing perhaps even more admirably than he had done, and so he became very anxious. There is a Pawnee way to say this, "Siks ti tu te wu kis." In this state he began to worry about what was going to happen when his turn came.

When it came, he got up and stood before the other doctors. He had by this time elevated his thoughts to a stage above normal. This stage comes after concentration and praying. Then individuals began to make the noises and the motions of the animals who had entered into their mind, and whose parts or roles they were now playing.[5] He turned to the headman and asked for clay. The headman then asked the two fire men who sat by the door to go out and get clay from someplace in the village. They soon returned with a block of clay, which they placed on the skin in front of him. He then turned to the young men with him, the other apprentices, and said, "Make clay horses as I am making," and he made one.

They watched and made others just like it. He then took the clay horses to the center where the circular fire pit was, and he lined them up facing the headmen. The number of horses is not remembered, perhaps, six or seven. He then took a whip he carried, which was about a foot and a half long. He hit it on the ground, saying certain things. The horses moved out and around the fire. Each time he hit the ground they moved a little farther, until they completely circled the fire place.

Then he returned to his place. In the quietness in the mudlodge, he sensed that something was wrong. Then he realized that he had overstepped himself, because he had not done what he was supposed to do. In becoming a doctor, the ability increased, and he had done something that was far, far beyond what he should have done as a second-year apprentice. And all the older doctors knew that he had.

In a given group of apprentices, each one would know more or less what the other was going to do. They practiced together, and they sang and learned together, so that an older doctor instructing them knew what each man could do. It would be an organized effort when they finally came to perform their rites of magic. This young man had not informed anyone of what he was going to do. He had run counter to custom. Therefore, in spite of the fact that what he had done was a tremendous feat, he was never allowed to practice again or continue with his training.[6]

So when the Pawnees say "remember the little clay horses," they are thinking of this story. It was not so much that the man overreached, but that he had let anxiety lead him into something that was not supposed to happen. The Pawnee expression above means "Do not act upon thoughts that are happening under pressure or anxiety."

There was a definite ranking of individuals in the ceremonies and dances that Garland remembered and took part in. Each society he knew had two headmen seated on the west side. Kitkahahki, Chawi, and Pitahawirata members sat all around the circle, and each man had a designated place. Their protégés made up the rest of the participants, except for two old men who sat on each side of the east doorway. They were called "Old Men of High Rank." Robert Taylor filled that role in one ceremony. In any deadlocked discussion, they made decisions. Near them by the door sat the Fire Makers. For the societies of which he was a member, Wichita Blaine, his protégés, and his grandson usually sat in the northwest quadrant of the lodge. During the early years in Indian Territory, the south and north bands did not share ceremonial occasions, but occasionally when Skidi society members were invited, they sat on the east or entry side on each side of the Fire Men.

The headmen made the decision to have a ceremony according to the time of the year or special need. After it was decided, a herald or messenger took the announcement to each member. If a nonmenber wanted to sponsor a dance, he first went to a leader and asked if the society would honor him by allowing him to do so. Then he held a small feast and invited other society members, the band chiefs, and singers. Before the meal began, the man would stand and solemnly explain why he wanted to have the dance. Anyone could stand and comment on this request. Usually approval was unanimous, and the time and place were determined. But if someone rose and disclosed that the man had been dishonorable in some way, the request was denied.

If the dance was to be held outside, it might be at a time when the ground was muddy. Then the old men scraped off the top surface, poured coal oil over the dirt, and set it afire, drying out the ground enough so that dancing could be done. If the place was dry, weedy, or grassy, Effie Blaine said that women scraped it clean with their hoes, then poured water on the area and had the children pack it down with their feet. The Pawnees constructed an arbor of slender poles and tree branches around the dance ground for warm weather events. Cold weather events took place in a mudlodge or later in the wooden round houses.

Smoking the sacred pipe was an integral part of rituals. Each man prepared his own tobacco-sumac mixture, but sometimes the protégés, who were uncertain of the mixture, would go to an older man and ask for some. Wichita Blaine grew his tobacco and picked and dried sumac of the right kind in the nearby fields. Young men would come and ask him if he had any of the old mixture left over that they could have. They usually arrived after he had just finished mixing the new batch, and they were expected to help the old man in payment for the tobacco. Wichita usually had them cut or chop wood for him. At other times young men who were not protégés came – they wanted to add his dried sumac to their Bull Durham. They usually said, "Oh, I didn't know how to do it, or I tried, but it scorched." He shared what he had with them, but he asked them to help with some chores because he did not want them to learn to get something for nothing.

Once in a great while, a ceremonial leader decided to build a mudlodge in which to hold his organization's dance. John Ruwalk or Luwalk, Chawi, lived west of Pawnee on his allotment near Black Bear Creek. In the early 1920s he decided to build a new house and to construct a mudlodge nearby. People came and camped there to help in the construction.

One day we all knew that John was going to pick out the site. All the children were encouraged to run down to the creek and play. I had to stay to lead my grandpa, and he said to me, "Be sure you look at everything and be quiet. Don't make any noise. He is going to pick out the place where our mudlodge is going to be. Stand still and don't wiggle around."

The older people prepared themselves for the selection of the spot. John and some of the Buffalo Dance members walked into the field while the other people waited back near the house. Grandpa and I went with the other members about halfway. Then they told Grandpa to stay in one spot; they did not want him to fall down on the uneven ground. I watched, and in my mind I can see John walking by himself with his mouth moving a little bit. I imagine he was praying. He stopped, looked a certain place over, and moved back and forth and around. I think he was going through some ritualized steps. Finally he walked to one spot, raised his foot up, and put it down very abruptly. In Pawnee he said, "This is where the mudlodge is going to be. This will be the place. This will be the land. This will be the area." His words had connotations of holy, serious, ritual activities.

He then pointed to a young man; I don't remember who it was, but he said, "Right over there will be the door." One man drove a stake right where he had stamped his foot, and another man placed a stake where the door would be. I could not see the stakes because the grass was about knee high or taller.

Then everyone faced the east and blessed themselves by raising their arms with hands up, palms together, then bringing them down, rubbing them on their head, then down their chests, down their thighs, shins, feet and finally touching the ground. They, Grandpa, and I did this four times. Some faced in other directions; it depends on whether your knowledge is from a sacred bundle. John faced the west, the place of death, to bless himself because his wife had just died. He continued to stand there alone, facing west. Soon someone started over toward him, saying these things in a loud voice, "We don't understand what God does. We can only feel sorry, and we can only cry and weep with our hurt." By this time several more people, men and women, walked toward him. They all were more or less weeping, like my grandmother, who was a close relative to Rena, John's wife. They took John by the arms and slowly turned him around to face the east. During this time they said: "Tirawahat takes people, and we are told this [east] is where life begins, and this is where life is forever. This direction is facing life. There Father Sun comes up." These were little short prayers that you could hear at funerals when someone is trying to console someone who has lost somebody.

Later I asked Grandpa why John had faced the west, and he explained that when John picked out that place for the mudlodge, he was still in sorrow with the loss of his wife. Possibly John thought, "Tirawahat, we are at the tail end of our culture and our dances. I have picked this place. You have taken my wife. Now I am putting my life in your hands. If there is a purpose for this, good. You may let me live. If there is no purpose, then you are going to take me." That is how Grandpa explained John's facing west to bless himself.

Members from the south bands built the lodge. I remember a lot of young men helping. Not all of them had folks who had seats in the lodge now, but whose families in the past had them. I saw no Skidis there. My uncle Elmer helped, and he would come home and tell Grandma what had been done if we were not there at that time. When we went out we stayed maybe a weekend or a week. They started building it in the early spring, maybe March – I didn't know months then – and they wanted to finish it so we could have our dances there after the corn ripened in the late summer.

When the mudlodge was completed, the members and their families gathered and camped, and we prepared to hold our first Buffalo Dance in it. One morning we went in to have breakfast in John's new house. After we all were through eating, John began to talk. He said, "I dreamed that I woke up and that I went outside, and it was night. I dreamed that I looked down to the mudlodge, and the pole was still standing in the smoke hole." There was a bright halo around the pole."[7] I cannot remember what else he said, but everyone sat without moving and cast their eyes down and listened, because John had received a vision.

There is one memory of the mudlodge there that is not so serious, yet it could have been. That is the time that Mickey Akers tried to start fire to it. One day we boys were playing around there – Cecil Ruwalk, Austin Real Rider, Mickey, and I. Mickey was the son of Martha Akers. She was the youngest daughter of Eagle Chief of our band and had married a white man. Mickey was playing around and found some matches inside the mudlodge. He started lighting them and setting the grass on fire at the door. I went over there and told him not to do it, but he kept on, so I ran up to the house and told my grandmother and grandfather. They hollered at John and told him that kids were setting the place on fire. There were long bunches of hay used, and there was always one that hung down by itself, and this was what Mickey was setting on fire. The fire could have gone up the grass sod sides that were very dry by then.

Everybody came tumbling out of the house. Well, somebody caught Mickey "right now" and spanked him good. I don't know whether Austin did any lighting or not, but he had matches in his hand. His grandmother picked up a little stick and made little half-hearted swipes at him, saying, "I'm going to whip you," in the way some people say, "Now don't do that," and kids keep right on doing it. Austin stayed about fifteen feet away from her during all this. Austin was two years younger than me, and he could really run. He was tremendously fast. Well, his grandfather War Ruwalk came down there. He was considered an old man then.[8] He looked at Austin and said, "Come here, I am going to whip you." And Austin backed off and giggled, like, "An old man is going to catch me. Ha."

War picked up a switch about a yard long and about a half inch wide at the handle end. And he took in after Austin. Austin just took off across the country. War ran after him but kept his distance. I can see why now. He let Austin run and run and run until he got to the fence corner which was probably a good three hundred yards away. Here Austin stopped because he couldn't run any farther. And old War started swatting him across the back and legs. Austin turned and started running back to the house, and with every step Austin took, War hit him with that switch – all the way back to the house. And that is why he let him run, because he was going to whip him all the way back. He was thinking, Austin, you run as far as you want, you are making it hard on yourself. He ran him all the way back, switching him all the way. Austin was so exhausted that he was barely moving when he got to the house. The old Pawnee warriors had been great runners, so that little run was nothing for War.

We were getting ready to have the Buffalo Dance there. Horses came up so close they could be seen outside the entrance. There must not have been any boys around, or the horses would not have come so close. Hawk Norman looked out and told me to go chase the horses away. So I ran out and chased them a good distance. On my way back Effie Little Eagle stopped me and said, "Let me take your picture." It's the only one I have from that time.

BUFFALO DOCTORS DANCE

In the Buffalo Doctors Dance of the Pitahawirata, Wichita Blaine or Overtakes His Enemy held a seat.[9] He and Effie Blaine were related to Young Bull or Captain Jim, for whom Wichita had served as a protégé. He learned the ritual, and when he became a mature man he became a leader and sat on the right-hand side of Young Bull, the principal leader.[10]

In the 1900–1920s the other men in the leadership were White Horse, Fancy Rider, and Fancy Eagle. By this time the members came from all four bands, and they bore the title of doctor.

The sacred buffalo, represented by a buffalo skull, served as a central object in the four-day ceremony that included talks, prayers, songs, dances, and feasting. It was believed that the Buffalo People sent an emissary to visit the dance to see if the people were following the old ways. The Pawnee doctors believed that when the emissary spirit came it entered the buffalo skull to be present with the people.[11] The occasion reinforced and restated their allegiance and connection to the powers resident in the skull and their medicine bundles. During the ceremony a buffalo hide was placed on the floor and spoken to by the head men. This hide is referred to as *Tah ri re rah ku* (as written by Garland Blaine). He explained this expression: "*Tah*, Being, *ri*, here, *re*, formless, *rah ku*, sitting, or, Being here formless sitting. The deeper meaning was that the hide signified a formless being [the buffalo spirit] whose soul or presence we cannot see."

Kuruks awaki retained certain memories of the four-day ceremony. About three in the morning, just as grayness showed in the east, the leaders summoned all the doctors to come to the mudlodge. At this time, they could "stretch out," pray, and smoke. The Fire Watcher examined the skies for the rising sun. To do this, from time to time he rose from the spot where he sat and in quick, short steps ran to the entrance, then outside to observe the constellations' locations. Their position presaged dawn and the coming sunrise. He returned to tell what he had observed. This early morning ritual act portrayed the events in the origin story that said, "In the beginning, the people were in a darkness. There was a cold night wind. They were afraid. They had no memory of what had happened before, but they could recognize family members in the light as it began to show gray as it does between three and four in the morning. Later, just as the sun came up, God spoke to the people in the thunder. Simultaneously, a flash of lightning went across the sky to the west. Tirawahat told them that there had been evil beings, but they were all drowned. There had been giants too, but they were all gone. Now the people could live."

In the mudlodge, the instant after the first shaft of sunlight advanced across the fields and came through the entryway, the Fire Watcher announced the day. The headman then proclaimed in a loud voice, "Life has come." This shaft of light symbolized the lightning. At this moment the doctors held their black eagle feather fans in front of their mouths and, moving them rapidly back and forth, would say in deep voices, "Hu a Hu a, Hu a, Hu a." This sound represented the voice of Tirawahat in the thunder at the time of our people's coming to life. His grandfather held his eagle feather fan and did this, but Garland had no fan, so he used his hand. Then the tall, narrow drums began to beat quickly, and someone could be heard praying through the sounds.

The participants wore paint on their bodies. The old men painted their faces and chests. Wichita applied black paint to his face, covering his lower face and nose. There were other individual ways of painting.[12] The old men applied the paint heavily, but the young men would sit with a mirror and carefully apply it with one finger, using very little paint.

At one point in the ceremonies Kuruks awaki watched as the leader, Old Man Captain Jim, or Young Bull, rose from his place.[13] He described the vivid memory:

> He began to pound his chest rhythmically, as he moved out on the floor to begin his dance. Whenever he stopped, he pawed the earth and imitated the movements of a buffalo. When he did this spurts of white, red, or black dust flew out behind his feet as he moved them, pawing the ground. The drums took up the rhythm of his chest pounding and the buffalo sounds he made. Then the doctors keeping time to the drums also made the sounds as he moved around the floor until the lodge seemed filled with the sound of buffaloes. When he finished, two younger men went along to help him dance back to his place. I sat near my grandfather, who sat next to him, and I saw Captain Jim sit down exhausted. His dance and the magic puffs of colored dust showed that he maintained his power as a buffalo doctor that Tirawahat had blessed.

During the dances the doctors moved around the circle clockwise, following the sun's light-to-darkness movement across the earth's surface. The motion the dancers used was called "to hoist the stomach on bones" (as written by Garland Blaine, *Tu ra wi kis Ka ra tsa wu*). It meant the way they imitated the movement of the buffalo. It was a jumping up with knees bent, arms bent out in front, hands in fists, while the shoulders, neck, and head turned in time to the singing and the drum. During one performance the whole group moved like a herd of buffalo as they swirled in an earth-pounding group around the floor.

The paraphernalia for each dancer consisted of an eagle-feather fan, a wooden whistle with one hole, rattles made of small hoof pieces from buffalo or deer attached to a stick or bone, a shag of buffalo hair worn on the head, a buffalo tail worn at the back of the hips, a breechcloth, black moccasins wrapped up shin high, and a buffalo robe.

John B. Dunbar described an important feast and ceremony that took place in the Nebraska villages where his father was a Christian missionary. It took place in several lodges at the same time, and a buffalo skull was central to each ceremony. The skull was painted, and Dunbar told of the use of five rods, "about a yard long, whittled and painted." During the course of the event one was set up directly in front of the skull, and the other four were taken outside the lodge and stuck in the ground at the four cardinal directions, "with a bit of a scalp at the top." Later, pieces of buffalo heart and tongue were placed on faggots around each of the four rods and set on fire" to consume the offerings.[14]

At John Ruwalk's dances, Garland remembered a "little fence of rods" placed inside. Four rods were taken out by Louis Matlock and others, who wore buffalo robes. The rods were stuck in the ground. The rods were about the size of short broom handles and were new each year. The four rods stood at the four directions, and the fifth one, which remained inside, signified Mother Earth. Beef was burned instead of buffalo meat. Then the men went back into the mudlodge. Talks were given, after which the men went outside and retrieved the rods. Garland said old scalp sections may have been on the rods; he was not sure, but he did see some on the mudlodge's center posts.

Although Garland's age and immaturity precluded a total recall of the events he observed, there was one aspect that did not escape the hungry child's memory. That was the food that accompanied the ceremonies. He recalled that soup was made in a large iron pot in the mudlodge. Two months before a dance, a cow was killed and the meat jerked and dried. Each day during the dance, enough dried meat was cooked for the participants. If there was leftover soup, new meat added to it the next day gave it a rich "deep" flavor. When it was time to eat, the headman told the two Fire Watchers to serve the food. Soup was served in large wooden bowls with buffalo horn spoons. Each member took two or three spoonfuls before it was passed to the next member. Since his grandfather sat in the west near the headman, Garland said, he was lucky not to have to wait too long to eat.

After this the cooked meat was laid out on a skin or a canvas tarpaulin spread on the floor. The servers placed the food in rows with a portion for each member. At a signal from the headman, one Fire Watcher served the meat, starting with the headmen in the west on the left, while the other Fire Watcher started serving the other leader on the right. They both served around the circle until they came to the members seated near the east entryway. After that, if there was an audience seated behind the members, they received portions of meat.

Eating was done in silence. If a baby cried, it would be carried outside. At other times the headman would say, "It makes my heart glad to hear that sound. It means that we are still here, that our people are still living [continuing to increase in numbers]."[15] Then the child could stay, but it was still considered good manners to go outside the mudlodge until the child became quiet. Garland said, "I was very aware of this because when I was very young, about three, my grandparents had to admonish me sometimes. Grandmother did this by pushing lightly on the top of my knee with one finger. Then if I continued to disturb, the push was slightly harder. If I persisted, it was a little gouge. If this didn't work, Grandfather would turn his head ever so slightly and look down at me. Then I got quiet."

Garland remembered seeing one of the doctors attempt to remove a woman's cataract during the Buffalo Society ceremonies. He later thought it was either High Eagle or Captain Jim, but he could not be sure.[16] He knew the man was very old, and when he began he asked for milk from a young nursing mother. Old women removed the milk in a black cup, which might have been a buffalo horn. Then they "scooted" across the floor and handed it to the doctor. He then began to put it drop by drop into the eye with the cataract. After a time he took a copper shell, the size of those used in the old buffalo guns, and wrapped a handkerchief around the pointed end. Then, dipping it in milk, he proceeded to gently abrade the top of the eye where the cataract showed. He repeated the process with the shell as long as he could. Then, not having removed all of it by this method, he lowered his head and removed the rest with his tongue. There were songs and prayers before and during this long process.

Garland recalled another vivid childhood event. He said there had been a Buffalo Dance the night before. The next day he was told to go to the mudlodge where it had been held and bring back the matches that had been left there. He went into the long entryway, and as he got into the interior he looked across to the west wall and saw a buffalo standing on its hind legs, with its head bowed, holding a black bowl or buffalo horn spoon in its hooves. It had shiny black horns and hooves. It seemed to be praying, and as he watched he noticed that it was transparent because he could see the wall of the mudlodge behind it. Frightened, he ran out, then stopped. He realized he should not have run away, and he went back. When he told his grandparents, they said that the buffalo would watch over him, and although things might go badly for him, eventually things would be right.

There were other Buffalo Dance societies. The *A ri ka*, or Buffalo Horn Dance, belonged to the Pitahawirata band. Wichita Blaine's uncle performed it, but his two wives owned and kept its sacred bundle. Effie's father was their cousin. When their husband died, Wichita Blaine inherited the right to his uncle's place. In this dance Effie Blaine, as a chief's daughter, related to the owner, led the women into the dance. The men carried short lances that had hooked tops with black crow and eagle feathers fastened on them. At about four in the morning, when the morning star reached a certain point in the sky, the members trotted into the lodge to their seats and talked and prayed in whispers.[17]

After Wichita became blind, his uncle's remaining wife said, "If I had the money to have the dance, he could take his place as leader, but now he cannot see." She put her hand on Garland's head and said, "Where else would I put my hand to lead the dance but you?"[18] He was just a little boy, however, and she knew that his father was dead and his uncle, too, so they could not lead it. So this particular dance was never performed again in the Pitahawirata band.[19]

The Skidis had a similar dance. Harry Coon's grandmother had a vision, and through this the Skidi danced it.[20] It followed the pattern of the Pitahawirata dance. Each time the Skidis held it, they invited Wichita Blaine to take part as a singer. His son James had married a Skidi, Maggie Box, daughter of John Box, the brother of White Eagle, the old chief, so there was friendship and kinship across band lines. In the second half

Wichita would sing songs from his family's Pitahawirata Arika dance. One of them said,

> Father gave me his stick [pipe]
> Father gave me his stick,
> And it is good.[21]

During the dance his Skidi kinsmen invited the young Kuruks awaki to dance with them. He said that at that time he saw only two lances like those carried in the Pitahawirata dance. The dance lasted all afternoon. There were "smokes" between the requisite song sets. The men used long pipe stems, and different men rose to pray. Certain rituals were performed then. Garland claimed it was a warrior society dance, and the last time he saw it was in the early to mid-1920s.

> I can remember that we went to John Ruwalk's place every summer for five or six years. We attended both the Buffalo Dance and the Doctor Dance, where my grandfather had seats. Later I heard that some of the old men went out there in the thirties and saw that the mudlodge had collapsed, and they cried.
>
> During the time when we had our dances in the mudlodges or later in the round houses, we had "sings" in between times at our homes. Our family, or another family, would invite relatives and friends to come. Each family would take some food, like meat, potatoes, flour, and canned peaches, knowing that they would probably stay overnight.

After supper the women would gather in the kitchen, clean up the dishes, and talk. The men would go into the living room, sit around, smoke, and talk briefly. Then they got out the drum and began to sing, usually Buffalo Dance songs, but sometimes songs of other dances they belonged to. One man would start his song, others joined in, and they'd sing each other's songs until about midnight. Some people might go home, but maybe one couple or a family would ask to stay several days. Garland remembered when sleeping people on pallets covered the living room floor and the porch. These were good times. Everyone enjoyed them.

THE DOCTOR DANCE

The ceremonies associated with the Pawnee bands' Doctor Dances originated in Nebraska long before the people migrated to Indian Territory.
They continued until the 1920s, when the older leaders died and there
were not enough protégés, or men interested enough, to continue their
performances. At this time acceptance of nontraditional healing as pro-
moted by agency doctors, the curing ceremonies of the Native American
Church, and Christian teachings also diluted the traditional rituals.

Many sacred bundles, integral to ceremonial maintenance, had been
sold, stolen, put away, or buried with their owners. Subsequently generations of English-speaking students at government Indian boarding
schools could not attend the old ceremonies, or were taught that their
religion was evil and belief in Jesus and the Bible was good. These and
other factors began the inevitable loss of this and other Pawnee ceremonies.

Garland Blaine, accompanying his grandfather, observed the Doctor
Dance in its last days. Other elderly people still living in the 1980s
and early 1990s also remembered attending dances in the 1920s and
recalled some of the events they had witnessed. They remembered that
the Pawnee bands held their Doctor Dances at different places. One Skidi
remembered that she participated in one at Henry Shooter's place. She
remembered that they got cottonwood poles and stood them in a circle to
make a place to dance. She believed that the last Doctor Dance was held
there.[22] Speaking of the same site, another Pawnee said, "This site was
near John Smith's place south of Pawnee. A little south and east, Henry
Shooter had a camp, called the Little Kitkahahki Camp." He claimed that
the last Doctor Dance took place there in 1932. There was no mudlodge,
and they held it outside in an arbor made of bent saplings.[23]

Pauline Jake Murie remembered that she had seen the Doctor Dance
and the Pipe Dance when she was young. The Doctor Dance she attended
took place at a low place in the willows east of the present Goodfox farm
west of Pawnee. There was also a mudlodge on her grandfather Jake's
place. What she remembered from the Doctor Dance was the man who
danced as a white horse with a flowing mane and tail. Henry Stoneroad
recalled going to the mudlodge with his grandmother Fannie Chapman
and seeing a Doctor Dance about 1926.[24]

Viola Blaine McIntosh remembered that she used to go with her parents, Effie and Wichita, to Doctor Dances in the mudlodge on the John Rice place south of town. His place was next to Spotted Horse's allotment. They built an arbor for some of the dances. Only the men, including her father, a doctor, could go in. She recalled a huge canvas with all the dried meat stacked on it. The pile was about three feet high. Her mother and the other women would begin cooking it so that the soup would be ready after midnight. She said it smelled so good, and there was never anything that tasted better than soup made from dried meat. She said she attended the last or one of the last Doctor Dances there. "Wonderful things were done at the dances in those days. But when those old men died all was forgotten. It's all gone now."[25]

Today most Pawnees who talk about the Doctor Dance have forgotten its origins – the involved rituals, meanings, and purposes of the dance. Most remembered are songs and the magic feats performed by the different doctors. There are many legends of its origin. One tells that after various adventures a Pawnee boy entered a cave under the hill Pa: huk on the Platte River. He had found the animal lodge. Beaver and otter were the lodge leaders, and many other animals and birds were also there. After a time the animals blessed the boy and taught him the mysteries of the animals and how to present their ceremony to his people when he returned to them.[26] In August 1914 White Eagle, revisiting his homeland, pointed out the site of Pa: huk or, as Garland Blaine named it, Pa hu ra Wa ruks ti.[27]

According to Clark Wissler, the shamanistic feats of the Pawnee "far [surpass those of] any other tribe that we have investigated."[28] It is these feats that present-day Pawnees remember, often with disbelief, as they describe what they saw. The dance was called *Ke hah rut* (as written by Garland Blaine). He then wrote *Tu ra kah is tu,* which he translated to mean "they are going to dance, when they perform a ritual such as making something disappear." *Ti tu hu rah wah ris ta* or "they are going to perform." When a member does his individual act, you say, *Ti tah wah ru kah,* or "he performed magic."[29]

Harking back to the society's origin, each doctor represented an animal. Members, selected from all bands, could be a deer, raccoon, otter, beaver, owl, bear, and others. The beaver was the most important and held the highest rank. "In my time," Garland said, "he was John Ruwalk or Raruhwaku."[30]

The members brought their sacred bundles, and their protégés came with them. Only men participated in the ceremonies the first four days. At the beginning of each day's events, the headman of the dance would talk for a while, telling the members why they were there, explaining their sacred obligations to Tirawahat, his creatures, and the people, and asking for a blessing on them. When he was through, he would say, *Ra wa;* then all the men there would say *Ru wa, Ru wa.* (In some ways, it is comparable to the Christian "amen.") Then the men would rise, bless themselves, and hold up their arms to pray. Wichita Blaine would pray, "My dear Atius Tirawahat, Father above, I have lived to see this dance again. This dance you caused, you gave to us. It seems there is more than one fate. All the things you have seen me do, make them good. All the things I have done wrong, I will try to get something good out of them. I will try to turn it into something good. All the things that were bad that were done to me by others, may I get something good out of it. I pray I am sitting here again, and fate will see me though the days by your doing. *Ra wa.*"[31]

After the fourth-day ceremonies, a man came out of the lodge and, in a voice loud enough to carry, announced to the people camped nearby that the dance would begin. He said that when they sat down in the mudlodge and observed the ceremonies they should react wholeheartedly. If they felt sad, they should not hold back sadness. If happy, they should not hesitate to be truly happy. Before he allowed the people to enter, he told them that the men inside were already with the animals. They were no longer merely men, but were the animals whose spirits were inside them now. In other words, their minds and bodies were filled with the minds and actions of the bear, the horse, the buffalo, and others.

Then the people came in quietly, placing themselves behind the members who were their relatives – their grandfathers, husbands, uncles, brothers, and sons. Some men who were not members could have a place, but not in the inner circle of doctors. Old Man Sun Eagle's uncle had a special seat because he possessed the pipe bundle that could make a tornado avoid the mudlodge and the people.[32] He did this by rising from his place, then circling to the southwest as he sang his song. With the motions of his body, he imitated fierce tornadic winds. As he danced with his pipe, he jabbed at the heavens with the long stem thrust upward. It was believed that this prevented a tornado from descending to harm the people.

Garland observed that when it was a doctor's turn to perform, the following sequence usually occurred. Two drums passed around the circle to him. Then with his protégés he would get ready. He sang his song through once, then the chorus that followed each verse. His protégés kept time with the drums. After this he arose and danced during the chorus. Then he would kneel on one knee and sing the next verse. This part described the animal that he was and what his dream or vision revealed. Then, on the chorus, he would continue to dance, exhibiting the animal's behavior as told in the preceding verse. As he danced, his protégés sang, beating the drums to keep the rhythm of his dancing. Sometimes there could be as many as seven or eight stanzas. After the protégés had been with their leader longer and knew the songs, the kneeling for each stanzas would be eliminated and the chorus continued while the doctor performed.

Ah-set-kah-ru, Bill Mathews, Kitkahahki, became the horse.[33] He sat with his protégés near by. There were four, two in front or by his side, and two behind his seat. When his turn came, two drums were passed along the circle to his place. He got up on his knees and told his protégés what he was about to do. He fastened his robe, which he slipped from his shoulders, around his waist and with their help affixed a horse's tail to it. Next he sang his first song in a low voice so that the protégés could be sure of it. Then he rose to his feet and sang his song, and his apprentices drummed and sang the chorus. As he chanted, his movements portrayed the significance and actions of the horse as he moved from east to west, back and forth across the floor. As the firelight flickered in the semidarkness, the scene became charged with the feeling that the man was the horse. This awareness among the watching people became a mystical experience.[34]

Other animals Kuruks awaki observed during this period were:

Beaver – John Luwalk
Buffalo – Hawk Norman
Bear – Wichita Blaine, Sam Horse Chief
Horse – William Mathews
Deer – White Eagle

Crane – Old Man Buffalo
Owl – Philip (Brigham) Young
Otter or mink (?) – High Eagle
Cardinal – Henry Shooter
Blue jay – ?

As a young girl in Nebraska, Effie Blaine attended Doctor Dances with her family and saw many miraculous events. Once a member showed a mark on his leg above his knee. During his performance, he stamped the ground again and again. As he did this his foot went deeper and deeper until he came to the mark on his leg and stopped.

Then he began to pull his leg out slowly, while the other doctors made the noises of their animal counterparts. When he finally pulled his foot out, a geyser of water came up from the hole. It rose high in the air, then cascaded down, splattering the people.[35]

Effie Blaine's family came with the first group of Pawnees that left Nebraska in the 1870s to go to the Wichitas in Indian Territory. After they had been there for a time, they heard that the Wichitas were going to have a Doctor Dance and the Pawnees were invited. One performer in the dance, said, "*Wi ti re wi Ti ki tah ki pu*" (as written by Garland Blaine). It meant that he gathered himself, picking up things nearby belonging to him, as he is thinking about what he going to do.

Then Effie said he began his song. "*Ah ski ra Ti wah ku.*" This is similar to the starting phrase in many Pawnee Doctor Dance songs. Effie believed the two phrases were almost the same, and the Pawnees were surprised by this. While living there, Wichita Blaine also went with his uncle to a Doctor Dance. One Wichita performer wore a black handkerchief around his face. When he danced he took it off and laid it on the ground, then danced around it. He stopped and slowly lifted it. Lying there was a huge black snake. Then he covered it up, danced around again, and bent and lifted the handkerchief. The snake was gone. Then, as he continued dancing, the snake slowly emerged from his mouth. People said when he later died he had a large stomach. Even when people came to mourn for him, his stomach moved slowly, and never stopped. This, it was said, was the snake inside – or all the snakes he had swallowed.[36]

Old Man Uncle John Smith, Chawi, who came from Nebraska, was a member of the Doctor Dance. In his presentation he had a flat rock that he had heated in the mudlodge fire pit until it was almost red hot. When it was his turn to perform, his assistants would go to the fire with sticks and push the rock out onto the floor. Then, during his dance, he would stand on it and dance without being burned.[37]

About this time a young man came back from Carlisle and began to stay around Old Man. He finally said that he wanted to learn from him, to be his protégé. The Old Man agreed, and the young man began to learn his duties. One day he was out at Old Man's house. He had a sweat lodge, and he had his rock in there with other rocks getting hot. He asked the young man to go in with him for a sweat. After they had been in there a while, he asked the young man if he really wanted to learn his ways. The young man said yes, he did. Then Old Man said, "Pull the rock out of the fire and stand on it." The young man could not do it – would not do it. He refused. Old Man looked at him and said, "You do not really want to learn. I cannot teach you. You do not have the faith."[38] When a man can perform this type of feat, the Pawnees say, "Tirawahat spoke to him," and this young man had not been blessed, so that he could not perform this exploit.[39]

An elderly Skidi, still living in the 1990s, remembered seeing a similar feat at a Skidi performance. She said that the rock remained in the fire and the doctor danced on it there. After such a performance, the man would go into one of the little individual half houses and be treated and return to dance. These little houses belonged to individual doctors and were made of saplings bent over and covered with branches or hides. They were built around the wall inside the Skidi north round house.[40]

Her mother told her about other Doctor Dances held in Oklahoma. One doctor, Dog Chief (Simon Adams), would dance, and the other doctors would pull a piece of sinew through his ears, through his head, from side to side. She indicated a piece about twenty-four inches long as she illustrated the movement. Another man was seen to have his tongue cut off and restored, and another was shot with an arrow.[41]

Rosanna Yellow Calf Turnbull, the cousin that Garland visited as a child, described a feat her mother Addie Troth Yellow Calf saw at a Doctor Dance. They brought a large cowhide into the lodge and and wet it. Then they laid it on the floor, and a man lay down on it. They then tied it all up into a bundle with him inside it and hung it over the fire. When this happened it got dryer and begin to steam, shrink, and burn. Everybody watched without saying a word. As it got smokier and blacker and tighter, they raised it through the smoke hole in the roof. Soon after they brought it back in through the door and walked with it all around the lodge, so that the people could see it. Nobody said a word. They just knew that man had to be dead in that burned, shrunken hide. The doctors then laid it on the floor, and someone brought a large buffalo robe and placed it over the burned bundle. Suddenly they pulled the robe off and the man jumped up, all right and alive. But his ankle had been hurt somehow; it was twisted, and he always walked with a limp after that.[42]

Rosanna's mother's mother told her of a Doctor Dance in Nebraska that Capt. Luther North attended. The lodge floor was moistened, then the doctors stamped on corn seeds they had buried in it. Their dancing continued, and as it did, the corn sprouted and grew and grew, and ears appeared on it. That corn just came out of that floor that was hard as cement. Then the doctors cooked it and gave some to North. Addie's grandmother saw this with her own eyes.[43] Captain North described the inexplicable exploits he observed at the Pawnee Doctor Dances in Nebraska. Later he and George B. Grinnell went to Oklahoma to determine the performers' methods, but they were unable to do so. After one impressive event Grinnell said, according to North, "It simply cannot be explained."[44]

One member of the Doctor Dance, whom young Blaine saw, cured people who had been struck by lightning. He previously had a vision that told him what he must do to cure them. His medicine came from something he found in the dirt he dug from the base of a tree struck by lightning. It was said to be a shiny object. When he danced he had zigzag lines down his cheeks that shone or glowed during the ceremony. People called for him whenever lightning struck someone. He took the victims to a creek into the water to heal them. Sometimes they were limp before he treated them. The man's name is not remembered.[45]

Doctors performed their magical curing acts during the Doctor Dance, but they could also cure people at other times. Once Wichita Blaine was hesitant to treat a relative who fainted and frothed at the mouth because it was not usually appropriate to doctor a member of your family. This was an emergency, however, and his grandson led him to the cornfield, where they got certain things for temporary curing. After that the family took the boy to Hawk Norman, who was younger and therefore a stronger doctor.[46]

Captain Jim was Garland's grandmother's cousin in the Pitahawirata band. When he was old he was asked to doctor a man with a broken leg. Whether it was broken by a fall from a horse, or in another manner is not remembered. When asked if he would treat the man, Captain Jim replied, "I don't know if I can; I am an old man now and my mind is not strong." He meant he did not have the strength needed to produce the state of mind required for curing or the physical stamina needed for the Doctor Dance.

In spite of his age, Captain Jim agreed to doctor the man. The ceremony took place at the family mudlodge, which was between Effie's allotment and that of the two old sisters, wives of Wichita's uncle. Different south band doctors came and took their seats. They did their dances, and finally Captain Jim got up. The others, now seated, sat with heads bent but with eyes watching each movement. He sang his song twice while dancing. Then his protégés, having heard it, joined in. Now each time he moved around the circle he left an item of regalia at his seat. He left his fan, his gourd rattle, and other things until he had nothing left but a short stick, painted red. At this point he knelt at the man's side and talked in a low voice, while inspecting the broken bone in order to set the course for the final curing. Then he arose, danced at the north side of the lodge, then reached up with his stick and hurled it with tremendous force at the man on the pallet. The stick hit the heel of the foot lying useless to one side below the break. The impact caused the leg to recoil, and it went straight up in the air and fell back to the ground, whereupon Captain Jim knelt by the man again and proceeded with the curing.

Before this, as Captain Jim danced, the cadence of the drums and the singing accelerated, more and more while each doctor emitted the sound of the animal he *was* at that moment. Effie Blaine saw this happen and sang a song that had been composed about this event.[47]

During the ceremony, several doctors became infused with their bird spirits. Some were the owl, cardinal, and blue jay. The owl was Brigham Young, Chawi, and the cardinal was Henry Shooter. When he danced he wore a red feather in his hair on top. During his song he crouched on the ground and held his arms out, up, then down, like wings. He moved his body and head in such a manner that he looked just like a cardinal. His song said,

Look. Here it comes
Here it comes.[48]

Pawnee songs are short, like the one above, but they tell a story that is not evident to the uninformed listener. Many or all Pawnee songs have a deeper meaning than is evident in the words one hears. As an example, the blue jay doctor sang about the blue jay or Ti it, as it was named.

Ti it, Ti it,
He is making sound in flight
Ti it, Ti it
He is audible as he arrives.

This song mentions only the flight and sound of the bird. Its true meaning reveals that Tirawahat created the bird and blessed him with the ability to fly. He is flying for a purpose, to get food, to get to safety, to find a mate, to make a nest, to increase his species.

In the same manner, Tirawahat made man. When a man is about, one can say he is "flying," moving, making sounds, seeking food, making a nest, creating children, and protecting his people by being aggressive. All the basic behaviors of life are the same for the bird and the man. Tirawahat made it so, as Garland explained it.[49]

BEAR DANCE

When Wichita Blaine and his grandson attended the Bear Dance, it had almost ceased to be performed. Many members were dead, and few people had learned the rituals or had rights to the songs. James R. Murie described the Pitahawirata Bear Dance in the early twentieth century as completely as it will ever be known.[50] According to Garland Blaine, "The bear was considered a medium between the people and God. The people recognized the bear as a creation of God, something that represented power and was significant of the wonderful works of Tirawahat. During a man's vision, the bear would come to him and he received certain powers, certain knowledge of certain roots to use, and how to doctor people."

The cedar tree, called Mother by the Pawnees, held a revered place in the ceremonies. It was said that long ago a man had a vision in which he saw a cedar tree and thought it was like a woman. It stands in a beautiful way and is everlastingly green both winter and summer. In the man's dream the "woman tree" made noises like the bear.[51]

> Grandfather Blaine told me that back in Nebraska, the doctors in the Bear Lodge sang a song to call the bears. They gathered at night, and one member went out and sang this song. It starts high and ends in a low voice. The song came from the time when the Pawnees lived near the mountains where the bears lived. As a child I heard this song. I cannot forget the men's voices, so deep at the end of this song with the drum emphasizing the rhythm. At the end the suspense was raised further by the men tapping their mouths with their eagle-feather fans. It was an eerie sound. Although they had no bears to call in Oklahoma, the oldest men wanted to have the Bear Ceremony and call the bears once again.[52]

When the Blaine family attended the ceremony, it occurred in the fall and lasted the traditional four days. Garland recalled that the first three days in the mudlodge consisted of songs, prayers, talks, and lectures. The doctors walked short distances around the lodge praying or lecturing. This activity described and represented the acts of the creation and the things that had taken place when Tirawahat and the sacred animals, particularly the bear, spoke to the doctors through dreams and vision. Garland's account continued:

> When I was a child, we attended one Bear Dance in the new mudlodge south of Pawnee on Roan Chief's place. The mudlodge was surrounded by tipis and "half houses" built of saplings and covered with canvas. It seemed it was maybe in late August or September. The first three days, ceremonies took place. During that period no women were allowed in the mudlodge. Men did the cooking and served the members.
>
> One day everyone waited in great anticipation. Several Bear Lodge members had been chosen to go south toward the Cimarron River to find the cedar trees used in the ceremonies. They had been gone for several days. This day one member stood on a hill about a half mile from the camp, scanning the horizon toward the south. I don't remember what time of the day it was. The people were all out standing around, waiting. It could have been in midafternoon when

he suddenly started running down the hill toward us. That was the signal. The women immediately ran to their campfires and got small pails or pots of food. Then they came up to the mudlodge where we stood. The runner announced to all that the men were coming and they were bringing Mother Cedar. Then he went into the mudlodge and announced this to the headmen.

Just as the men came over the hill's summit, the women all started running up there to give the men some of their food. I was small, but I could see all these women running up the hill, and I could hear some of the old men walking around with their arms up in the air praying. Every once in a while you could hear a woman's voice, but it was mostly the old men.

The men came down the hill eating the food the women had carried to them. Everyone seemed to be rejoicing. Then, as they came nearer, the Bear Society doctors came out of the mudlodge and stood outside in a solemn line. When the men arrived they carried the two cedar trees inside and laid them down.[53] They could have been eight to ten feet tall. It seems to me that the following morning they erected the trees inside, where ceremonies continued.

On the last day, the families of the members came into the mud-lodge to participate. I sat with my grandfather, and Grandmother sat behind us. Across the mudlodge and to the left were Grandpa John Box and his brother, my great-uncle White Eagle.

After we sat down, Grandfather carefully placed his sacred bundle in front of him. It was wrapped in red wool broadcloth and tied with woven horsehair rope. He untied it. The contents were in the middle with the sides folded over and rolled toward the middle. Inside was a bearskin, a large one. It too was rolled, and the remaining contents were in there. When you rolled it out on the earth floor, the red broadcloth was under the bear robe. He would let me have one small corner where he would spread my little bear hide. Then he spread the bundle's contents in front of him, including his bear claw necklace, fan, white clay, branch of cedar, sweetgrass braids, medicines, a bag of cedar, black moccasins, a wooden whistle with one hole, and some gourds. Then he brought out the pipe, the one that came down in our family had been the head pipe of the Bear Dance. When they decided to have a Bear Dance, some men came to my grandparents and asked if it could be used. They would say, "*We wi ta ra ku Kuruks. Ti ra ku Kuruks*" (as written by Garland Blaine). It is comparable to saying there is going to be a Bear Dance and the pipe is needed. After my grandparents consented, the members who came held a small ceremony at our place.

Grandfather said the white clay in his bundle signified the silver tinge of the fur on the top of the grizzly's neck, as well as the fog that is found in the mountains where he lives. The Pitahawirata said the bear and fog and the cedar lived and came together from high mountainous country. When Grandfather painted himself, he streaked white clay in his hair and had two- to three-inch vertical marks that went up and down his chest, arms, and face.

On the last afternoon, I remember the four drums. They were painted gray with that chalky white paint. Each doctor and his protégés sang the doctor's family songs. There could be as many as eight songs that the man could sing at one time. The drumbeat continued to maintain the emotional level as one group's singing ended and another's began. They would start off with the headmen, and then they would go to the south side. Then they went down the seats from a doctor on that side to a doctor on the north side. Most of the doctors got up when the songs started, and they would dance. They would have on a breechcloth, leggings, and bear claws. They wore a bear hide around the shoulder or shoulders.[54] Some did not have bear robes, just bear claw necklaces. All the dancers had a sprig of cedar, and the paint on their bodies was white, a chalky color, like Grandpa's. When they danced, they bent over a little bit and extended their fingers, not straight out, but bent in the form of a bear's claws. They would jump up and down in time to the drum. And they made a motion, extending their arms forward and pulling them back in repetition with the beat of the drum. When they moved there was a sort of sideways movement of their feet. It's like a bear running. Some songs are a little faster than the others according to what the song was about.

There was one set of songs belonging to my Skidi grandfathers, John Box and White Eagle. When they would dance, they carried cedar branches with white paint on them. As they came around, they would say something to my grandfather, and he would say to me, "Go out and follow them." I would go out and follow them a little ways, then I'd go back to Grandpa. After a while, I got a little braver and would dance completely around, following after them. At the end they would look down, pat my head, and smile at me.

It was really wonderful to watch the old men. When they danced, they would make grunting noises like a bear. They would make motions with their bodies, because these men had seen bears in the wild. They had hunted them and many times had tried to get away from them, too.[55] These old men, they really had their profound belief in Tirawahat; especially those that had a vision believed that Tirawahat was in the bear. When they danced they were on a different level in their minds than ordinary people. I know that in their actual minds, they were bears, performing the dance. Some of the men I remembered dancing were George Little Sun, Hawk Norman, Roan Chief, John Ruwalk, John Box, White Eagle, and Charlie Wood. One man, whose name I cannot recall, would go out to dance and he had nothing to dance with. Then he would stop his dance. He would open his mouth wide, like a bear, and from it came a dense fog of white. There were about thirty men on each side, from all bands. This was our band's dance, so the Skidis sat in a special place, in the southeast quadrant.

Grandfather sang songs about Mother Cedar during the ceremonies. I learned my grandfather's songs, and here is one about when Mother Cedar is brought into the lodge and erected. [Sings.] These songs tell certain things the man did who made the song. They say, "We have put up the tree," then, "Would there be a lady, Mother Cedar, among us. There she stands." The singer could add other verses, such as "My mother is my mother. She has come to a stop." "How beautiful are the trees. She is my mother." "I have profound, deep respect and love. She is my mother." "I listen intently to the wonders of Tirawahat. She is my mother."

During the ceremony, I wore my little bearskin robe and held a cedar twig. I would stand beside my grandfather, who could not see to dance. I would imitate the movements I could see the doctors make as they danced. At a certain time the headman, Roan Chief, said, "Here is a song for little boys." He would start singing and make motions for me to go out on the floor to dance. Of course I knew the song, I had heard it many times. So I would go out and lead the dance. It says,

> There are three.
> And the mother is guiding them.
> They are running and passing each other.[56]

The story behind this song is that at one time there were some hunters and they saw a mother bear. And she had three little cubs. They would play a bit, and they would fall, tumble. And the mother was walking behind them and she patted them around, you know, to get them to stay together. Every time they would separate, she would bring them back together, then they would tumble over each other, bite each other, then they'd run, and stop and bat each other around a little bit. Anyway, they were playing. It just happened that the little bear hide that I had on when I danced was the bear hide of one of these little bears, killed by one of my ancestors, perhaps my great-grandfather, Leading with the Bear, or his father. When I danced as Little Spotted Bear, I could see smiles of satisfaction from the older men and women, because I was such a small boy taking part. I guess they were remembering my role with my blind grandfather and grandmother. Maybe they were thinking about my being an orphan. Maybe they thought, "If his mother and father were living, he might be like other small boys." I might not be taking part, but out playing. Maybe there might have been mixed emotions, mixed thinking about the things that were and the things that might have been. Before these years there must have been other young boys to learn these things, but now they had been taken away to school, or didn't want to dance, like my uncle Elmer.[57]

During the intervals in the dance, they smoked. Each man had his own pipe. During these times someone could request certain songs, so they would give a drum to those people to whom the songs belonged. During these periods they were always requesting grandfather's songs. For one thing, he had a wonderful voice.

This was the last of the two Bear Dances that my grandfather and I attended and that he talked to me about. It was in the late 1910s or early 1920s. I still have the picture of my father in our Bear Claw necklace [see fig. 9].

Throughout his life with his grandparents, Blaine attended the different dances with them. After he started to attend the Pawnee Indian School, it was discovered that his eyes were in serious condition:

I had trachoma, and the agency decided to take me to the government Indian hospital at Shawnee. Frank Long, the agency's Indian farmer, came to the house and took me and William Taft Eaves, who was tubercular, to the hospital. They operated on my eyes and kept me there. In early December I received a letter that someone had written for my grandparents. Bill read the letter to me. It said there would be a Buffalo Dance. I knew that my grandparents needed me, and I went to the doctor and asked to go home, but the doctor refused to release me, even though my eyes were well. I went outside and sat down under the doctor's office window, where I could hear the nurse talking to the doctor. I heard him say that the Pawnee agent wanted me to stay there because my grandparents kept me out of school. This angered me because I knew that my grandparents wanted me to go to school even though my Prairie View experience had been so bad. I thought they were blaming my grandparents. So right then I decided to go home. I got up, found my friend Justus, and asked if he wanted to run away, because he had wanted to run away before. But this time he hesitated, so I went to the pecan grove and filled my jacket pockets with pecans and started north toward Pawnee. I didn't know exactly where it was, but I knew it was north, because that is the direction they brought me from in a car. I got about a mile down the road toward town, when there came Justus. By that evening we had gone north of Shawnee all the way to Meeker. We got north of Meeker a little ways and stopped at a farmhouse where there was a nice old couple.

We stayed all night and went on walking. We walked along the side of the road and would hide whenever anyone came by. There were very few cars in those days. When we got hungry we ate pecans and walked and ran north to Chandler, then on to Agra to the road that crossed east and west from Cushing. We left the road and went cross-country until that evening, when we got a few miles north of Glencoe.

That was quite a stretch. We then stayed at Mr. Boyle's house. I knew him. He had a store in Pawnee. On Sunday we walked the rest of the way to Pawnee and home. We walked about eighty miles from Shawnee home. Back in those days I could go anywhere just one time and remember all the landmarks. This is the training I got from my blind grandfather, who said, "Always notice where we are going so you can always bring us home."

In about a week they came after me and said they were going to send me to another Indian hospital in Laguna, New Mexico. But I spoke up and said if they did, I'd run away again. They said it was hundreds of miles away – too far away, but I said I would leave anyway. So they left me there, and I went to the Buffalo Dance with my folks.

On 29 July 1925 a letter to H. M. Tidwell, signed Garland Blaine, requested money that was needed "very bad." According to a letter from A. W. Leech at the Shawnee Indian agency to the Pawnee Indian agency, Garland had one dollar in funds there. Leech sent the dollar back to the Pawnee agency because Garland had returned home. If Garland said he left in December, it would be 1925, and he was ten years old when he made his journey.[58]

During this period when the Pawnees were attempting to hold their traditional ceremonies and other dances not described here, the United States government maintained a steady opposition to such efforts. In 1920 the commissioner of Indian affairs wrote in response to a Pawnee inquiry, "It is injurious to permit such gatherings to run four or five days at a time because of the tendency – of some of the Indians at least – to neglect their stock or crops. One day or evening should, as a general rule, be sufficient for a celebration or ceremony." He advised superintendents of Indian schools and reservations to prevent Indians from holding dances and celebrations of "an injurious or immoral nature."[59] In 1923 the commissioner sent "a message" to all Indians, informing them that dances and celebrations caused neglect of their farms and advising them to give them up voluntarily during the months of "seed time, cultivation of crops and the harvest," and to gather only for a short period at other times of the year.[60] The next year the Pawnee superintendent reported that "the older and uneducated men and women are passing from the scene rather rapidly and when they are gone the present gatherings will largely disappear."[61] He was correct, except for a few dances, such as the Young Dog Dance, Pipe Dance, Ghost Dance, and others given intermittently in the years to follow.

Even the traditional vision experience became rare, except for the trances during Ghost Dances. Sometimes Garland and his grandfather talked about the times when the sacred animals appeared in a dream or a vision. Garland would retell his experience of seeing the buffalo in the mudlodge, with its head bowed, standing on its hind legs holding a black bowl in its hooves. Wichita solemnly told him, "That is what Tirawahat wanted you to see, but he is taking these things away from us now. But revere it and do not forget it. What is more in line for you will be the white man's church. Tirawahat gave us the old ways, but now it's time, and he is taking them away from us."

After Garland moved away from the tribal area and lived and worked successfully in the white man's world, he continued to return to attend tribal gatherings and ceremonies. He honored the old ways, and until their deaths he accompanied his grandparents to the old ceremonies and dances. Each year on Memorial Day it was customary for each Pawnee family to clear the weeds and tall grass from family graves. Once, before his death, his grandfather said, "Grandson, will you come here after I am gone?" Garland continued to do so all the years of his life.

APPENDIX A:
BLAINE GENEALOGY CHART

Wichita Blaine talked about his uncles when Garland was a child, and the boy began to learn their names and the names of others in his paternal line. He was expected to be able to repeat their names as far back in time as his grandfather knew them. On 4 September 1978, for the first time, Garland Blaine wrote down their names, as follows.

BLAINE PATERNAL ANCESTRAL RECORD

Garland James Blaine, born March 25, 1915

My father – James G. Blaine, born in 1888

My paternal grandfather – Wichita Blaine, or Tu-tu-ra-wi-tsat, Man Caught His Enemy or Overtakes His Enemy.

Wichita Blaine's father – Ti-ra-wa-hat ra-ra-hu-re-sa-ru or He Who Reveres the Universe.

Wichita Blaine's paternal uncles.

    Ruh-ra-ru-re-sa-ru or He Who Reveres Goals

    Ti-kits-ka-sa or Water along the Trees

    Re-sa-ri-tsa-riks or Worthy Man of Regal Wisdom

    Re-sa-ri-tsa-rak-su or Worthy Man Unruly

These five brothers were born approximately in the 1820s and 1830s.

The brothers' father's name was Kurauspukskats or Old Man Gray Hair. This was my great-great-grandfather, born approximately 1790.

Old Man Gray Hair's father was Pita-kisatski, or Man of Meat, born approximately 1760.

Man of Meat's father's name was Pita-kisu, or Tall Slender Man, who was my great-great-great-grandfather, born approximately in the 1730s.

Tall Slender Man's father's name was Tsa-tska-ra-ra-kiri-ka-wa-wi, or Only One with Eyes, born approximately 1700.

His father's name was Ti-ra-wa-hat ra-ra-hu-re-sa-ru, or He Who Reveres the Universe, my great-great-great-great-great-grandfather, born approximately 1670.

[There appear to be thirty-year intervals between generations, which may be too long – MRB.]

APPENDIX B:
PAWNEE INDIAN GUARDIANSHIP RECORD

Pawnee County Clerk's Office, 1895–1920 (the years 1910–12 are missing). An asterisk indicates the guardian was a Pawnee Indian.

Guardian	Ward	Date
Bagby, A. H.	Benjamin White	4-10-02
Bagby, A. H.	Lucy Pritchard	4-10-02
Bagby, A. H.	Mack Harris (or Murie?)	4-9-02
Bagby, A. H.	Nellie Pratt, 18	12-3-02
Bagby, A. H.	Mabel Pratt, 4 months	12-3-02
Bagby, A. H.	Charlie Adams	4-3-02
Bagby, A. H.	Emma Kester, 13	4-20-06
Bagby, A. H.	Elmer Echohawk, 14	1-23-06
Bagby, A. H.	Harry Mad Bear, 11	1-23-06
Bagby, A. H.	James G. Blaine	2-21-06
Bagby, A. H.	Ida Osborne Ridge	3-27-07
Bagby, A. H.	Lucy Little Chief, 15	4-20-06
Bayhylle, Louis*	Edwin, Rachel, Battiste L. (children)	9-9-18
Biddison, A. J.	Gertie and Joseph Esau, 6	9-15-95
Bowman, James*	Alice Leader, 14	8-26-19
Bowman, James*	Jacob Leader, 20 (in service)	9-14-19
Brave Chief*	Stah kau, 13, and Sarah Manchief, 14	1-28-98
Bruington, Wm.	Mary, 17, Wm., 8, Lulu, 11, Real Rider	2-15-06
Bruington, Wm.	Clifford Taylor, 16	2-15-06
Bruington, Wm.	Jobie Taylor, 17	2-6-06
Bruington, Wm.	Burris Curly Chief, 8	1-23-06
Capstick parent	Children	1907?
Carrion, Joseph*	Kit Carrion	10-13-99
Carrion, Kittie C.*	Goldie May Carrion, 8 months	9-29-05
Chapman, Charles*	Kit Carrion, 11 (blind)	9-7-00
Chapman, Charles*	Kit Carrion, 12	4-17-99
Chasteen, Robert	Julia Tennyson, 12	1-23-03

Guardian	Ward	Date
Chasteen, Robert	Lucy West, 8	1-23-03
Chasteen, Robert	Albert Pappan	1-9-02
Chasteen, Robert	Bertha Eagle Chief	12-22-02
Chasteen, Robert	Kit Carrion, 11	1-22-01
Chasteen, Robert	Gordon Shaw, 14	12-29-99
Chasteen, Robert	Wm. S. Crow, 11	12-1-99
Chasteen, Robert	Jane Fox, 11	11-3-99
Chasteen, Robert	Edith, Annie,	11-3-99
	Lucy Sitting Eagle	
Chasteen, Robert	Walter O. Hunt, 13	11-3-99
Chasteen, Robert	Hiram Good Chief	11-15-99
Chasteen, Robert	Starry Sun Chief, 14	4-30-00
Chasteen, Robert	Hiram Goodchief	11-15-99
Chasteen, Robert	Rousen [?] Crow, 14	9-19-01
Chasteen, Robert	Lucy Cummings, 14	9-18-01
Chasteen, Robert	Lida White, 16	12-1-99
Chasteen, Robert	Gordon Shaw, 14	12-29-99
Chasteen, Robert	Emma, 16, Jennie, 11, Shaw	12-1-99
Chasteen, Robert	William Lincoln, 15	9-19-ol
Chasteen, Robert	Kate,17, Eva,13, Samuel,	9-17-01
	12, Annie, 9, Walker and	
	Emmett Carrion, 7	
Chasteen, Robert	Nellie Pipe Chief, 9	9-17-00
Chasteen, Robert	Virginia Weeks, 14	5-7-00
Chasteen, Robert	Mary E. Carrion, 3	11-4-01
Chasteen, Robert	James Peters, 5	1-20-01
Chasteen, Robert	Susie Bear Chief, 12	2-26-00
Coons, Belle*	Arthur, Harry, Cyrus	8-17-99
Coons, Harry*	Earnest Bayhylle, 3	3-18-99
Daniel Pappan*	Children	5-14-19
Eagle Chief*	Martha Eagle Chief, 6	9-6-04
Eagle Chief*	Alice Jake, 8	6-19-99
Eagle Chief, Henry*	William Crow, 18	5-25-00
Eagleton, W. L.	Jamie Mason, 14	4-25-02
Evarts, Isabella*	Louisa, Mary, Julia Bayhylle	9-7-99
Fox, Webster*	Gordon Shaw, 14	6-10-99

Guardian	Ward	Date
Gillingham, David*	May, 10, Hattie, 7, Lillie, 5, Wilde	1-19-03
Hailman, W. H.	Wm. S. Crow Chief, 10	5-24-99
Hailman, W. H.	Charles Riding Up, 11	6-17-99
Hailman, W. H.	Jennie Shaw	4-17-99
Hailman, W. H.	Will Barker, 13	6-17-99
Hailman, W. H.	Mary Shaw, 15	12-26-98
Hand, Alex*	Howard Lushbaugh, 14	4-26-95
Hanna, H. C.	Arthur, 5, Willis, 6, Mathews	6-3-03
Hanna, H. C.	Rollie Weeks	6-26-03
Hanna, H. C.	Belle, 8, Stella, 6, Joseph, 3, Weeks	12-15-04
Hosick, D. D.	Jesse, 9, Nora Moore, 49	1918
Howell, George*	Charles Riding Up, 12	12-1-99
Howell, Joseph*	Viola Wilde, 15	3-1-95
Hudson, Frank	Anna, 11, Alex, 9, Jennie, 6, Adams	1-23-06
Hudson, Frank	W. E. Wheeler (incompetent) Pawnee?	6-29-19
Hudson, Frank	Violet, 16, Elijah, 4	1-12-06
Hudson, Frank	Ernest Wichita	2-5-14
Jay, Palmer C.	James Smith, 14	3-19-02
Jay, Cecil D.	Nathaniel Charles Wilson, 4	7-2-21
Jay, Cecil D.	May Smith	8-1-14
Jay, Cecil D.	Henrietta Wilde	1-13-14
Jay, Cecil D.	Stella Weeks	8-31-14
Jay, Palmer C.	John J. Jake	3-20-02
Jay, Palmer C.	Henrietta Rice, 3	4-25-02
Jay, Palmer C.	Annie Brown, 3 (blind)	3-20-02
Jay, Palmer C.	Jennie, 9, Myrtle, 6, Pollak	12-16-04
Jay, Palmer C.	Allen Moses	4-3-02
Jay, Palmer C.	Josie Washington	4-3-02
Jay, Palmer C.	John Jake	4-3-02
Jones, J. D. (grandfather)	Cleve and Oscar Wilde	7-17-14
Krow, A. D.	Mary, 5, Andy 1, Smith	12-03
Krow, A. D.	Andy K. Smith, 15	6-29-18

Guardian	Ward	Date
Krow, A. D.	Andy K. Smith, 15	6-29-19
Lancaster, O. M.	George Hunt, 9	10-22-04
Leading Fox*	Virgil Fox, 5,	5-14-21
	George Howell, 7	
Lehew, B. A.	Julia Mathews	2-16-06
Lehew, B. A.	Eva Blue Hawk	1-25-06
Lehew, B. A.	Wallace Mathews	2-16-06
Lehew, B. A.	John Smith, 1	9-2-02
Lehew, B. A.	Thomas, 12, Grace, 15,	9-1-02
	High Eagle	
Lockley, May*	Dolly Garcia	5-18-19
Lone Chief*	A. B. Manchief, 17	12-18-96
Mason, B. F.	John C. Smith	1-22-14
Mason, B. F.	Lena Weeks	1-22-14
Mason, B. F.	William Real Rider	1-22-14
Minor, Jerry	Gertie Esau, 11	2-26-95
Morgan, Thomas*	Alexander Eagle, 9	8-21-97
Moses, John*	Charlie Adams, 11	5-10-98
Murie, James R.*	James (Robert) Smith, 14	10-2-99
Murie, James R.*	Gertie Esau, 14	2-22-96
Murie, James R.*	Will Barker, 13	7-18-99
Murie, James R.*	Gertie Esau, 14	12-22-96
Murie, Alfred*	William Murie, 2	2-27-95
Murie, James R.*	Nora Rider, 10	1-28-98
Murie, Alfred*	Harry Mad Bear, 19	9-1-14
Murie, Alfred*	Wm. Simon Murie, 12	2-27-97
Murie, Alfred*	Wm. Murie, 11	2-25-95
Murie, James R.*	Howard Lushbaugh, 18	2-8-99
Murie, James R.*	Susie Lushbaugh 15	3-1-94
Murie, James R.*	James or Robert Smith, 14	10-2-99
Nellis, Geo. W	Mattie, 17, Flora, 15,	8-13-07
	Eagle Chief	
Nellis, Geo. W.	Gilbert Wichita, 6 months	3-27-09
Nellis, Geo. W.	David Wright, 8	3-27-09
Nellis, Geo. W.	Ernest Wichita, 13	3-27-09
Nellis, Geo. W	George Taylor	7-19-07

Guardian	Ward	Date
Nellis, Geo. W	Edith Minthorn, 5	11-23-06
Nellis, Geo. W.	Mattie Leading Fox	10-25-06
Nellis, Geo. W	Cecilia Matlock, 12	9-1-06
Nellis, Geo. W.	Sarah Wichita, 19	9-1-06
Nellis, Geo. W.	Mary B. Rice, 17	10-6-06
Nellis, Geo. W.	Thomas B. Chapman, 3	4-21-09
Nellis, Geo. W.	Mabel Fancy Rider	7-26-06
Nellis, Geo. W.	Bertha Eagle Chief	11-23-06
New Rider*	Hiram Good Chief, 12	7-15-95
Nield, J. W.	May Riding In, 14	1-25-06
Nield, J. W.	Delbert Spotted Horse Chief, 13	2-1-06
Nield, J. W.	Harry Richards, 15	1-23-06
Nield, J. W.	John C. Smith, 12	2-1-06
Nield, J. W.	Susan Wilson, 4	2-1-06
Nield, J. W.	Charles Richards	2-8-06
Pappan, Addie*	Eight Pappan children, 1-21	7-29-98
Pappan, L. & C.*	Juanda E. 3, James Pappan, 1	2-26-19
Pappan, Fred*	Margaret Louise, 3, Rousseau, 1, Polite	8-16-21
Parent (mother)*	Emmett Carrion, 19	10-30-14
Paulter, J. F.	Frank Young Eagle, 3½	4-20-01
Paulter, J. F.	Henry Adams, 12	2-19-01
Paulter, J. F.	Kate Hawk Chief, 9	2-5-01
Paulter, J. F.	Alexander Eagle, 12	4-18-01
Pearson, Emmet*	Wm. Allen, 18	1895?
Phillips, G. H.	David Wood, 15	1902/3
Phillips, G. H.	Julius, 5, Francis, 12, Flora Smith	6-26-03
Phillips, G. H.	Thomas, 14, Grace, 16, High Eagle	9-30-03
Phillips, G. H.	Harold Curly Chief, 12	1904?
Phillips, G. H.	Maud New Rider	9-30-03
Phillips, G. H.	Henry Fox, 10	8-1-04
Phillips, George	Lottie Phillips, 13	12-8-96

Guardian	Ward	Date
Phillips, G. H.	Julia Young Hawk	6-24-03
Phillips, Frank M.	Burris Curly Chief	8-39-14
Phillips, G. H.	Irene, 15, Sarah, 10,	8-13-04
	Lena, 6, Knifechief	
Rappuie parents*	Gertrude, 13, Estelle L.	1-27-07
Real Rider, Addie*	Dorothy, 12, Ruth, 9,	7-7-19
	Rosanna, 6, Yellow Calf	
Roberts, Henry*	Children	10-26-18
Roberts, Rush*	Ed Howell Roberts, 17	1-22-06
Roberts, Rush*	Lena, 13, Henry, 17	1-22-06
Roberts, Rush*	Vivian, 12, Rush, 10	8-13-19
Running Scout*	Lizzie Esau, 12	1896?
Seeing Eagle*	Ora Running Scout, 15	4-19-95
Shaphard, C. J.	Wilbur, 17, Fannie, 15, Eaves	6-19-06
Shaw, Webster,*	Gordon Shaw, 14	12-99
Sun Chief*	Starry, 10, Wiley, 2,	1-24-96
	Sun Chief	
Thompson, H. E.	Grant White	6-5-02
Thompson, H. E.	Maud Blue Hawk, 15	6-14-02
Thompson, H. E.	Clarence Fields, 12	6-14-02
Thompson, H. E.	Mack Harris (or Murie?)	6-2-02
Thompson, H. E.	Dora Rutter, 16,	8-1-04
Thompson, H. E.	Dollie Sherman, 6	6-12-02
Townsend, Samuel*	Gertie, Joseph Esau	3-20-95
Turner, Joseph D.	Will Justice, 13	12-17-01
Turner, Joseph D.	Benjamin Gover, 12	12-17-01
Turner, Joseph	Helen Lockley, 13	11-4-01
Turner, J. D.	Fred Duncan, 15	1902
Turner, Joseph D.	Clara Mannington, 16,	11-4-01
	James, 14	
Turner, Joseph D.	Mollie, 15, Thomas, 14,	11-4-01
	Maud, 12, Hand	
Turner, J. D.	Nervin, Murray, 11	1-23-06
Turner, J. D.	Henry Goodfox, 16	2-3-06
Turner, J. D.	James Wilde, 10	11-2-95

Guardian	Ward	Date
Vandervoort, C. E.	Mabel Manchief, 1	3-4-05
Vandervoort, C. E.	Eva Blue Hawk	8-25-05
Vandervoort, C. E.	Cecil Riding In	11-8-19
Vandervoort, C. E.	Robert, 18, Samuel, 6, Osborne	2-15-06
Vandervoort, C. E.	Nannie Davis, 13	4-5-06
Vandervoort, C. E.	Gus, 8, Austin, 2, Real Rider	8-30-19
Vandervoort, C. E.	Nellie, 9, Arthur, 8	1-23-06
Vandervoort, C. E.	Maggie Box	1-22-06
Vandervoort, C. E.	Katie Tilden, 14	1-22-06
Vandervoort, C. E.	Warren Leader, 14	1-23-06
Vandervoort, C. E.	Jennie Fancy Rider, 1	1-22-06
Vandervoort, C. E.	Sherman Ricketts, 1	1-16-06
Vandervoort, C. E.	Walter Keys, 11	1-23-06
Vandervoort, C. E.	James Earl Bowman, 16	2-23-06
Vandervoort, C. E.	Eugene Haymond, 3 (property, $10,000)	9-7-18
Washington, Lizzie*	Josie Washington, 17	1902
Waters, G. A.	Harry Coons, 17	12-30-13
Waters, Geo. A.	Simond Fancy Eagle	2-8-06
Waters, Geo. A.	George Haymond, 18	1-22-06
Waters, G. A.	Sarah, 17, and Henry, 16, Chapman	1-2-06
Webb, W. B.	Bessie Blaine, 6	11-2-02
Webb, W. B.	Kate, 10, Annie, 8, Lena, 5, Weeks	12-19-01
Webb, W. B.	Nora Rider	11-4-01
Webb, W. B.	Mary E. Carrion, 3	11-4-01
Webb, W. B.	Henry E., 16, Gertie, 13, James, 8, White	1-22-06
Webb, W. B.	Fred Pappan, 18	8-29-02
Webb, W. B.	Cora, 7, Viola, 5, Jim	8-25-02
Webb, W. B.	James G. Blaine, 15	11-2-02
Weil, Barney	Robert, 4, Rose, 2, Pappan	8-16-18
Wheeler, E. C.	Paul Little Eagle, 16	2-5-06
Wilde, Fearing Bear*	James Wilde, 10	11-2-95
Wilson, John W.	Belle Weeks	1-23-14

Guardian	*Ward*	*Date*
Wilson, John W.	Myrtle Pollack	1-13-14
Wilson, John W.	Hattie Wilde estate	1-13-14
Wilson, Reuben*	———— White, 7	9-30-97
Yellow Horse*	Charles Wheeler, 19	2-4-99
Young Eagle*	Alexander Eagle, 10	1-19-99

NOTES

ABBREVIATIONS

BRN Garland J. Blaine and Martha R. Blaine Research Notes
CIA Commissioner of Indian Affairs
CIA AR Commissioner of Indian Affairs Annual Report
IPH *Indian and Pioneer History Collection*
NA RG M R National Archives, record group, microcopy, roll
OHS Oklahoma Historical Society
OHSAMD Oklahoma Historical Society Archives and Manuscripts Division

PREFACE

1. Waldo R. Wedel, *An Introduction to Pawnee Archeology*, Bureau of American Ethnology Bulletin 112 (Washington DC: Government Printing Office, 1936). Roger T. Grange Jr., *Pawnee and Lower Loup Pottery*, Nebraska State Historical Society Publications in Anthropology 3 (Lincoln: University of Nebraska Press. 1968).

2. Skiri is correct linguistically, but in common usage Skidi has been used by tribal speakers and continues to be used. This can probably be traced to the early interpreters who used this form, even though the language has no *d* sound.

3. Alice C. Fletcher, "The Hako: A Pawnee Ceremony," asst. James R. Murie, music trans. Edwin S. Tracy. *Twenty-second Annual Report of the Bureau of American Ethnology*, part 2 (Washington DC: Government Printing Office, 1904).

4. Martha Royce Blaine, "The Pawnee and Sioux Relationship," in *Pawnee Passage: 1870–1875* (Norman: University of Oklahoma Press, 1990).

5. All Pawnee treaties are given in Charles J. Kappler, comp., *Indian Affairs: Indian Laws and Treaties, 1902–1941*, vol. 2 (Washington DC: Government Printing Office, 1904–41; reprint, New York: Interland, 1972).

6. See bibliography for works by these authors.

7. Selected works by these authors include Walter R. Echo-Hawk and James Botsford, "The Legal Tangle: The Native American Church v. the United States of American, in *One Nation under God – the Triumph of the Native American Church*, ed. Reuben A. Snake Jr. and Huston Smith (Santa Fe NM: Clear Light, 1996); Walter R. Echo-Hawk, guest ed., preface to special edition, "Repatriation of American Indian Remains," *American Indian Culture and Research Journal* 16, 2 (1992); Walter R. Echo-Hawk and Roger Echo-Hawk, *Battlefields and Burial Grounds: The Indian Struggle to Protect Ancestral Graves in the United States* (Minneapolis: Lerner,

1994); Walter R. Echo-Hawk and Roger Echo-Hawk, "Repatriation, Reburial and Religious Rights," in *Handbook of American Indian Religious Freedom,* ed. Christopher Vecsey (New York: Crossroads, 1991); Roger C. Echo-Hawk, "Pawnee Mortuary Traditions," *American Indian Culture and Research Journal* 16, 2 (1992); Roger C. Echo-Hawk, "Exploring Ancient Worlds," *Society for American Archaeology* 11, 4 (1993): 5–6; Roger C. Echo-Hawk, "The Saga of Kiwaku Taka," prepared for the Repatriation and Reburial Committee of the Pawnee Tribe of Oklahoma, July 1994; Roger C. Echo-Hawk, "At the Edge of the Desert of Multicolored Turtles: Skidi Pawnee History on the Loup River," prepared for the University of Nebraska Bureau of Reclamation Archaeological Project, February 1994; James Riding In, "Report Verifying the Identity of Six Pawnee Scout Crania at the Smithsonian Institution and the National Museum of Health and Medicine," prepared for the Native American Rights Fund, Boulder CO, April 1990; James Riding In, "Keepers of Tirawahut's Covenant: The Development and Destruction of Pawnee Culture" (Ph.D. diss., University of California, Los Angeles, 1991); James Riding In, "Six Pawnee Crania: Historical and Contemporary Issues Surround the Massacre and Decapitation of Pawnee Indians in 1869," *American Indian Culture and Research Journal* 16, 2 (1992); James Riding In, "Twentieth-Century American Indian Cultural Survival: A Pawnee Case Study, 1994," unpublished manuscript; Ann Lee Walters, "The Pawnees," in *Talking Indian: Reflections on Survival and Writing* (Ithaca NY: Firebrand Books, 1992); Ann Lee Walters, *The Sun Is Not Merciful* (Ithaca NY: Firebrand Books, n.d.); Ann Lee Walters, *The Sacred: Ways of Knowledge, Sources of Life* (Tsaile AZ: Navajo Community College Press, 1977); Ann Lee Walters, *Ghost Singer, and The Spirit of Native America* (Flagstaff AZ: Northland, 1988).

CHAPTER 1

1. Garland Blaine related all the stories about his family and wrote their names as they appear here and in appendix A.

2. His childhood name is not known. Wichita was a name given later in his life.

3. Wichita Blaine account as told to Garland Blaine.

4. Addison E. Sheldon, *History and Stories of Nebraska* (Chicago: University Publishing, 1913), 157–59.

5. The hoop game was a game of skill that men played with spearlike wooden sticks. A small hide-covered hoop about four inches in diameter was tossed so as to roll along the ground, and as it passed the spears were thrown to go through it. The game had sacred significance but also helped develop accuracy in throwing projectiles. Betting on the outcome became a part of it.

6. Martha Royce Blaine, "Surrounded by Strangers," in *Pawnee Passage*, 11–15. Although the Indian agent made some attempts to stop the intrusion, timber stealing continued as long as the Pawnees lived on the Nebraska reservation.

7. Garland Blaine account, BRN.

8. Family names can be repeated from generation to generation, as in this case.

9. The Pawnees say that in battle the warriors that withstood the enemy for a long time would dodge, maneuver, and trample the ground in one place so that it looked like a grassless buffalo wallow. On a journey, warriors would point out such places where fierce battles had taken place. Once in a while human bones could be found on the surface.

10. Wichita Blaine account as told to Garland Blaine.

11. See Martha Royce Blaine, "The Last Days, Pawnee Removal from Nebraska," in *Pawnee Passage*, chap. 9, for a detailed account of the removal.

12. General Allotment Act, 8 February 1887, *U.S. Statutes at Large* 24 (1888): 388–91. This legislation is commonly called the Dawes Act.

13. The 1913 Pawnee Annuity Roll lists her birthdate as 1869. Like other birthdates of these early years, it may be inaccurate. Pawnee Agency – Census, OHSAMD.

14. John Dunbar, a Pawnee missionary in the 1830s, said the Pawnees would point out the site of a former village on this river, but its location is not yet certain.

15. Alice C. Fletcher studied and described the rituals and songs of this event in "Hako." One of its important purposes was to serve as the means by which amicable interband and intertribal relations were fostered by establishing bonds of kinship. The Pipe Dance, as the Pawnees in Oklahoma called it, continued to be performed as late as the 1920s and 1930s. As a child, one elderly Skidi Pawnee in her nineties (in 1991), daughter of Lone Chief, was adopted by the Chawi band in this ceremony.

16. Possible Pitahawirata village sites that would fit this family's history were near the confluence of Willow (Cedar) Creek and the Loup River and on Plum Creek. They are identified by Elvira Platt in "Some Experiences as a Teacher among the Pawnees," *Transactions of the Nebraska Historical Society* 3 (1892): 125–43, Grange, *Pawnee and Lower Loup Pottery*, 5, 22, and James H. Carleton, *The Prairie Log Books: Dragoon Campaigns to the Prairie Villages in 1844, and to the Rocky Mountains in 1845*, ed. with intro. Louis Pelzer (Chicago: Caxton Club, 1943; reprint, Lincoln: University of Nebraska Press, 1983), 64.

17. Gene Weltfish, *The Lost Universe, with a Closing Chapter on "The Universe Regained"* (New York: Basic, 1965) (reprinted as *The Lost Universe: Pawnee Life and*

Culture [Lincoln: University of Nebraska Press, 1977]), 403 ff., discusses Pawnee weaving techniques (page numbers refer to 1965 edition).

18. Gene Weltfish, *Caddoan Texts: Pawnee, South Band Dialect,* Publications of the American Ethnological Society 17 (New York: G. E. Steichert, 1937), 29–41, gives and translates an Effie Blaine account of the procedures for planting and processing food crops.

19. The rider must have been another type of courier, because the Pony Express system terminated in October 1861, before Effie was born.

20. There appear to have been two men with this name in the Pitahawirata band, one of whom was called "uncle" by Effie Blaine.

21. Blaine family records.

22. Although Skiri is linguistically correct, Skidi is in common usage among the Pawnees and others.

23. For a history of this battle and other references to it, see Garland J. Blaine and Martha R. Blaine, "Paresu Arirake: The Hunters That Were Massacred," *Nebraska History* 58, 3 (1977): 342–58.

24. United States and Pawnee treaty councils were held in 1818, 1825, 1833, and 1848.

25. Effie Blaine account given to Garland Blaine, BRN.

26. In Pawnee Agency Volume "Misc. 1880–1881," OHSAMD, 141, 166, the name "Coo-ruks-ce-rah-ke-tah-we" is listed with other Pitahawirata band members. Garland Blaine believed that was his great-grandfather. He also added that a sacred bear came in a vision and revealed what his name should be.

27. Horses were wealth and a symbol of status. Men who acquired them by stealth from other tribes were considered brave and successful. See Martha Royce Blaine, "Horse Stealing: An Economic Necessity," in *Pawnee Passage,* chap. 5.

28. These are the words Gene Weltfish attributed to Effie Blaine, who spoke only Pawnee. They were translated into English by that author in *Caddoan Texts,* 18. According to Garland Blaine, there are errors in the translation.

29. Captain Luther North said of his visit to the Pawnees: "The tribe was in very bad shape. They were miserably poor, nearly all of them had ague, and many of them were dying." Donald F. Danker, ed., *Man of the Plains: Recollections of Luther North, 1865–1882* (Lincoln: University of Nebraska Press, 1961), 197.

30. Major North was ill, and his brother reported that on the return trip, at Coffeyville, Kansas, "he shook so hard he seemed he would shake to pieces, then he had a terrible fever and was delirious." Danker, *Man of the Plains,* 198.

NOTES TO PAGES 9-13 229

31. "Major Frank North received the name Pawnee La Shar [Pari resaru] after his first fight on the Powder River Expedition of 1865." Danker, *Man of the Plains,* 46.

32. One of his names was Warrior Horse, but this name does not appear in Scout rosters, or if written there in English-spelled Pawnee, it cannot be recognized.

33. Blaine family account. According to Luther North many men followed in case they could take the places of those who were ill and might die on the way. Danker, *Man of the Plains,* 197.

34. His death date is not recorded; it may have been during the years when so many of the tribe died and many deaths went unrecorded. He did not receive an allotment in 1892, so presumably he was dead at that time.

35. This was said when she was eighty years old and had been taken to a place where there were many horses.

36. Her exact kinship relation to High Eagle has not been determined. However, "grandfather" is also a term of respect that now can be used even if there is no relationship.

37. Garland Blaine told this story to his cousin, Rosanna Yellow Calf Turnbull. They decided that Effie received the horses because she was the daughter of an honored chief.

38. Although his grandmother may have told him more about this event, this is all that Garland Blaine said about the ceremony.

39. James R. Murie gave John Box's last two names in a letter regarding pension claims. James R. Murie to J. C. Hart, Superintendent, Pawnee Agency, 27 January 1921, Pawnee Agency – Pensions, OHSAMD.

40. An elderly Skidi woman accompanied me to the place where she remembered seeing earth mound circles at the old village site when she was a girl. Because the area is now overgrown with thick brush and trees, we did not find any of the mounds or depressions.

41. This is affirmed in James R. Murie, *Ceremonies of the Pawnees,* ed. Douglas R. Parks, vol. 1, *The Skiri,* Smithsonian Institution Contributions to Anthropology 27 (Washington DC: Government Printing Office, 1979), 123.

42. Tape 76.4.2, BRN.

43. The Cunningham site is described in Grange, *Pawnee and Lower Loup Pottery,* 4, 5, 22.

44. According to James Mooney, "the winter that the stars fell," could be identified from Sioux and Kiowa pictographic calendars as occurring in 1833. Mooney,

Calendar History of the Kiowa Indians, intro. John C. Ewers, Classics of Smithsonian Anthropology (Washington DC: Smithsonian Institution Press, 1979), 261.

45. Wichita Blaine account, BRN. The Morning Star Ceremony has been extensively researched. See Ralph Linton's *The Sacrifice to the Morning Star by the Skidi Pawnee,* Department of Anthropology, Leaflet 6 (Chicago: Field Museum of Natural History, 1922), and idem, "The Origin of the Skidi Pawnee Sacrifice to the Morning Star," *American Anthropologist* 28 (1922): 457–66.

46. This song was recorded by Garland Blaine on tape 75.7.2, Blaine Pawnee Music Collection.

47. In addition to this Pitahawirata account about Pitaresaru, other South Band accounts about the event exist.

48. Leading warriors and chiefs could change their adult names when they had been brave in battle, after a successful vision-seeking experience, or after some other notable event. The number of names was one indicator of status.

49. Charles Hill to D. J. M. Wood, 14, 15 September 1892, Pawnee Agency Volume 10, OHSAMD.

50. In later years Mr. and Mrs. W. H. Custer leased three tracts of land from John Box. When he visited them he said his first wife had died and he had had to marry her nearest relative in line, a customary practice. He told them his present wife, Lizzie, did not like white people, and he was not too fond of her. In *Indian and Pioneer History Collection,* 114 vols. (Oklahoma City: Oklahoma Historical Society Archives and Manuscripts Division, 1936–38), 2:406 (hereafter cited as IPH).

51. Author's interview with Maude White Chisholm, 19 September 1990. Her father, Barclay White, was Lizzie's son.

52. Ibid.

53. John Box, Pawnee Agency – Individual Indian Files, OHSAMD.

54. Maude White Chisholm story.

CHAPTER 2

1. Blaine, *Pawnee Passage,* 231–32.

2. Charles Tatiah to CI, 30 May 1878. NA RG 75 M234 R666.

3. Wichita Blaine as told to Garland Blaine, BRN.

4. Among those committing suicide was the son of the Pitahawirata Two Chiefs. Yet this band believed that "people who commit suicide never enter this entrance [to the place were the dead live on in the village of the dead]." George A. Dorsey, *The Pawnee: Mythology,* part 1 (Washington DC: Carnegie Institution, 1906), 419.

5. Martha R. Blaine Field Notes, Pawnee interviews.

6. Wichita Blaine information, BRN.

7. Spelling by Garland Blaine.

8. Ibid.

9. Ibid.

10. Once I accompanied my husband to find a certain plant that St. Elmo Jim, an elderly relative, said he needed to cure an ailment he had. We spent an afternoon searching in the type of terrain he had described, but the plants we took to him were not suitable. When St. Elmo looked at them he said, "Nephew, I don't know these. That plant I want may not grow in this country."

11. The Pawnees prefer the term doctor to medicine man or shaman, anthropological terms they have never used.

12. CIA *Report of the Commissioner of Indian Affairs*, 1876, xx; 44 Cong. 1 sess., H.R. Ex. Doc. no.80; "Pawnee Indians in Nebraska, Letter from the Secretary of the Interior Transmitting Correspondence upon the Present Necessities of the Pawnee Indians in Nebraska, January 15, 17, 1876."

13. Joseph Stanley Clark, "Irregularities at the Pawnee Agency," *Kansas Historical Quarterly* 12 (1943): 367.

14. J. D. Miles to E. A. Hayt, 2 February 1878, NA RG 75 M234 R666.

15. Tom McHugh, *The Time of the Buffalo* (Lincoln: University of Nebraska Press, 1979), 271–87.

16. Joseph S. Clark, "The Ponca Indian Agency" (Ph.D. diss., University of Wisconsin, 1940), 97. Clark did not give the date or source for this information.

17. T. E. Berry to E. A. Hayt, 1 October 1878, and Samuel Ely to CI, 8 July 1878, NA RG 75 M234 R666.

18. Before allotment of the reservation in severalty to individual Indians, cattlemen leased portions of the Pawnee reservation and other Indian reservations and ran cattle on the land (John Scott to CIA, 14 March 1884, Pawnee Agency Volume 5, OHSAMD, and E. C. Osbourne to CIA, 29 May 1889, Ponca Agency Volume 11, OHSAMD). In the latter 127,265 acres were leased to the Fairmount Cattle Company of Greeley, Colorado, for one year for $5,000.

19. BRN.

20. J. L. Williams to Charles H. Searing, 28 December 1877, NA RG 75 M234 R666.

21. C. H. Searing to CIA, 1 January 1878, ibid.

22. This story has no single known source; the Pawnees tell it from time to time to illustrate the difficulties their grandparents faced in the early days. They add the expression, "All four bands know this."

23. Ibid.

24. Joseph Hertford to CIA, 7 November 1877, NA RG 75 M234 R666.

25. Ibid.

26. Joseph Hertford to CIA, 7 February 1878, NA RG 75 M234 R666. Annuity goods and foods obtained by agency employees were to be paid for, and the money was to be placed in a fund to pay for Indian subsistence. But the beef described above should have been distributed to the destitute Pawnees rather than sold to the employees.

27. Joseph Hertford to CIA, 6 November 1877, NA RG 75 M234 R668.

28. J. Hertford to Barclay White, 15 June 1878, NA RG 75 M234 R666.

29. BRN.

30. Houghton and McLaughlin to Pawnee agent, 8 March 1878, NA RG 75 M234 R666.

31. James Bowman to CIA, CIA AR, 1881, 89. Much of the clothing ordered each year did not fit or was unsuitable.

32. Roster of Employees, Pawnee Agency, 1 July 1878, NA RG 75 M234 R666.

33. Estimate of Funds, Pawnee Agency, 3d quarter, 1878, NA RG 75 M234 R666.

34. Apparently after his discharge John Box was not paid for his service, and he requested compensation later. Agent Charles Searing to CIA, 26 February 1878, and Agent Samuel Ely to CIA, 9 September 1878 (NA 75 M234 R666) were letters requesting payment.

35. Joseph Hertford to CIA, 22 November 1877, NA RG 75 M234 R668.

36. Bond of W. F. Cody and John F. Ford, 10 and 21 September 1878, NA RG 75 M234 R666.

37. Clark, "Ponca Indian Agency," 99.

38. Ibid., 100.

39. An asterisk indicates that more than one band had this name for a leader.

40. Clark, "Ponca Indian Agency," 100.

41. The purpose of the Cheyennes' visit was not recorded. At this time conditions at their reservation were unsettled and difficult, particularly among some Northern Cheyennes, who wanted to leave and return to their lands in the north. The Cheyennes made several visits to ask the Pawnees to return their sacred arrows captured in battle years before.

42. Clark, "Ponca Agency," 101. No date is given for this meeting.

43. Ibid.

44. When she told her grandson about this event, Effie Blaine did not say what her immediate family did. Little is known of her life at this time in the late 1870s. BRN.

45. This probably included Effie Blaine's father; I do not know the date or the circumstances of his death.

46. I discuss these issues in *Pawnee Passage*, in several chapters concerning land cessions, annuity, white depredations, removal to Indian Territory, and other topics.

47. In Volume 1884, "Leasing of Indian Lands in Indian Territory," 756, OHS Library.

48. Garland Blaine married a Ponca woman, and close friends and cousins married into the Osage, Comanche, Creek, and Otoe tribes, among others. In most instances contact at Indian boarding schools, attended by members of different tribes, fostered the relationships. BRN.

CHAPTER 3

1. There are few family stories of this period, leaving gaps in their history. Effie Blaine's brother had died, and it seems there was no one to take her father's position in his part of the band.

2. Several band villages were established after the Pawnees' arrival on the reservation, but their precise location is uncertain. Nor is it certain how the agent defined a village – whether it consisted of mudlodges or tipis or a mixture of the two. At times the word camp was used to define a group of dwellings near one another where members of one band or another lived together.

3. The idea of Indian land allotment was not new. In 1826 Thomas L. McKenney, first United States Indian commissioner, suggested that individual allotments be given to Indians who could read or write or, as he said, were educated.

4. Jacob M. Troth, 8 September 1871, CIA AR, 451.

5. Pawnee Council Volume, 25 September 1871, OHSAMD.

6. Kappler, *Indian Affairs*, 1:159–61.

7. Samuel S. Ely to CIA, 28 June 1878, NA RG 75 M234 R666.

8. Samuel S. Ely to CIA, 9 September 1878, NA RG 75, M234 R666.

9. Blaine, *Pawnee Passage*, 159–60.

10. CIA AR, 1880, xxxii.

11. E. H. Bowman to CIA, 30 August 1880, CIA AR, 77, 79.

12. E. H. Bowman to CIA, 15 August 1881, 88.

13. BRN.

14. Pawnee Agency Miscellaneous Volume 1881–91, 28, OHSAMD. This volume is a journal and not a record of correspondence. The Skidi and Kitkahahki villages are also mentioned, although their locations are not given.

15. See IPH, 106:354.

16. Pawnee Agency "Occasional Issues" Volume, 1881–91, 76.

17. Ibid., 293, 304, 313, 321. Charles Hill to D. J. M. Wood, 9 October 1892, Pawnee Agency Volume 7, OHSAMD.

18. John W. Scott to CIA, 25 February 1884, Pawnee Agency Volume 5, OHSAMD.

19. John W. Scott to CIA, CIA AR 1884, 87.

20. This combined agency was established by congressional act of 27 May 1882 with headquarters at the Ponca agency. The Pawnee agency became a subagency. E. C. Osborne, CIA AR, 1886, 137.

21. CIA AR, 1889, 196.

22. E. C. Osbourn to CIA, 8 July 1889, Ponca Agency Volume 2, OHSAMD.

23. D. J. M. Wood to T. J. Morgan, 1 May 1890, Ponca Agency Volume 14, 155, OHSAMD.

24. The tribes were the Cherokees, Choctaws, Chickasaws, Creeks, and Seminoles.

25. B. B. Chapman Collection, "Pawnee Allotment," 3, NA Indian Office Special Cases, no.147, 33751–1890.

26. Joel Bryan Mayes to the Cherokee Commission, 16 December 1889, Cherokee Volume 715j, 238–44, OHSAMD.

27. When the Pawnees were to be removed from Nebraska, the government planned to settle the tribe on the small Quapaw reservation in the upper northeast corner of Indian Territory, an area much smaller than the Pawnees' Nebraska reservation. Resident tribes included the Quapaws, Senecas, Miamis, Wyandots, Peorias, Ottawas, and others, who would have had to cede land to make room for the Pawnees. See Blaine, "The Last Days," in *Pawnee Passage*, 263.

28. One Skidi woman's father born in Nebraska had a "brother" in the Omaha tribe. Once he took his family and other Pawnees from Oklahoma to Nebraska on the train to visit him and his family. John Box accompanied the group and pointed out former Pawnee sites as they went along.

29. Garland Blaine had a "brother" in the Otoe tribe and another in the Wichita tribe. According to him, his grandmother selected his brother from the latter tribe in conjunction with the boy's mother during a tribal visit there when he was a young man.

30. Garland Blaine pointed out the campsite on a ridge on the south side of State Highway 15 about four miles west of the intersection with U.S. Highway 77 on the old Pawnee reservation.

31. Adam LeClair, Ponca, also remembered these visits to Eagle Chief's camp and told Garland Blaine about them. BRN.

32. Clark, "Ponca Indian Agency," 397.

33. Roaming Chief is known by this name as well as Roam Chief and Roan Chief. Now and in the past his name has been written all three ways. Today he is known by both of the last two names. Garland Blaine used Roan Chief, but in his youth he called him by his Pawnee name.

34. Clark, "Ponca Indian Agency," 398.

35. Dawes Act of 1887, sec.5, in Wilcomb E. Washburn, comp., *The American Indian and the United States: A Documentary History* (Westport CT: Greenwood, 1979), 3:2190.

36. F. P. Prucha, *The Great White Father: The United States Government and the American Indian* (Lincoln: University of Nebraska Press, 1984), 2:746.

37. The Cherokee Outlet was a strip of land fifty-seven miles wide containing some 6 million acres. In an 1828 treaty the Cherokees exchanged their land in Arkansas for land in Indian Territory. The outlet was included to provide access to buffalo hunting grounds to the west.

38. Report of Councils held by Cherokee (Jerome) Commission and Several Indian Tribes, National Archives, NA RG 75, Indian Office file no.4738, part 1, Pawnee Agency, 31 October–24 November 1892. Transcript in OHSAMD, 15. The complete transcript is over 150 typed pages; only a small portion of it has been used in this chapter. Hereafter cited as Jerome Commission Transcript.

39. Ibid., 1–7.

40. E. E. Dale and Jess Lee Rader, *Readings in Oklahoma History* (New York: Row Peterson, 1930), 503.

41. Jerome Commission Transcript, 19.

42. The Pawnee leaders continued to repeat what the others said and to make their own points, thus showing unanimity and reinforcing their arguments by reiteration.

43. Some years before their deaths, I talked to St. Elmo and Susie Jim, Pitahawirata relatives of the Blaines. They said they were cheated and their folks were cheated. According to the allotment record of 1893, St. Elmo was ten years old and received 100 acres. Susie Bearchief, age four, received 120 acres, and her father received the same amount.

44. Jerome Commission Transcript, 31.

45. This was an inaccurate statement as to land type and description.

46. Jerome Commission Transcript, 43.

47. In total, the Pawnees ceded to the United States 23,512,343 acres in Nebraska, Kansas, and Oklahoma. Blaine, *Pawnee Passage*, 213.

48. An idea that the government gives the Indians "something for nothing" became part of the non-Indian mind-set in United States relations with the native population, particularly after the treaty period. Many of the general population today erroneously believe that Indians are getting free handouts in medical care and education, don't pay taxes, and so forth. There is a misconception that the non-Indian taxpayer is paying for these services, and some resentment over it. Few people understand that many Indian benefits result directly from treaties in which the government promised to assume certain obligations, stemming from Indian land cessions that allowed westward expansion of the non-Indian population.

49. Jerome Commission Transcript, 77.

50. Kappler, *Indian Affairs*, 1:764.

51. Jerome Commission Transcript, 89a–90. See Debo, *And Still the Waters Run*, 126–34, for confirmation and discussion of this situation among the Cherokees and members of other tribes.

52. Garland Blaine said that when he was young the old men chiefs always claimed they had been tricked or misled, and that what they requested and agreed to was never what happened afterward. For instance, the government led them to believe that when they left Nebraska they would live near their old friends the Wichitas. Instead they received a reservation several days' journey away.

53. Jerome Commission Transcript, 102.

54. Ibid. 126–27.

55. Ibid., 129.

56. Ibid., 130–32.

57. E. C. Osbourne to CIA, 8 July 1889, Ponca Volume 11, OHSAMD. Previously, when the Indians had great amounts of land that the government wanted, it granted their requests to consult with the heads of government in Washington. But as their land decreased in area and government control over their lives increased, officials in Washington refused their requests to come and talk about their problems and needs.

58. Benjamin Harrison, in *Messages and Papers of the Presidents, 1789–1902*, ed. James D. Richardson (Washington DC: Bureau of National Literature and Art, 1907), 9:203.

59. At annuity payment times, paper warrants were issued to the Pawnees instead of cash. "The traders, knowing the amount and time of payment extend a credit to the Indians accordingly, so that in effect, the Indian receives goods from the trader instead of the money provided by law and treaties." T. J. Morgan to Secretary of Interior, 9 December 1892, Senate Exec. Doc., 16, 52–2 [30551] 4.

60. Jerome Commission Transcript, 139.

61. Ibid., 141.

62. Ibid., 143–44.

63. Ibid., 142, 147.

64. Ibid., 148–49.

65. Ibid., 150–51.

66. Ibid., 150–52.

67. Report of Jerome Commission; Senate Exec. Doc. 16, 52–2 [3055], 23 November 1892.

68. Act of 3 March 1893, 27 State. 612, "Agreement with the Pawnee Indians," 4 January 1893. The official transcript says the Pawnees signed the agreement on 24 November 1892.

69. Garland Blaine speculated that his grandfather chose this wooded area because it offered good hunting, whereas Effie's land was treeless, hilly grassland except along the border of a creek that crossed it.

70. D. S. Otis, "The Application of Allotment," in *The Dawes Act and the Allotment of Indian Lands* (Norman: University of Oklahoma Press, 1973), 82–97, discusses the reasons for resistance to allotment and the means taken for resolving it.

71. Berlin B. Chapman, "Pawnee Allotment," manuscript, Chapman Collection, OHSAMD, 8–9.

72. Grover Cleveland Proclamation, in *Messages and Papers of the Presidents*, 9:441.

73. Prucha, *Great Father*, 2:747.

74. BRN.

75. Addie Troth Yellow Calf told this story to her daughter, Rosanna Yellow Calf Turnbull. BRN.

76. Ethel Riding In, Lulu's granddaughter, told this story. She and Viola Blaine, Effie's daughter, grew up together and were "close relatives," she said. She told me their families often stayed in Eagle Chief's camp together and went to ceremonies.

77. The specific number cannot be given. Each year additional allotments are offered for sale by their owners through the Pawnee Indian agency.

CHAPTER 4

1. Wichita Blaine account as told to Garland Blaine.

2. Alexander Lesser, *The Pawnee Ghost Dance Handgame: A Study of Cultural Change*, Columbia University Contributions to Anthropology 16 (New York: Columbia University Press, 1933; reprint, Madison: University of Wisconsin Press, 1978), 56.

3. David H. Miller, "Wounded Knee," in *Ghost Dance* (New York: Duell, Sloan and Pearce, 1959; reprint, Lincoln: University of Nebraska Press, 1985), 218–44.

4. D. J. M. Wood to T. J. Morgan, 21 January 1891, Ponca Volume 16, 64–65, OHSAMD.

5. Ibid.

6. Max Lerner, *America as a Civilization: Life and Thought in the United States Today* (New York: Simon and Schuster, 1957), 13.

7. Ralph Linton, "Nativistic Movements," *American Anthropologist* 45, 2 (1943); 230.

8. Lesser, *Pawnee Ghost Dance Handgame*, 63.

9. Dorsey, *Pawnee: Mythology*, 342.

10. BRN.

11. Lt. H. L. Scott to Post Adjutant, Fort Sill, 5 January 1891, NA RG 75 "Documents relative to the Ghost Dance Religion and the Sioux Outbreak of 1890 (1890–1898)," Bureau of Indian Affairs, Land Division, Special Cases, no.188, roll 1.

12. H. L. Scott to Post Adjutant, Fort Sill, 30 January 1891, ibid.

13. Ibid. 10 February 1891.

14. James R. Murie, "Pawnee Indian Societies," *Anthropological Papers of the American Museum of Natural History*, 2, pt. 7 (1914): 634–35.

15. Ibid.

16. *Guthrie Oklahoma State Capitol*, 25 August 1891, 2.

17. Charles Hill to D. J. M. Wood, 7 November 1891, Pawnee Volume 7, 322, OHSAM.

18. Murie, "Pawnee Indian Societies," 634–35.

19. Garland Blaine observation, BRN.

20. James Mooney, "The Ghost Dance Religion and the Sioux Outbreak of 1890," in *Fourteenth Annual Report of the Bureau of Ethnology*, pt. 2 (Washington DC: Government Printing Office, 1896), 902; Frances Densmore, *Pawnee Music*. Bureau of American Ethnology Bulletin 93 (Washington DC: Government Printing Office, 1929), 78. Lesser, *Pawnee Ghost Dance Handgame*, 61.

21. Murie, "Pawnee Indian Societies," 633.

22. Ibid.

23. Mooney, *Ghost Dance Religion,* 902.

24. This account was told to Garland Blaine by Wichita Blaine. He repeated it in his own words. BRN.

25. Garland Blaine comment, BRN.

26. Garland Blaine disagreed with Alexander Lesser that the sacred societies were revitalized by the Ghost Dance. They functioned from the earliest days in Indian Territory, although they were weakened by loss of members from illness and death.

27. Densmore, *Pawnee Music,* 83–84, no.57.

28. This feather still exists in the Blaine Collection.

29. Lesser, *Pawnee Ghost Dance Handgame,* 75.

30. Composed by Effie Blaine, BRN.

31. NA RG 75 "Documents relative to the Ghost Dance," Special Cases. no.188, roll 1, frame 0091. One of the early Arapaho Ghost Dance songs written down by a Carlisle Arapaho student said, "Crow holloa at me. When God sends for me, I hear his voice." Another said, "Crow holloa me. To make me get up and dance." Sitting Bull gave these songs to each tribe after it was "given the feather."

32. Murie, "Pawnee Indian Societies," 636. Alexander Lesser's *Pawnee Ghost Dance Handgame* gives a detailed development and description of the various games that developed in the bands.

33. Wichita Blaine was nominated to be an agency police private on 14 September 1892 (Pawnee Volume 10, OHSAMD). His experience during the epidemics described above occurred at a different time not dated by family accounts.

34. Charles Hill to D. J. M. Wood, 9 January 1892, 6 June 1892, Pawnee Volume 7, OHSAMD.

35. Maude White Chisholm told me that James Murie lived at the home of her paternal grandmother (Lizzie Washington Box) while married to Maude's aunt, Lizzie's daughter. Maude used to see him working with his papers at his desk. After he died she saw her grandmother gather up his papers and burn them.

36. Murie states that the Prophet was a young man. According to the 1889 Pawnee census the older Frank White was forty-four years old, and the 1892 census said the younger man was twenty-five. NA RG 234 M595 R386.

37. James R. Murie to D. J. M. Wood, 6 December 1891, Ponca Volume 19, OHSAMD.

38. BRN.

39. D. J. M. Wood to Frank White, 18 December 1891, Ponca Volume 18, OHSAMD.

40. The Kiowa agency had jurisdiction over the Kiowas, Comanches, Wichitas, and other tribes. A careful search of the Wichita tribal rolls did not reveal White's name. It is possible he was using another name not known to me, or that he was not on the rolls as Wood believed.

41. Charles M. Hill to D. J. M. Wood, 22 December 1891, Ponca Volume 18, 461, OHSAMD. Blaine Kent, Iowa, told me in 1964 that whenever his tribe had a Ghost Dance on their reservation south of the Cimarron River, they asked the Pawnees to come. His father, Frank Kent Nawanoway, the chief, led the dance, sang, and shook the gourd. In turn the Iowas attended Pawnee Ghost Dances.

42. D. J. M. Wood to John Noble, 25 January 1892. Ponca Volume 18, OHSAMD. Agent Wood believed that Superintendent F. Conway of the agency school wrote this letter. Conway wrote to the secretary of the interior and denied doing so. Pawnee Volume 8, 460, OHSAMD.

43. D. J. M. Wood to John W. Noble, Secretary of the Interior, 25 January 1892, Ponca Volume 18, OHSAMD.

44. According to Pawnee agency family history charts, she is listed as Lucy Kuhns Leader Keys White Lewis, indicating a series of marital alliances, apparently not listed in order. She was born in 1873 and was about seventeen or eighteen years old at the time of her marriage to Frank White (Family History Chart, fiche 837, Pawnee Agency, Pawnee, Oklahoma).

45. D. J. M. Wood to Secretary of the Interior, 25 January 1892, Ponca Volume 18, OHSAMD.

46. D. J. M. Wood to T. J. Morgan, 26 January 1892, Ponca Volume 18, OHSAMD.

47. It has been said that the god the Pawnees referred to in the Ghost Dance was always the Christian God. This was not true in all cases. The Blaines and many others were not Christians, and the deity they appealed to or mentioned in the Ghost Dance songs was the Pawnee supreme being. Garland Blaine.

48. D. J. M. Wood to T. J. Morgan, 26 January 1892. Ponca Volume 18, OHSAMD.

49. Ibid.

50. Charles M. Hill to D. J. M. Wood, 7 March 1892, Pawnee Volume 7, OHSAMD.

51. Several Pawnees told me this happened.

52. D. J. M. Wood to F. W. Miller, 23 March 1892, Ponca Volume 19, OHSAMD.

53. The Organic Act, passed by Congress on 2 May 1890, created Oklahoma Territory. The Pawnee reservation became part of this area, and the Pawnees and

other nearby tribes were subject to arrest, trial, and sentencing under the United States court system. Indian Territory now contained the Five Civilized Tribes and the reservations of smaller tribes in the territory's northeast corner.

54. Charles Hill to D. J. M. Wood, 25 March 1892, Pawnee Volume OHSAMD.

55. Blaine, *Pawnee Passage*, 17–23.

56. D. J. M. Wood to CIA, 29 March 1892, Ponca Volume 19; and Wood to CIA, 20 August 1892, CIA AR, 396; John W. Boles to Wood, 1 April 1892, Ponca Volume 19, OHSAMD.

57. D. J. M. Wood to Clerks F. W. Miller and C. M. Hill, 9 April 1892, Ponca Volume 19, OHSAMD.

58. Ibid.

59. Ponca Volume 19, 16 May 1892, OHSAMD.

60. Traditional Pawnee doctors also used their hands to cure their patients.

61. C. M. Hill to D. J. M. Wood, 30 June 1892, Pawnee Volume 10, OHSAMD.

62. In seeking to avoid using Pawnee-language names in records, government employees gave military titles and names of United States officials to several Pawnees, such as Colonel Moore and Captain Jim. The real Col. A. B. Meacham, who died in 1882, was a United States peace commissioner, editor of *Council Fire*, and a superintendent of Indian affairs.

63. Fort Reno was established in 1874 near the Cheyenne and Arapaho agency on the North Canadian River, approximately one hundred miles from the Pawnee agency.

64. C. M. Hill to D. J. M. Wood, 7, 8 September 1892, Pawnee Volume 10, OHSAM.

65. Lesser, *Pawnee Ghost Dance Handgame*, 62.

66. Frank White is said to have used peyote while on the Wichita reservation. Benjamin R. Kracht, "The Kiowa Ghost Dance, 1894–1916: An Unheralded Revitalization Movement," *Ethnohistory* 39, 4 (1992): 462. The Peyote religion, later called the Native American Church, made its appearance on the Pawnee reservation at about the same time as the Ghost Dance.

67. Weston LaBarre, *The Peyote Cult* (New York: Schocken, 1971), 43.

68. Lesser, *Pawnee Ghost Dance Handgame*, 76.

69. Ibid., 76–77.

70. Ibid., 77–78.

71. L. G. Moses, "Wovoka: The Ghost Dance Prophet," *American Indian Quarterly*, summer 1985, 344.

72. N. Hammons, Farmer in Charge, Walker Valley Reserve, 22 November 1892, NA RG 75, "Documents relative to the Ghost Dance," Special Cases, no.188, roll 2.

73. Lt. H. L. Scott to Post Adjutant, Fort Sill, 22 February 1891, NA RG 75 "Documents relative to the Ghost Dance," Special Cases, no.188, roll 2.

74. *Edmond (Oklahoma) Sun Democrat*, 24 January 1896, 31 July 1897, OHS Newspaper Archives.

75. Fred Winterfair, Clerk in Charge, Cheyenne and Arapaho Agency, Cantonment, to Maj. Geo. W. H. Stouch, Agent, Darlington, 13 October 1900. Cheyenne and Arapaho Agency, microfilm roll 51, frame 113, OHSAMD.

76. Superintendent of Schools to CIA, 17 May 1902, Pawnee Volume 18, OHSAMD.

77. Ibid.

78. Author's interview with Viola Blaine McIntosh in 1982, Pawnee, Oklahoma.

79. Author's interview with Ethel Riding In, born in 1906, 14 November 1988, Pawnee, Oklahoma.

80. Densmore, *Pawnee Music*, 79–80.

81. Lesser, *Pawnee Ghost Dance Handgame*, 102. Hand games are frequently held today, and songs are sung all during the games' playing. Ghost Dance songs are rarely heard unless requested during the games' intervals. Usually the round dance and war dance songs are sung at this time, and people dance.

82. James Murie to Alice Fletcher, 20 July 1900, Smithsonian Institution, National Anthropology Archives, MS 4558 (1) 1900.

83. J. G. Brendel, "A Memorable Week among the Pawnee Indians – Opening the New Church," in Contributed Articles, *Our Home Field*, Home Mission Board, Southern Baptist Convention. n.d. In Vertical File, Oklahoma Historical Library.

84. BRN.

85. Murie, "Pawnee Indian Societies," 636.

86. BRN.

87. During the Pawnee Doctor Dance the doctors assumed the mannerisms and sounds of their spiritual animal counterparts. Brave Chief and others had remarked that at traditional Pawnee dances, the actions of the Ghost Dance took place, regardless of the dance's purpose. The dance Garland observed may have been an example of this.

88. BRN.

89. Author's taped conversation with Maude White Chisholm, 1992, Oklahoma City, Oklahoma.

90. BRN.

91. BRN. Author's taped interview with Garland Blaine, 5 May 1979, Oklahoma City, Oklahoma.

92. Author's observation, BRN.

93. BRN.

CHAPTER 5

1. Effie Blaine account told to Garland Blaine, BRN.

2. BRN.

3. BRN.

4. Interview with Sadie Hughes, 13 March 1937, IPH, 5:242.

5. Ibid., 5:225.

6. Jeff Briley of the Oklahoma Historical Society said that such hunters salted and dried game and sent it to St. Louis, Wichita, Kansas, and Kansas City (personal communication, 27 February 1994).

7. Interview with John H. Conley, 16 March 1937, IPH, 100:173. In the 1890 Guthrie city directory, a Thomas Conley appears as a land claimant in Logan County. Game hunters listed in this directory did not include a Benjamin Conley. No Bushyhead quarry is known in that area. Some other information in the article cannot be verified, according to Helen F. Holmes, Guthrie historian (personal communication, 19 March 1994).

8. Act of Congress, 4 Stat. 730, sec.2139, 30 June 1834.

9. Interview with William E. Aikman, 10 June 1937, IPH, 12:154.

10. Author's interview, March 1991 (Pawnee name withheld by request).

11. *New York Times,* 26 December 1901, p.1. No Guthrie newspapers *(Daily Leader, Oklahoma State Capitol)* for 25 December and several days before reveal any news about the Pawnees.

12. Interview with Mrs. W. H. Custer, 29 April 1937, IPH, 2:407.

13. Author's conversation with Maude White Chisholm, whose paternal grandmother married John Box, 18 September 1990, Oklahoma City, Oklahoma.

14. According to Pawnee census records, Susie was born in 1842 and Julia in 1849.

15. The onset of Wichita and Effie Blaine's blindness from trachoma began in the middle 1900s.

16. Garland Blaine account, BRN.

17. BRN.

18. In the 1900s and later, times became difficult for many farmers, who could not, or said they could not, pay their annual lease money. The agent

made lists of the debtors' names and sent them to Washington. In the Dust Bowl days in the 1930s defaulting on Indian lease payments came to be a serious problem.

19. C. C. Graham opened the Midway Restaurant in 1907 on the south side of the Pawnee courthouse square. Kenny A. Franks and Paul F. Lambert, *Pawnee Pride: A History of Pawnee County,* Oklahoma Heritage County History Series, ed. O. B. Falk (Oklahoma City: Western Heritage Books, 1994), 132.

20. BRN.

21. BRN.

22. BRN.

23. Testimony of Charles E. Vandervoort, 5 October 1891, NA RG 75 M234 R39. "Report of Inspections of the Field Jurisdictions of the Bureau of Indian Affairs, 1873–1900."

24. Interview with Leslie W. Webb, IPH, 73:348. In 1899–1902, W. B. Webb held the position of clerk-in-charge at the Pawnee subagency.

25. Personal communication, Hazel Walker, 12 July 1994.

26. Berry's government license expired in May 1882. In the discussion of whether it should be renewed Agent Bowman said he did not care who the trader would be, except he did not want a "copperhead" (a northerner who had sided with the South in the Civil War). E. H. Bowman to CIA, 4 August 1882, Pawnee Volume 4.

27. Interview with H. M. Thompson, n.d., IPH, 10:447.

28. Interview with J. M. Herd, 9 December 1937, IPH, 28:497.

29. On 21 February 1887, Congress provided for investigation of Indian trade licenses. "Resolution of Senator Platt," Senate Misc. Doc. 73, 49–2, vol.2 [2451]. Congress received "A Report on Indian Traders," 2 March 1889, Senate Rept. 2707, 50–2, vol.5, 635 [2623].

30. Washburn, *American Indian and the United States,* 1:459.

31. This apparently is a reference to the act of 27 May 1902 (32 Stat. 245) that stated that the Indian heirs to lands inherited from a deceased Indian "to whom a trust or other patent containing restrictions upon alienation has been or shall be issued" may sell and convey such lands.

32. Interview with David N. Hatfield, 23 April 1937, IPH, 4:469.

33. W. A. Jones, CIA AR, 1 October 1900.

34. Washburn, *American Indian and the United States,* 2:806–7.

35. F. E. Leupp, CIA AR, 30 September 1905.

36. Superintendent and Special Disbursement Agent to CIA, 24 May 1912, Wichita Blaine, Pawnee Agency – Individual Indian Files, OHSAMD.

37. F. E. Leupp to Agents and Superintendents, 24 January 1906, circular 182, Pawnee Agency – Circulars, OHSAMD.

38. Washburn, *American Indian and the United States,* 2:807.

39. When I asked other Pawnees the expression used for the merchants, several older individuals repeated this term to me.

40. Garland Blaine account, BRN.

41. BRN.

42. BRN.

43. BRN.

44. BRN.

45. Recently a group of Pawnee women told me they found the town of Pawnee prejudiced against Indians. "People there treat you different." One said she never buys anything there; she buys her gas in Hallett and her groceries in Stillwater. She refuses to put up with some Pawnee merchants' attitudes, saying, "It's damaging to self-esteem."

46. BRN.

47. BRN.

48. *Portrait and Biographical Record of Oklahoma* (Chicago: Chapman, 1901), 1252–54.

49. "Pawnee Pioneers," *Pawnee Chief,* 1 January 1994.

50. Author's interview with Henry Stone Road, 28 January 1994, Oklahoma City, Oklahoma. I have paraphrased his account.

51. Ibid. A few of these men are remembered today with scorn as cheating their people for their own gain.

52. Roam Chief, 1 May 1910, Pawnee Agency – Individual Indian Files, OHSAMD.

53. Superintendent's Annual Narrative and Statistical Report, Special Agent's Report, 30 June 1914, NA RG 75 M1011 R100.

54. Wichita Blaine, Pawnee Agency – Individual Indian Files, OHSAMD.

55. Ibid. There is no record of Anna as wife of Wichita according to family information. She may have been a cousin, aunt, or some other relative. No Anna Wichita was allotted, nor does she appear on any census of the period.

56. Wichita Blaine, Pawnee Agency – Individual Indian Files, OHSAMD.

57. Effie Blaine, Pawnee Agency – Individual Indian Files, OHSAMD. Superintendent to Commissioner of Indian Affairs, 5 August 1924, OHSAMD.

58. Kappler, *Indian Affairs,* 1:56. This act was an amendment to the 1887 Dawes Act, and it was passed before many Indians were allotted.

59. Chapters 4 and 5 of Janet McDonnell's *The Dispossesion of the American Indian: 1887–1934* (Bloomington: University of Indiana Press, 1991) give an excellent description of the problems, views, and outcomes of Indian land leasing.

60. Report of the Secretary of the Interior, 1896, 264.

61. George Harvey to Commissioner of Indian Affairs, 28 January 1902, Pawnee Volume 18, 194, OHSAMD.

62. Department of the Interior circular 181, 9 January 1908, Pawnee Agency – Circulars.

63. George Harvey to Commissioner of Indian Affairs, 28 January 1902, Pawnee Volume 18, 194, OHSAMD.

64. McDonnell, *Dispossesion of the American Indian*, 88–89.

65. Ibid., 98.

66. Ibid., 89.

67. Annual Narrative Report, George W. Nellis, 13 March 1911, NA RG 75 M1011 R100.

68. Pawnee Agency – Agents' Reports, 1923, OHSAMD.

69. By 1994, one hundred years after allotment, only about 10 percent of the original allotment acres remained under Pawnee ownership. Each year sees a few more Pawnee land sales.

70. Garland Blaine account and explanation, BRN.

71. Author's interviews with several Pawnees who agreed that problems with lessees continue from generation to generation.

72. From a tape recording I made with Myra Eppler and her cousin, 14 May 1994, Pawnee, Oklahoma.

73. Washburn, *American Indian and the United States*, 1:388–91.

74. Organic Act [51 Cong. 1 sess., chap. 182, 26 Stat. 81].

75. Kappler, *Indian Affairs*, 1:971.

76. *The Statues of Oklahoma, 1890, . . . from the Laws Passed by the First Assembly of the Territory*, comp. Will T. Little, L. G. Pitman, and R. J. Baker, under direction of Robert Martin, Secretary of the Territory, 1891 (Guthrie OK: State Capital Printing Company, 1891).

77. *U.S. Statutes at Large*, 1906, chap. 3335, sec.3, 269.

78. "Selection Docket," Pawnee County Court Clerk's Office, Pawnee, Oklahoma.

79. "Guardian Record – County Q," now "Guardian Record vol.1," Pawnee County, Oklahoma, County Clerk's Office.

80. *Consolidated Statutes of Nebraska, 1891,* comp. J. E. Cobbey, Esq. (Lincoln: Nebraska State Journal Company, 1891). *Statutes of Oklahoma, 1890,* Courts, chap. 19, art. 13, "Of Guardian and Ward," secs.1–58, 357–67.

81. *Statutes of Oklahoma, 1890,* chap. 19, sec.8., 359.

82. Ibid., secs.18, 20, 22.

83. An attorney employed by an Oklahoma Indian legal aid services group to represent Indians in court cases told me, as an example, that an unscrupulous guardian would pay the bill for $1.50 for an Indian child's shoes, then charge the child's account $10 for his services for taking care of the matter. Guardianship cases continue, he said.

84. Angie Debo, "The Grafters' Share," in *And Still the Waters Run,* describes this situation. Debo found opposition to the book's publication in Oklahoma.

85. I. J. Talbott, of the City Trust, Safety Deposit and Surety Company of Philadelphia, in Kansas City, Kansas, to Indian Agent, Pawnee, Oklahoma Territory, 30 May 1904, Pawnee Agency – *Agents and Agency,* OHSAMD.

86. "Guardians Record No.2," 36, 37, Pawnee County, Oklahoma. County Clerk's Office.

87. Listed in and compiled from "Guardian Record – County Q," "Administrator – Guardian Record No.1," "Guardians Record No.2," "Guardianship Record vol.4," Pawnee County, Oklahoma, County Clerk's Office.

88. Superintendent and Special District Agent to Judge Graves, 1 August 1904, Pawnee Agency – *Agents and Agency,* OHSAMD.

89. George Harvey to Robert Chasteen, 9 January 1904, and George W. Nellis to H. F. Thompson, 10 September 1904, both in Pawnee Agency – Volume 27, "Miscellaneous," OHSAMD.

90. A. D. Krow became the guardian of Mary Smith, age five, and Andy Smith, age one, in 1903. The 1912 Pawnee County map that includes Indian allotments shows that the lands they inherited now belonged to their guardian.

91. "Guardians Record No.2," 95, Pawnee County, Oklahoma, County Court Clerk's Office.

92. Ibid., 111.

93. See 57 Cong. 1 sess., 32 Stat. 174, sec.7. in Kappler, *Indian Affairs,* 1:120.

94. "Guardians Record No.2," 2–24, 37, Pawnee County, Oklahoma, County Clerk's Office.

95. Ibid., 26. After Captain Jim's death, St. Elmo Jim became band chief in 1921. He selected Garland Blaine to succeed him in 1964. I had the pleasure of knowing St. Elmo, a wise and respected man.

96. *Shawnee Herald,* 14 February 1906, 4, col.2, Newspaper Department, OHS.

97. *Daily Oklahoman,* 25 July 1905, col.3, Newspaper Department, OHS.

98. *Shawnee Herald,* 17 March 1905, 2, col.3, Newspaper Department, OHS.

99. C. F. Larrabee, Acting Commissioner to the Superintendent of the Cantonment Indian School, 9 February 1907, Cheyenne and Arapaho Agency, Cantonment, OHSAMD.

100. *Kingfisher Free Press,* 28 June, 12 July 1906, Newspaper Department, OHS.

101. C. F. Larrabee to Superintendent, 9 February 1907, Cheyenne and Arapaho Agency, Cantonment, OHSAMD.

102. Ibid.

103. *Daily Oklahoman,* 20 August 1907, 3, col.3, Newspaper Department, OHS.

104. *Oklahoma Enabling Act (Hamilton Statehood Bill),* 14 June 1906, sec.13.

105. "Guardians for Minor Indians," *Shawnee Herald,* 13 December 1907, microfilm, Newspaper Department, OHS.

106. "Powers and Duties of Guardians," in *Compiled Laws of Oklahoma, 1909,* comp. Henry G. Snyder, 1910, art. 38, pp.581, 738 ff. *Revised Laws, State of Oklahoma, 1890–1910,* vol.2, comp. C. R. Bunn, 1911. *Supplement to the Revised Laws of Okalahoma of 1910,* comp. C. R. Bunn, 1915.

107. 60 Cong. 1 sess., Act of 27 May 1908, chap. 199, secs.3 and 6.

108. *Revised and Annotated Statutes of Oklahoma,* 1903, chap. 22, art. 14 (1816), sec.340.

109. His actual signature is found on several documents in Pawnee agency records and in his son's collection.

110. "Guardians Record No.2," 146, Pawnee County, Oklahoma, County Clerk's Office.

111. Ibid.

112. James Murie had guardianship of eight minors and Alfred Murie had guardianship of four, according to Pawnee County guardianship records.

113. Author's taped interview with Myra Eppler 14 May 1994 at Pawnee, Oklahoma. Myra Eppler died in 1996.

114. Ibid.

115. Maggie Box Blaine, Pawnee Agency – Individual Indian Files, OHSAMD.

116. Angie Debo, *Oklahoma, Foot-Loose and Fancy Free* (1949; Norman: University of Oklahoma Press, 1987).

CHAPTER 6

1. There are four bands in the Pawnee tribe: Pitahawirata, Chawi, Kitkahahki, and Skiri (Skidi).

2. Garland J. Blaine and Martha R. Blaine Research Notes. In this chapter, all quoted segments are from Garland's taped remarks or notes dictated to me. Some other portions are paraphrased from his comments on the subject discussed.

3. Brackets added by author.

4. The Skidis believed that the first twins known were the offspring of a warrior and Deer Woman, the changeling. All subsequent twin births were said to be her descendants. James R. Murie and George A. Dorsey, *Notes on Skidi Pawnee Society*, ed. Alexander Spoehr, Anthropological Series, vol. 27, no. 2 (Chicago: Field Museum of Natural History, 1940), 89.

5. Several Pawnees volunteered this information when I heard that James Blaine had died in the Pawnee jail and asked questions. L. W., alive at the time, said it was talked about in a "hush-hush" manner. He said a lot of bad things happened in that jail. He had been in there himself when he drank too much and knew it was true. He said the standards of justice were different for whites and Pawnees. Once a local attorney, who repeatedly got drunk, was driving his car over a bridge. He struck L. W.'s parents, and their buggy tipped over. Although they were hurt, nothing was done to the attorney. Another time he struck an Indian in the street, hurting him seriously. Nothing was done. Author's interview with L. W., 25 August 1993, Oklahoma City, Oklahoma.

6. This among other reasons explained Garland Blaine's devotion and attention to his grandchildren. It was a warm and caring relationship expressed by both sides whenever I observed it. Small grandchildren clustered around him, and as they got older and measured their height against him, they put their hands on his shoulders and their arms around him, kissed him, and showed their admiration. In many of their lives he was the polestar – steady, firm, always supportive, sometimes critical but in a kind way. He used parables to teach them some of the hard lessons he had learned. Several of them spent much of their childhood living with him when family circumstances made this necessary.

7. Effie Blaine also gave Gene Weltfish this information. See Weltfish, *Caddoan Texts: Pawnee South Band Dialect*, Publications of the American Ethnological Society 17. (New York: G. E. Steichert, 1937), 22.

8. Author's interview with Maude White Chisholm, 1992, Oklahoma City, Oklahoma. Once in a great while in the 1990s one sees a baby on a cradle board. The young parents are attempting to carry on tradition.

9. This battle occurred in 1829 or 1830, according to George E. Hyde, *The Pawnee Indians* (Norman: University of Oklahoma Press, 1974), 180–81.

10. Author's interview with granddaughter of Skidi family holding arrows, 1981, Pawnee, Oklahoma.

11. Sam Horse Chief was born in 1877.

12. John Knife Chief, in his seventies, told me in 1991 that he and other young men still used to get up in the morning and ride all over the countryside on their horses. Before the turn of the century, the Indian agent criticized what he considered the Pawnees' wasteful riding of horses. Their animals should be used only for farmwork, he said.

13. After adoption, James Blaine became Benjamin Peters. He was called by both names during his life. The Pitahawiratas called him by the former name, and the Skidi band, in which he was adopted, by the latter.

14. Today older Pawnees continue to say "that was when I had no sense," meaning a time before they were able to reason comprehensively.

15. Expression written by Garland Blaine.

16. At this time there was intermarriage between the Otoe and Pawnee people, so the two women may have been related to Garland in some way. Usually teasing behavior is well defined and confined to certain kinsmen.

17. Adjacent Indian reservations in Indian Territory and Oklahoma were homes to tribes that may have been enemies in their traditional homelands, such as the Otoes and Missourias, Poncas, Kaws, Sacs and Foxes, Iowas, and Osages. For a short time the Osages and the Pawnees continued sporadic hostile acts after settling on adjacent reservations. This consisted of the Osages' crossing the Arkansas River, which divided the two reservations. Once in Pawnee country, they would sometimes find a hapless Pawnee and cut off some of his hair – for ceremonial uses, it was thought. Other times they stole horses and set fire to the prairies. Of course the Pawnees claim they never did a thing to cause those Osages to act like that.

18. Although homosexuality was accepted as normal behavior by some tribes, to Garland Blaine's knowledge Pawnees discouraged it. In one family, a man told of his brother's homosexuality threatened to kill him but was persuaded not to do so. Although this might not have been a universal reaction, other present-day examples of negative Pawnee attitudes toward it are known.

19. According to Garland Blaine, the Kawarakis were said to have been the first Pawnees to receive the sacred teachings from Tirawahat, and thus they carried a responsibility to maintain moral standards in many aspects of behavior. George A. Dorsey said that in Pawnee legends, the Kawarakis were said to be the first band

of the Pawnees. From it the Chawi and Kitkahahki split off, forming two distinct bands that migrated to different places. The Pitahawirata emerged from the Kawarakis. Dorsey, *Pawnee: Mythology,* part 1, 8. Garland's people told him that the original home of the Kawarakis was in the far north, "the origin place," Puk siks tu, where Tirawahat, the supreme being, first spoke to the Pawnees and gave them consciousness. After the separation of the Chawi and Kitkahahki, there were separate divisions of the Pitahawirata band, each of which contained some Kawarakis who were among the elite rulers and religious figures. This group always lived farthest east, where the sun rises and life begins each day. The name translated means roughly, "into, amid, to go into the core, to be part of the center of life, to be complete." This group attempted to intermarry so as to maintain their uniqueness. In some older ceremonies, the Pitahawirata chiefs sat in the north, toward the place of origin, affirming their original role. Both Wichita and Effie Blaine were descended from the Kawarakis. Very few descendants are known today.

20. BRN.

CHAPTER 7

1. Aunt May took care of many orphans and other children during her lifetime and was considered a kind and caring mother surrogate. Blaine continued to visit her during her long life.

2. I consulted a medical doctor about the baby's appearance. He said he believed that it would be normal considering his recent illness and that bruising occurs more easily with malnutrition.

3. It was common practice for the Pawnees to visit one another for extended periods. For many centuries they lived close to each other in villages. Later when they lived on allotment farms, they no longer had the close relationships that village life fostered. Therefore visiting families and friends for days or weeks became a way of maintaining relationships.

4. Garland Blaine said "Roan Chief." I have heard this as well as Roam Chief used. His name translated from Pawnee as Roaming Chief. Garland, speaking Pawnee as a child, probably called him by his Pawnee name.

5. Effie and Wichita Blaine legally adopted Garland Blaine on 10 February 1917. "Probate Appearance Docket," vol.2, 194. Pawnee County, Oklahoma, County Clerk's Office.

6. Ethel Wilson Riding In, who saw Effie at this time, told me that she was not completely blind and could prepare meals, although awkwardly and slowly.

7. Gordon Lillie, or Pawnee Bill, a local entrepreneur, owned a Wild West show that traveled the country at this time. Local Indians sometimes took part in the acts.

8. Pawnee Superintendent to Alex Adams, 10 October 1918, Pawnee Agency – Individual Indian Files, OHSAMD.

9. Garland Blaine, Pawnee Agency – Individual Indian Files, 10 October 1918, OHSAMD.

10. Ibid.

11. Ibid.

12. Superintendent to Commissioner of Indian Affairs, 31 January 1921, Pawnee Agency – World War I, OHSAMD.

13. Densmore, *Pawnee Music,* 65–66.

14. The narratives Densmore heard may have been the soldiers recounting their battle exploits in the recent conflict or older men, like Wichita Blaine, telling of their battle experiences.

15. Traditionally a song created for a special event would not use an older melody; the singer would create a new song for the new words. It is possible that Densmore did not hear the often minor differences as she listened in these circumstances.

16. Pawnees today talk about the old times when gift horses were brought and people walked up and placed blankets and shawls on their backs for the honoree.

17. Densmore, *Pawnee Music,* 64.

18. The latter seems true because he and Wichita came from the same Pita-hawirata village in Nebraska.

19. The Pawnee 1913 Annuity Roll says he was born in 1839. Another source said he was born in 1828. He died in Pawnee on 26 June 1929. He claimed to be over one hundred years old. He had been a first sergeant in Company A, Pawnee Scouts, and had served in eleven campaigns. See "Years Take Their Toll of Pawnee Scouts," interview by Clayton G. Seward, 18 July 1939, OHS Library, Vertical File.

20. The belief in "witching," as it is called, continues to be held by a few older Pawnees.

21. The Pawnees say that the Union Pacific Railroad Company allowed the Pawnees to ride free on the tops of cars or on flatcars as a reward for their service as Indian scouts during the railroad's construction.

22. Blaine and Blaine, "Paresu Arirake," 342–58, gives the Pawnee account of this encounter between the Brulé and Oglala Sioux and a Pawnee hunting group, as well as the government records that differ from the Pawnee accounts.

23. Blaine Pawnee Music Collection, album 1, record 11, side 2.

CHAPTER 8

1. Acting Commissioner to Superintendent in Charge, 10 April 1906. Wichita Blaine, Pawnee Agency – Individual Indian Files, OHSAMD.

2. Ibid., 19 June, 21 July 1906.

3. Ibid., 21 July 1906.

4. Ibid., 23 February 1907.

5. Elmer Blaine, Pawnee Agency – Individual Indian Files, 10 October 1918, OHSAMD.

6. Ibid., 26 October 1918, Request for Funds.

7. Wichita Blaine was "almost or quite totally blind." J. C. Hart, Pawnee Agency Superintendent to CIA, 20 March 1922, NA RG 75 LR 1881–1927, Office of Indian Affairs.

8. In the 1980s and 1990s, after decades of absence, bald eagles have returned to winter along the Arkansas River, Keystone Dam, and the lake area not far from the Blaine allotment near Maramec. The *Pawnee Chief,* 21 March 1985, noted that Oklahoma ranked fourth out of forty-two of the continental states in bald eagle population, with 794 birds counted.

9. In Oklahoma City, when a door would suddenly blow open in a hard wind, Garland would turn to me, smile, and say, "There's Uncle, he has come to visit."

10. A wooden structure built in the shape of a mudlodge where ceremonies and other band or tribal events were held. Both the Skidi or North Band and the South Bands had one. I photographed the stone foundations of the latter, which can be found some distance from the road in a field south of Pawnee.

11. Explanation by Garland Blaine.

12. In a letter to Herbert Welsh, of the Indian Rights Association, from M. C. Collins, 15 April 1891, she states that the Indians with Wild Bill Cody in Chicago have been reported as being in deplorable condition and "terribly neglected, and it is a disgrace that men can be so treated." NA RG 75, "Documents relative to the Ghost Dance Religion," Special Cases, no.188, roll 2.

13. In Pawnee Scout rosters, Blaine's name was Ta Ka II.

14. He attended that school in 1923, according to the Pawnee census of that year. Pawnee Agency – Census, OHSAMD

15. When Garland first married me, his friends would come up, laugh, and ask in Pawnee if he got enough salads. If you married a white woman, you'd be sure to have to eat those salads.

16. Garland remembered mispronouncing "appooh" (apple), "peetsees" (peaches), "too rahts" (doughnuts), and "tanky oo" (thank you).

17. Garland Blaine observed that Indian children become silent and often do not do well in school because of some of the same conditions he experienced. A recent study says cultural conflicts and language differences/difficulties can promote bias. Minority children generally seem to receive less positive feedback (e.g., verbal praise, smiling) and more negative feedback (e.g., interruptions, nonverbal signs of disdain) from teachers than do nonminority children . . . relationship problems with teachers were cited as a reason by 25% of Indian students who were considering dropping out of school." Keith James, Ernie Chavez, Fred Beauvais, Ruth Edwards, and Gene Oetting, "School Achievement and Dropout among Anglo and Indian Females and Males: A Comparative Examination," *American Indian Culture and Research Journal* 19, 3 (1995): 186.

CHAPTER 9

1. All Pawnee words are written as Garland Blaine wrote and translated them. BRN.

2. Clark Wissler, *The American Indian: An Introduction to the Anthropology of the New World*, 3d ed. (New York: Oxford University Press, 1938), 220.

3. Murie, *Ceremonies of the Pawnees*, describes in great detail ceremonies involving different sacred bundles of the several bands.

4. Martha R. Blaine, *The Pawnee Sacred Bundles: Their Present Uses and Significance*, Papers in Anthropology 24, no.2 (Norman: University of Oklahoma Press, 1984), 145–55.

5. Garland Blaine, who observed this behavior, said it was an extraordinary experience to watch this transformation as the different doctors assumed their animal forms.

6. Story told by Garland Blaine, 1965.

7. This pole stood in the place where John stamped his foot and had the stake placed. It determined the center of the fire pit, and the circumference of the lodge was measured from that point. This lodge was approximately forty feet in diameter.

8. According to the 1913 Pawnee annuity roll, War Ruwalk was born in 1863. Pawnee Agency – Census, OHSAMD.

9. Overtakes His Enemy or Overtaker is cited as one of the "owners" of the Buffalo Ceremony in Dorsey, *Pawnee: Mythology*, part 1, 318.

10. Murie, *Ceremonies of the Pawnees*, 2:418. For a complete description of

Murie's description of the ritual, participants' roles, lectures, and songs, see 2:394–460.

11. Ibid., 2:413.

12. Ibid., 2:429.

13. The Pawnee Agency Records, Allotment File, says Captain Jim was fifty-three years old in 1892, born in 1849. The 1913 Pawnee annuity roll gives 1836 as his birth year.

14. John B. Dunbar, "The Pawnee Indians: Their Habits and Customs," *Magazine of American History* 5, 5 (1880): 326–27.

15. In these years the Pawnee population continued to decrease, so there was gratitude for each baby or young child.

16. According to the Pawnee Agency – Allotment File, OHSAMD, 1893, both High Eagle and Captain Jim were born in 1839.

17. Garland Blaine had given no further details of this dance before his death.

18. Garland Blaine account, BRN.

19. Garland Blaine recorded many songs from this dance, and they are in the Blaine Pawnee Music Collection.

20. James Murie names "the One Horn Dance" of the Skidis and gives a brief description in "Pawnee Indian Societies," 638.

21. This song recorded by Effie Blaine appears in Densmore, *Pawnee Music*, 115, with a slightly different translation.

22. Author's interview with Maude White Chisholm, Pawnee, Oklahoma, 14 May 1993.

23. Personal communication with Clifford Jim, 20 February 1992.

24. Personal communication with Henry Stoneroad, 28 January 1994.

25. Personal communication with Viola Blaine McIntosh, 7 September 1980.

26. Dorsey, *Pawnee: Mythology*, sec.3, gives versions of human and animal contacts where the animals impart powers to the person. Murie, "The White Beaver Ceremony of the Chawi," in *Ceremonies of the Pawnees*, 2:204–317, details the rituals and songs that existed at the beginning of the twentieth century.

27. Nebraska State Historical Society, Library and Archives, Photograph Collections, I 396:8, Additional Information File. White Eagle previously traveled to North Dakota in the spring of 1911 to visit friends and relatives. Pawnee Agency – Authority to Expend Inherited Land Funds, White Eagle, 20 May 1911, OHSAMD.

28. Clark Wissler, "General Discussion of Shamanistic and Dancing Societies," *American Museum of Natural History* 11, 2 (1916): 858–62.

29. Garland Blaine writing and translations of Pawnee phrases.

30. John Ruwalk had two white beaver pelts near him during the dance. When James Murie observed the ceremony he called it the White Beaver Dance or Lodge. "Well, it wasn't," said Garland Blaine. "It was simply our Doctor Dance, and these pelts belonged to John. I never heard any of our people call it that."

31. Garland Blaine account, BRN.

32. Historically, since records began, tornadoes have occurred with great frequency in Oklahoma, earning it the name "Tornado Alley."

33. Bill Mathews's Pawnee name was given to me by his grandson, Alex Mathews. He spelled the name for me and translated it as "Dust Coming off the Horse's Hooves."

34. BRN.

35. Effie Blaine account, BRN.

36. Ibid. I heard a similar story in more recent times. A woman who had been "witched" died, and after her death her stomach moved. People believed it was a snake that had been sent to make her ill, which had entered her body and caused her death.

37. BRN.

38. BRN. The handling and use of fire, such as fire walking, occurred among the Pawnees, Siouan bands, Arapahos, Cheyennes, and others. Wissler, "General Discussion of Shamanistic and Dancing Societies," 859.

39. Garland Blaine account, BRN.

40. Author's interview with Maude White Chisholm, 23 July 1991, Oklahoma City, Oklahoma.

41. Ibid.

42. Rosanna Yellow Calf Turnbull to Garland and Martha Blaine, conversation, 14 July 1975, Oklahoma City, Oklahoma.

43. Ibid. Maj. Frank North, who witnessed and described the miraculous events at several Nebraska Doctor Dances, said, "Many of their maneuvers equalled, and perhaps excelled, the best prestidigitory acts of Houdini and Herman, the great illusionists." Alfred Sorrenson, "Life of Major Frank North," *Columbus (Nebraska) Times*, 9 May 1896 to 30 January 1897, 27.

44. Luther North, "Fighting the Frontier Battles," *Nebraska Farmer*, 21 March 1931, 3.

45. Garland Blaine account, BRN.

46. Ibid.

47. Effie Blaine account, BRN.

48. Ibid.

49. Garland Blaine explanation, BRN.

50. Murie, "The Bear Dance of the Pitahawirata," in *Ceremonies of the Pawnees*, 2:319–85.

51. Wichita Blaine account in Densmore, *Pawnee Music*, 39.

52. Garland Blaine account, BRN.

53. Murie, *Pawnee Societies*, 604, said two piles of cedar brush in the lodge supplied the cedar sprigs the doctors used. The second tree young Garland saw might have been used for this purpose.

54. The Pawnees of this society hunted bears for hides and claws to use in their ceremonies. Before killing the animal, they would first address the spirit of the bear, as they did the spirit of buffalo before hunting it. Garland Blaine.

55. Wichita Blaine said that when a bear charged, if it stood up on its hind legs, a man shot arrows into its paws to impede its running.

56. In the Blaine Pawnee Music Collection are several Bear Dance songs recorded by Garland and his grandmother, Effie Blaine. Frances Densmore recorded two Bear Dance songs by Wichita Blaine in *Pawnee Music*, 37–40.

57. James Murie reported that sometimes two young boys with bearskins were asked to dance. "Pawnee Indian Societies," 604.

58. Garland J. Blaine, Pawnee Agency – Individual Indian Files, OHSAMD.

59. Cato Sells to Wm. Allen and Barclay White, 25 May 1920, Pawnee Agency – Indian Dances, OHSAMD.

60. Commissioner to All Indians, 24 February 1923, Pawnee Agency – Indian Dances, OHSAMD.

61. Superintendent, Pawnee Agency to CIA, 18 March 1924, Pawnee Agency – Indian Dances, OHSAM.

BIBLIOGRAPHY

UNPUBLISHED SOURCES

Author conversations with Maude White Chisholm, 1980–95, Oklahoma City, Oklahoma.

Author interview with Myra Eppler, 14 May 1994, Pawnee, Oklahoma.

Author interviews with Viola Blaine McIntosh, 7 September 1980 and 5 July 1981, Pawnee, Oklahoma.

Author interview with Ethel Riding In, 14 November 1988, Pawnee, Oklahoma.

Author interview with Henry Stoneroad, 28 January 1994, Oklahoma City, Oklahoma.

Blaine Pawnee Music Collection, Oklahoma City, Oklahoma.

Garland J. Blaine and Martha R. Blaine Research Notes, Oklahoma City, Oklahoma.

Chapman, Berlin B. "Pawnee Allotment." Manuscript, Chapman Collection, Oklahoma Historical Society Archives and Manuscripts Division.

Clark, Joseph Stanley. "The Ponca Indian Agency." Ph.D. diss., University of Wisconsin, 1940.

James Murie to Alice Fletcher, 20 July 1900. Smithsonian Institution, National Anthropology Archives, MSS 4558 (1), 1900.

Barclay White Journals. Vols. 1–3. Swarthmore College Library.

FEDERAL AND STATE DOCUMENTS AND PUBLICATIONS

Commissioner of Indian Affairs Annual Reports, 1877, 1878, 1880, 1881, 1884, 1885, 1886, 1889, 1891, 1892, 1896, 1897, 1900, 1905. Report of the Secretary of the Interior, 1896.

National Archives

INDian Office File 78120, Pawnee File no. 725.

NA RG 75 LR 1881–1927, Office of Indian Affairs.

NA RG 75 M234 R662, Pawnee Agency (1873).

NA RG 75 M234 R666, Pawnee Agency (1878).

NA RG 75 M234 R668, Pawnee Agency (1880).

NA RG 75, Report of Councils Held by Cherokee (Jerome) Commission and Several Indian Tribes, Indian Office File no. 4738. Part 1, Pawnee Agency, 31 October–24 November 1892 (a typescript is held in Oklahoma Historical Society Archives and Manuscripts Division).

NA RG 75, "Documents relative to the Ghost Dance Religion and the Sioux Outbreak of 1890 (1890–1898)." Bureau of Indian Affairs, Land Division, Special Cases, no.188, roll 1.

NA RG 75 M595 R386, Pawnee Census, 1886–96.

NA RG 75 M234 R39, "Report of Inspections of the Field Jurisdictions of the Bureau of Indian Affairs, 1873–1900."

NA RG 75 M1011 R100, Special Agent's Report, 30 June 1914.

Bureau of Indian Affairs, Pawnee Agency, Pawnee, Oklahoma. Family History Chart Fiche 837.

United States Congress

Senate Exec. Do c. 16, 52–2 [3055], T. J. Morgan to Secretary of the Interior, 9 December 1892.

Senate Misc . Doc. 73, 49–2, vol.2 [2451].

Senate Rept. 2707, 50–2, vol.5 [2623].

Act of 3 March 1893, 27 Stat. 612, "Agreement with the Pawnee Indians," 4 January 1893.

Act of Congress, 2 March 1907 (34 Stat L. p.1221).

Act of Congress, 4 Stat. 730, Sec.2139, 30 June 1834.

Act of Congress, 32 Stat. 245, 27 May 1902.

Act of Congress, 39 Stat. 126, vol.39, pt. 1, 127, 1916.

Organic Act, 51 Cong. 1 sess., chap. 182, 26 Stat. 81.

Oklahoma Enabling Act (Hamilton Statehood Bill), 14 June 1906, sec.13.

Act of 27 May 1908, chap. 199, secs.3 and 6.

State of Oklahoma

The Statutes of Oklahoma, 1890 . . . from the Laws Passed by the First Assembly of the Territory, comp. Will T. Little, L. G. Pitman, and R. J. Baker, under direction of Robert Martin, Secretary of the Territory, 1891. Guthrie OK: State Capital Printing Company, 1891.

The Statutes of Oklahoma, 1891. Chapter 19, "Courts," art. 13, secs.1–58.

Revised and Annotated Statutes of Oklahoma, 1903.

Compiled Laws of Oklahoma, 1909. Comp. Henry G. Snyder, 1910, article 38.

Revised Laws, State of Oklahoma, 1890–1910. Vol.2. Comp. C. R. Bunn, 1911.

Supplement to the Revised Laws of Oklahoma of 1910. Comp. C. R. Bunn, 1915.

State of Nebraska

Consolidated Statutes of Nebraska, 1891. Comp. J. E. Cobbey, Esq. Lincoln: Nebraska State Journal Company, 1891.

Pawnee County, Oklahoma. County Clerk's Office

"Probate Appearance Docket," vol.2.

"Selection Docket."

"Administrator – Guardian Record No.1."

"Guardian Record – County Q," now "Guardian Record Vol.1." "Guardians Record No.2."

"Guardianship Record Vol.4."

Oklahoma State Historical Society, Archives and Manuscripts Division

Cherokee Volume 715j.

Cheyenne and Arapaho Agency, Cantonment. Microfilm roll 51.

Pawnee Agency Files

Individual Indian Files Census, Pensions, Allotment File, Deaths, Vices, Agents and Agency, Field Matrons, World War I, Authority to Expend Inherited Land Funds, Circulars, Indian Dances

Pawnee Agency Volumes (letter press) 3, 4, 7, 10, 27

Ponca Agency Volumes (letter press) 1, 14, 16, 18, 19

Oklahoma State Historical Society Library

"Leasing of Indian Lands in Indian Territory, 1884."

"Years Take Their Toll of Pawnee Scouts." Interview by Clayton G. Seward, 18 July 1939. Vertical File.

Oklahoma State Historical Society, Newspaper Division

Sun Democrat. Edmond, Oklahoma.

Daily Oklahoman. Oklahoma City, Oklahoma.

Oklahoma State Capitol. Guthrie, Oklahoma.

Pawnee Chief. Pawnee, Oklahoma.

New York Times. New York, New York.

Shawnee Herald. Shawnee, Oklahoma.

Kingfisher Free Press. Kingfisher, Oklahoma.

Nebraska State Historical Society

Library and Archives Department. Photograph Collections, Pawnee I396.

Nebraska Farmer. Lincoln, Nebraska.

BOOKS AND ARTICLES

Blaine, Garland J., and Martha Royce Blaine. "Paresu Arirake: The Hunters That Were Massacred." *Nebraska History* 58, 3 (1977): 342–58.

Blaine, Martha Royce. *Pawnee Passage: 1870–1875.* Norman: University of Oklahoma Press, 1990.

———. *The Pawnees: A Critical Bibliography.* Bloomington: Indiana University Press, 1980.

———. *The Pawnee Sacred Bundles: Their Present Uses and Significance.* Papers in Anthropology 24, no.2. Norman: University of Oklahoma Press, 1984.

———. "The Pawnees." *Encyclopedia of Native Americans in the Twentieth Century.* New York: Garland, 1994.

Brendel, J. G. "A Memorable Week among the Pawnee Indians." In *Our Home Field.* Nashville TN: Home Mission Board, Southern Baptist Convention, n.d.

Carleton, James H. *The Prairie Log Books: Dragoon Campaigns to the Prairie Villages in 1844, and to the Rocky Mountains in 1845.* Ed. with intro. by Louis Pelzer. Chicago: Caxton Club, 1943; reprint, Lincoln: University of Nebraska Press, 1983.

Clark, Joseph Stanley. "Irregularities at the Pawnee Agency." *Kansas State Historical Quarterly* 12 (1943): 366–77.

Curtis, Natalie. *The Indians Book: Songs and Legends of the American Indians.* New York: Dover, 1968.

Dale, E. E., and Jess Lee Rader. *Readings in Oklahoma History.* New York: Row Peterson, 1930.

Danker, Donald F., ed. *Man of the Plains: Recollections of Luther North, 1865–1882.* Lincoln: University of Nebraska Press, 1961.

Debo, Angie. *And Still the Waters Run.* Princeton: Princeton University Press, 1940.

———. *Oklahoma, Foot-Loose and Fancy Free.* 1949. Norman: University of Oklahoma Press, 1987.

Densmore, Frances. *Pawnee Music.* Bureau of American Ethnology Bulletin 93. Washington DC: Government Printing Office, 1929.

Dorsey, George A. *The Pawnee: Mythology.* Pt. 1. Washington DC: Carnegie Institution, 1906.

Dunbar, John B. "The Pawnee Indians: Their Habits and Customs." *Magazine of American History* 5, 5 (1880): 326–27.

Dunlay, Thomas W. *Wolves for the Blue Soldiers: Indian Scouts and Auxiliaries with the United States Army, 1860–90.* Lincoln: University of Nebraska Press, 1982.

Fletcher, Alice C. "The Hako: A Pawnee Ceremony." Asst. James R. Murie, music trans. Edwin S. Tracy. In *Twenty-second Annual Report of the Bureau of American Ethnology,* pt. 2. Washington DC: Government Printing Office, 1904.

Franks, Kenny A., and Paul F. Lambert. *Pawnee Pride: A History of Pawnee County.* Oklahoma Heritage County History Series, ed. O. B. Falk. Oklahoma City: Western Heritage Books, 1994.

Gilmore, Melvin R. *Uses of Plants by the Indians of the Missouri River Regions.* Thirty-third Annual Report of the Bureau of American Ethnology, 1912; reprint, Lincoln: University of Nebraska Press, 1977.

Grange, Roger T., Jr. *Pawnee and Lower Loup Pottery.* Nebraska State Historical Society Publications in Anthropology 3. Lincoln: University of Nebraska Press, 1968.

Grinnell, G. B. *Pawnee Hero Stories and Folk Tales, with Notes on the Origin, Customs and Character of the Pawnee People.* New York: Forest and Stream, 1889; reprint Lincoln: University of Nebraska Press, 1961.

Hamilton, Robert. *The Gospel among the Red Men: History of the Southern Baptist Indian Missions.* Nashville TN: Sunday School Board, n.d.

Hittman, Michael. "The Ghost Dance in Nevada." *American Indian Culture and Research Journal* 16, 4 (1992): 123–66.

Hyde, George E. *The Pawnee Indians.* Norman: University of Oklahoma Press, 1974.

Identification and Description of the Lands Covered by Selections and Allotments under the Act of March 3, 1893 (27 Stat. 619) and the Agreements with the Cherokee Nation and Tonkawa and Pawnee Tribes of Indians Ratified Thereby. Washington DC: Government Printing Office, 1893.

Indian and Pioneer History Collection. 114 vols. Oklahoma City: Oklahoma Historical Society Archives and Manuscripts Division, 1936–38.

Kappler, Charles J., comp. *Indian Affairs: Indian Laws and Treaties, 1903–1941.* Washington DC: Government Printing Office, 1904–41; reprint, New York: Interland, 1972.

Kracht, Benjamin R. "The Kiowa Ghost Dance, 1894–1916: An Unheralded Revitalization Movement." *Ethnohistory* 39, 4 (1992): 462.

LaBarre, Weston. *The Peyote Cult.* New York: Schocken, 1971.

Lerner, Max. *America as a Civilization: Life and Thought in the United States Today.* New York: Simon and Schuster, 1957.

Lesser, Alexander. *The Pawnee Ghost Dance Handgame: A Study of Cultural Change.* Columbia University Contributions to Anthropology 16. New York: Columbia University Press, 1933; reprint, Madison: University of Wisconsin Press, 1978.

Linton, Ralph. "Nativistic Movements." *American Anthropologist* 45, 2 (1943): 230–40.

———. *The Sacrifice to the Morning Star by the Skidi Pawnee.* Department of Anthropology, Leaflet 6. Chicago: Field Museum of Natural History, 1922.

———. "The Origin of the Skidi Pawnee Sacrifice to the Morning Star." *American Anthropologist* 28 (1922): 457–66.

McDonnell, Janet. *The Dispossession of the American Indian: 1887–1934.* Bloomington: University of Indiana Press, 1991.

McHugh, Tom. *The Time of the Buffalo.* Lincoln: University of Nebraska Press, 1979.

Miller, David H. *Ghost Dance.* New York: Duell, Sloan and Pearce, 1959; reprint, Lincoln: University of Nebraska Press, 1985.

Milner, Clyde A. *With Good Intentions: Quaker Work among the Pawnees, Otos, and Omahas in the 1870s.* Lincoln: University of Nebraska Press, 1972.

Mooney, James. *Calendar History of the Kiowa Indians.* Intro. John C. Ewers, Classics of Smithsonian Anthropology. Washington DC: Smithsonian Institution Press, 1979.

———. "The Ghost Dance Religion and the Sioux Outbreak of 1890." In *Fourteenth Annual Report of the Bureau of Ethnology,* pt. 2. Washington DC: Government Printing Office, 1896.

Moses, L. G. "Wovoka: The Ghost Dance Prophet." *American Indian Quarterly,* summer 1985, 335–51.

Murie, James R. *Ceremonies of the Pawnees.* Vols.1 and 2. Ed. Douglas R. Parks. Smithsonian Institution Contributions to Anthropology 27. Washington DC: Government Printing Office, 1979.

———. "Pawnee Indian Societies." *Anthropological Papers of the American Museum of Natural History* 2, pt. 7 (1914): 545–644.

Murie, James R., and George A. Dorsey. *Notes on Pawnee Skidi Society.* Ed. Alexander Spoehr. Anthropological Series, vol.27, no.2. Chicago: Field Museum of Natural History, 1940.

Murray, Charles A. *Travels in North America during the Years 1834, 1835, and 1836. Including a Summer Residence with the Pawnee Tribe of Indians, in the Remote Prairies of the Missouri, and a Visit to Cuba and the Azore Islands.* New York: Harper and Brothers; reprint, New York: Da Capo, 1974.

Otis, D. S. *The Dawes Act and the Allotment of Indian Lands.* Norman: University of Oklahoma Press, 1973.

Portrait and Biographical Record of Oklahoma. Chicago: Chapman, 1901.

Prucha, F. P. *The Great White Father: The United States Government and the American Indian.* Vols.1 and 2. Lincoln: University of Nebraska Press, 1984.

Richardson, James D. *Messages and Papers of the Presidents, 1789–1902.* Washington DC: Bureau of National Literature and Art, 1907.

Sheldon, Addison E. *History and Stories of Nebraska.* Chicago: University Publishing, 1913.

Sorrenson, Alfred. "Life of Major Frank North." *Columbus (Nebraska) Times,* 9 May 1896 to 30 January 1897.

Thurman, Melvin D. "Skidi Pawnee Morning Star Sacrifice of 1827." *Nebraska History* 51, 3 (1979): 269–80.

Washburn, Wilcomb E., comp. *The American Indian and the United States: A Documentary History.* Vols. 1 and 2. Westport CT: Greenwood, 1979.

———. *Red Man's Land, White Man's Law: A Study of the Past and Present Status of the American Indian.* New York: Charles Scribner's Sons, 1971.

Wedel, Waldo R. *An Introduction to Pawnee Archeology.* Bureau of American Ethnology Bulletin 112. Washington DC: Government Printing Office, 1936.

Weltfish, Gene. *The Lost Universe, with a Closing Chapter on "The Universe Regained."* New York: Basic, 1965. Reprinted as *The Lost Universe: Pawnee Life and Culture* (Lincoln: University of Nebraska Press, 1977).

———. *Caddoan Texts: Pawnee, South Band Dialect.* Publications of the American Ethnological Society 17. New York: G. E. Steichert, 1937.

White, Richard. *The Roots of Dependency: Subsistence, Environment, and Social Change among the Choctaws, Pawnees, and Navajos.* Lincoln: University of Nebraska Press, 1983.

Wishart, David J. *An Unspeakable Sadness: The Dispossession of the Nebraska Indians.* Lincoln: University of Nebraska Press, 1995.

———. "The Dispossession of the Pawnee." *Annals of the Society of American Geographers* 69, 3 (1979): 382–401.

Wissler, Clark. *The American Indian: An Introduction to the Anthropology of the New World.* 3d ed. New York: Oxford University Press, 1938.

———. "General Discussion of Shamanistic and Dancing Societies." *American Museum of Natural History* 11, 2 (1916): 858–62.

INDEX

Printed in the USA
CPSIA information can be obtained
at www.ICGtesting.com
CBHW021032150824
13242CB00004B/18

9 780803 245273